D0966774

I Never Knew That ABOUT ENGLAND

Christopher Winn

I Never Knew That ABOUT ENGLAND

EBURY
PRESS

Title page illustration: Charleston Manor, Sussex

First published in Great Britain in 2005

9 10

First published by Ebury Publishing
Random House, 20 Vauxhall Bridge Road, London SW1V 2SA

Random House Australia (Pty) Limited
20 Alfred Street, Milsons Point, Sydney, New South Wales 2061, Australia

Random House New Zealand Limited
18 Poland Road, Glenfield, Auckland 10, New Zealand

Random House South Africa (Pty) Limited
Isle of Houghton, Corner of Boundary Road & Carse O'Gowrie, Houghton 2198, South Africa

The Random House Group Limited Reg. No. 954009
www.randomhouse.co.uk

A CIP catalogue record for this book is available from the British Library.

The map references in the gazetteer on pages 264-269 appear by kind permission of Ordnance Survey.

EDITOR: Judith Hannam
DESIGNER: Peter Ward
ILLUSTRATOR: Mai Osawa
PROOFREADER: Margaret Gilbey

ISBN: 009190207X (before Jan 2007)
ISBN: 9780091902070

Papers used by Ebury Press are natural, recyclable products made from wood grown in sustainable forests.

Printed and bound in Great Britain by Mackays of Chatham plc.

This book is dedicated to HUGH MONTGOMERY MASSINGBERD,
without whose advice, encouragement and inspiration
it would never have been written.

Also to my wife, MAI, who never lost her patience, grace
and good humour during the process. Her exquisite illustrations
lift this book beyond mere words.

Contents

Radcliffe Camera, Oxford

Preface

As Dr Johnson might have said, 'If I had no duties, and no reference to futurity, I would spend my life in driving briskly through England in a post-chaise with a copy of *I Never Knew That About England*.'

He, like me, considered 'exploring England' and a 'good story' to be two of the greatest pleasures in life, and this book is designed neatly to combine the two. I am never happier than when browsing through England. I have read the books, seen the films and done the tours, and yet still I find, down every lane, round every corner, in every town and village, new stories to surprise and inspire me.

The only criteria I have used for including stories in *I Never Knew That About England* are that they have England as their backdrop and that they have left me intrigued. I have endeavoured to ensure that there is something here for everyone, with a true miscellany of love stories, ghost stories, anecdotes, achievements, triumphs and disasters, inventions, mistakes and adventures, plus a smattering of fascinating facts and figures.

England packs an astonishing diversity of scenery and heritage into a tiny but ravishingly beautiful space and so, I hope, does this book. My aim is to enliven conversation, to enrich any journey, however mundane, to make anywhere you happen to find yourself a little more interesting. This book can be read on the train, in the bath, with a glass of wine, alone or in company, in a stolen moment. It can be used to impress your friends, to help you shine in the pub quiz or just to put a smile on your face. With *I Never Knew That About England* in your possession, time and time again you will experience the pleasure of hearing your friends exclaim 'Well, I never knew that!'

Although I have made every effort to get the facts right, many of these stories are not eternal truths but have been handed down through time, sometimes by word of mouth only. Details can vary according to different sources, but the essential substance and essence remains.

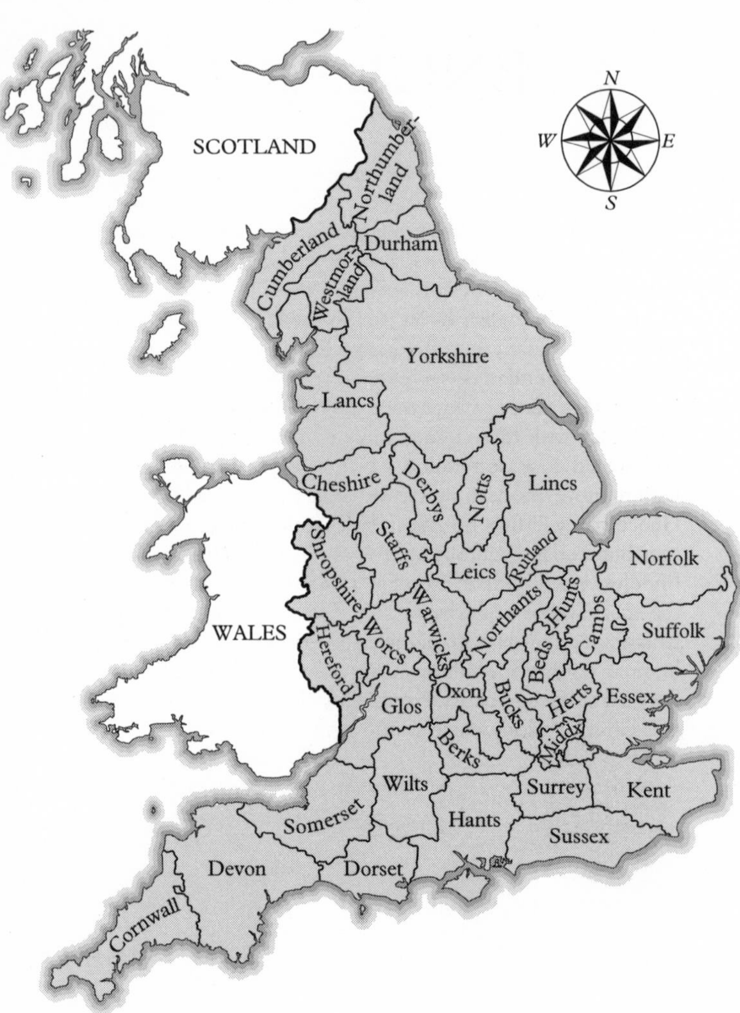
N
W
E
S
SCOTLAND
Northumber-
land
Cumberland
Durham
Westmor-
land
Yorkshire
Lancs
Cheshire
Derbys
Notts
Lincs
Shropshire
Staffs
Leics
Rutland
Norfolk
WALES
Warwicks
Northants
Hunts
Cambs
Suffolk
Hereford
Worcs
Beds
Glos
Oxon
Bucks
Herts
Essex
Berks
Middx
Wilts
Surrey
Kent
Somerset
Hants
Sussex
Devon
Dorset
Cornwall

The 39 Counties
of
ENGLAND

I Never Knew That About England is organised by counties, as these are the most natural, recognisable and manageable way of describing localities. Furthermore, I have chosen the 39 traditional English counties that have defined the map of England for many hundreds of years, since these are based on natural boundaries, such as rivers and hills, and still inspire loyalty and a sense of identity. Most of the stories in this book took place with these traditional counties as their background, and would lose something of their flavour if relocated to within more modern, yet meaningless, bureaucratic entities. Hence you will find no Avon, Humberside or Cleveland while Northumberland, Cumberland, Westmorland, Huntingdonshire, Middlesex and Rutland are all restored to their rightful place on the map. Major conurbations such as London, Birmingham, Bristol, Newcastle and Manchester are broken up into their original county identities. The Vale of the White Horse is covered at the end of the Berkshire chapter. The only omission is Central London, which would make a book in itself.

BEDFORDSHIRE

COUNTY TOWN: BEDFORD

'a brickworks in the middle of a cabbage patch'

ANONYMOUS

Elstow Moot Hall, standing on the green where John Bunyan set his Vanity Fair from 'The Pilgrim's Progress'

Cockayne Hatley

Long John Silver and Peter Pan's Wendy

Turn east off the A1 near Sandy and you find yourself in an empty landscape of big skies and open hills. Down a lonely lane, on the crest of a rise, embowered in trees, is the church of St John, Cockayne Hatley, slumbering at the gates of an ancient hall. Step inside the church and gaze at the startling interior, which is a feast of medieval woodwork, carvings and stained glass, all imported from the Continent by a 19th-century rector, a display unrivalled by any country church in England.

But what really turns this remote and lovely spot into a special place of pilgrimage is the simple, grey tomb of WILLIAM HENLEY (1849–1903) and his family, which stands beneath an ash tree in the churchyard. William Henley was a Victorian poet. As a boy, he suffered from tuberculosis, which led to the amputation of one leg. While recuperating in Edinburgh, he befriended another young writer who suffered from ill health, ROBERT LOUIS STEVENSON. When Stevenson wrote *Treasure Island*, he drew inspiration for his peg-leg villain, LONG JOHN SILVER, from the redoubtable Henley.

William Henley wrote these famous lines in his poem 'Invictus':

Under the bludgeonings of fate
My head is bloody but unbowed

and

I am the master of my fate
I am the captain of my soul

MARGARET HENLEY, William's much-loved daughter, was known to everyone as the 'golden child'. With her flaxen hair, merry laugh and bright eyes, she captivated all who met her. William, by now editor of the *National Observer*, was mentor and confidant to many of the prominent writers of the age, including J.M. BARRIE, who quickly fell under Margaret's spell. She noticed how her father would call Barrie 'my friend' and, whenever he visited, she would fling herself into his arms crying 'Fwendy, Fwendy!' It was thus that Peter Pan's Wendy came by her name.

Biggleswade

Birthplace of the Tractor

Few motorists speeding past Biggleswade on the A1 realise that this quiet market town can proudly claim a place amongst the pantheon of world heritage sites. For it was here, in 1902, 82 years before Band Aid, an invention was unveiled that truly did help to 'feed the world' – the WORLD'S FIRST PRACTICAL TRACTOR.

The IVEL AGRICULTURAL MOTOR was the brainchild of inventor 'GENIAL DAN' ALBONE, who was born in Biggleswade in 1860. In his workshop beside the River Ivel, the site of which is marked by a plaque, he produced championship-winning Ivel bicycles, motor bicycles and motor cars, as well as a host of other ingenious devices, but the tractor was his crowning achievement. Work on adapting traction engines to pull farm machinery had already been going on in America, but these proved too heavy and unwieldy for the light soil around Biggleswade. Dan's vision was for a light but powerful machine that could replace the horse for ploughing and harvesting, and could also be used to operate a whole range of other agricultural implements. After five years of experiment and research, he astonished the world by successfully demonstrating his tractor's abilities, on fields 3 miles (4.8 km) away near Old Warden. These fields are still there, just past the Jordans cereal mill, and are the FIRST FIELDS IN THE WORLD TO BE PLOUGHED BY TRACTOR.

Daniel Albone died, tragically young, in 1906. So brilliant was his design that modern tractors of today are still largely based on his blueprint. He was also responsible for inventing:

- the first ladies' safety bicycle
- the first practical tandem
- an early version of the motor bicyle (created by attaching a simple motor to one of his bicycles)
- and, for his Ivel motor car, independent spring suspension and electric ignition

Cardington

The World's First Air Disaster

Two vast green sheds, looming over the fields of Cardington village, stand as an eerie memorial to the WORLD'S FIRST AIR DISASTER. From this spot, the mighty R101 departed, on a blustery October morning in 1930, to meet a fiery end on a hillside in France.

In the 1920s, airships were considered to be the transport of the future. Comfortable, safe and twice as fast as steamships, they appeared to offer a new and efficient way of linking the Mother Country to her far-flung Empire – India in six days, Canada in three, Australia in ten. The technology was still experimental, but the project was rushed along. LORD THOMSON, the Air Minister, was keen to make a grand arrival on the R101 at the first Imperial Conference, to be held in India in October 1930.

At 6.30 am on 4 October 1930, the R101 slipped her moorings and set off for India. Three thousand people watched her leave from Cardington, with thousands more waving their encouragement as she passed over

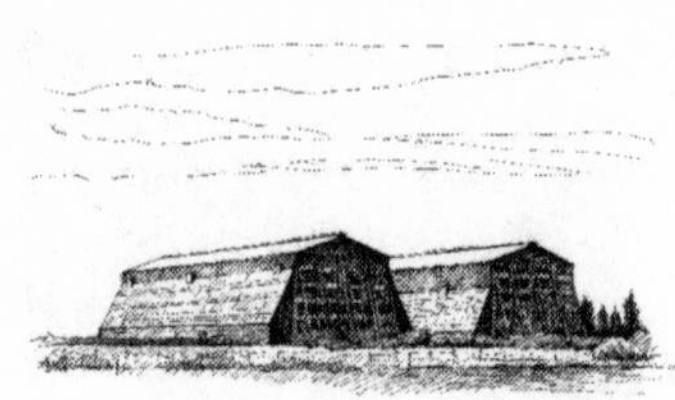

When it was built, the R101 was the biggest vessel in the world and the shed in which it was built the largest building in Britain. That same shed is now the largest enclosed laboratory in the world. The other shed is used to build small airships used by the police and in film work.

southern England. On board there were 54 passengers, including Lord Thomson. At 1.45 am the next day, from just north of Beauvais, and with the weather suddenly deteriorating, she sent out a call enquiring as to her whereabouts – the last thing ever heard from the doomed ship. The storm brought her down and she hit the hillside in a sheet of flame. There were only eight survivors, two of whom died shortly afterwards.

No one really knows why the R101 crashed. The weather became far worse than expected, the payload was heavier than recommended, and neither the crew nor the ship had been tested in adverse conditions. Somehow, the pride of the Empire had ended up as a pile of twisted and scorched girders in a French field. The country was stunned. The 48 dead lay in state at Westminster Hall and there was a memorial service held in St Paul's Cathedral attended by the Prince of Wales. All the victims were buried together in one grave, beneath a fine monument in the churchyard across the road from St Mary's church. In the church hangs the flag that flew proudly from the R101 and was recovered from the flames.

Twinwood

End of the line for the Chattanooga Choo Choo?

Was this eerie, barren airfield, on windswept flats above Bedford, the last place on earth that America's greatest band leader ever saw?

On 15 December 1944, GLENN MILLER (1904–44) boarded a Norseman transport plane at Twinwood airfield to fly to Paris, where his band was booked to perform for American troops. He flew off into the mist and was never seen again. No wreckage was ever found, nor was his body. Official records show that no planes took off that day, due to the foggy conditions. But Miller, who was a nervous flyer, apparently did take off, unofficially, uncharted and in appalling weather. Why? Was he on a secret mission? No-one knows.

However he died, Glenn Miller left a legacy of great music and the long-abandoned control tower at Twinwood has been restored to its original wartime appearance and turned into a museum dedicated to his memory. It is a haunting place and, just occasionally, a melancholy saxophone can be heard and the muffled beat of an old plane rising painfully into the sky . . .

Dunstable Priory was also the scene of the trial and divorce of Catherine of Aragon. It was here that Archbishop Thomas Cranmer pronounced the Queen's marriage to Henry VIII illegal and the document he issued to record this was the last ever to describe the Primate of England as an official of the Church of Rome.

Dunstable

Well Spring of the English Theatre

Standing at the crossroads of the Icknield Way and Watling Street, the ancient town of Dunstable is the unlikely BIRTHPLACE OF ENGLISH THEATRE. Here, in the 12th century, GEOFFREY DE GORHAM wrote and directed the FIRST PLAY EVER SEEN IN ENGLAND.

While he was waiting to become Prior of St Albans, de Gorham established a school in Dunstable, where he was living. The town possessed a large colony of weavers and he decided to compose a play as a way of teaching his pupils about St Catherine, the patron saint of weavers. For costumes, he used the robes of the choristers of St Albans Abbey and, for a stage, he used the cloisters of Dunstable Priory.

The play proved such a success that others copied his example and put on the first MYSTERY PLAYS, which tell stories from the Bible, and are still performed today in places such as Chester. Originally staged in churches, they became so popular that they spilled out on to the streets and, eventually, non-religious themes were introduced. Thus was sown the seeds of a tradition that grew into arguably the greatest theatre in the world – the theatre of Shakespeare and Dryden, Coward, Pinter, Stoppard and Ayckbourn.

Well, I never knew this
ABOUT
BEDFORDSHIRE

SIR JOSEPH PAXTON (1801–65), designer of the CRYSTAL PALACE, was born in MILTON BRYAN near Woburn. His first job was as gardener at the next door estate of BATTLESDEN PARK. The lake he created there can still be seen, as can the avenue of trees he planted to mark his walk to work.

MARGARET BEAUFORT (1443–1509), matriarch of all European royalty, was born in BLETSOE, north of Bedford. As mother to Henry VII, she was the forebear of every monarch in Europe, and direct ancestor of our own Prince William. Educated and self-confident, she was perhaps the first modern English woman.

JOHN BUNYAN (1628–88), author of the religious best-seller *The Pilgrim's Progress*, published in 1678, was born in the quaint village of ELSTOW, a tiny gem set amongst the industrial litter south of Bedford. Bunyan used many Bedfordshire landmarks in his novel, including a wonderfully boggy patch of weeds by the church at STEVINGTON – the SLOUGH OF DESPOND.

BERKSHIRE

COUNTY TOWN: READING

'Berkshire is like a tattered old shoe, kicking out eastwards'

Newbury Cloth Hall, a fine legacy from the days when Newbury was at the centre of England's wool trade.

Reading

Hidden Depths

Reading became the county town of Berkshire in 1867, displacing the former capital, Abingdon. On the surface this might have appeared a bad move for Berkshire as Abingdon is a town of ancient beauty while Reading is not. But there is more to Reading than meets the eye.

KING HENRY I founded Reading Abbey in 1121 and presented it with the Hand of St James, which ensured the abbey grew rich as a centre of pilgrimage. Henry is buried before the High Altar, reputedly in a silver coffin, the site marked with a plaque.

Nearby lies his daughter, the EMPRESS MAUD. And JOHN OF GAUNT was married here in 1359, setting off 14 days of celebrations.

In 1240, a monk from Reading Abbey, JOHN OF FORNSETE, who originally came from Norfolk, wrote down the music for a song called 'Sumer is icumen in'. This is the EARLIEST RECORDED ENGLISH SONG and there is a memorial plaque on the wall of the Chapter House which records the tune. The original manuscript is in the British Library.

It is possible to wander among the ruins of this once powerful abbey, although only the inner gateway remains intact. JANE AUSTEN attended the Abbey School here. In FORBURY GARDENS next door, stands the WORLD'S LARGEST LION, a memorial to the Afghan Wars of the 19th century.

In the 18th century, HUNTLEY & PALMERS set up what became the BIGGEST BISCUIT FACTORY IN THE WORLD, making biscuits that were sent across the globe. Tins of Huntley & Palmers Reading biscuits were found in Scott of the Antarctic's hut on Ross Island, where they still await his return. In 1975, just before the factory was closed, the bar scenes in *Bugsy Malone*, starring Jodie Foster, were filmed there. There is nothing left now, except for the recreation block beside the canal.

In 1892, OSCAR WILDE, a friend of the Palmers, visited the factory and, three years later, returned to serve two years in the prison next door, which was known to the inmates as the 'biscuit factory' because of its proximity to the real thing. This experience inspired *The Ballad of Reading Gaol*.

Bear Wood House

Sign of The Times

BEAR WOOD HOUSE, near Wokingham, was built in 1865 by the WALTER family, founders and owners of *The Times* newspaper. *The Times* was started by JOHN WALTER, a coal merchant and Lloyds underwriter, who began with a daily advertising sheet called the *Daily Universal Register*, which was first published on 1 January 1785. Walter was happy to negotiate secret deals to publish stories favourable to the government and this helped increase profits so that, in 1788, he was able to expand the paper to appeal to a larger audience. He renamed it *The*

Times, began to publish gossip about members of London society, and was sent to prison for two years for writing about the Prince of Wales.

He handed over a flourishing paper to his son, JOHN WALTER II, in 1803. This Walter introduced steam-powered printing and was soon selling 7,000 copies a day. He wanted to produce a paper free from government influence and, as a result, began to employ independent reporters who gathered their own stories. *The Times* was hugely influential in its support of the GREAT REFORM ACT of 1832, the first major shift of power away from the land-owning aristocracy.

In 1816, John Walter II bought 3,000 acres at BEAR WOOD, and laid out the grounds and a fishing lake. In 1822, he built a small classical villa in the park, with a village at the gates, adding a church across the road in 1846.

JOHN WALTER III further enhanced the reputation of *The Times* when he took it over in 1847 by employing the finest writers and reporters of the day, such as W.H. RUSSELL, whose dispatches from the CRIMEAN WAR were instrumental in getting FLORENCE NIGHTINGALE sent out to the front. He also invented the WALTER PRESS, the first machine to print newspapers at high speed from a continuous roll.

Bear Wood House was rebuilt by John Walter III in 1865 and his extravagance in constructing the monstrous Victorian pile almost drained the profits of *The Times*, even though it was now selling 65,000 copies a day, the LARGEST NEWSPAPER CIRCULATION IN THE WORLD. Walter III also rebuilt *The Times* offices in Printing House Square at Blackfriars, with bricks and wood from the Bear Wood estate.

In 1870, JOHN WALTER IV drowned in the lake at Bear Wood while trying in vain to rescue his brother and a cousin, who had fallen through the ice while skating. This tragedy, allied to falling profits, forced the sale of *The Times* to LORD NORTHCLIFFE.

The family still live in the grounds, although the house itself is now a boarding school, which can be visited during school holidays or by appointment. The lake is still there, and the

Walters are buried beneath four great trees outside the church. One famous descendant is the actress, HARRIET WALTER.

The Sounding Arch

The Widest, Flattest Brick Arch in the World

Built in 1838 by ISAMBARD KINGDOM BRUNEL, this bridge, constructed for the GREAT WESTERN RAILWAY over the River Thames at MAIDENHEAD, has the WIDEST AND FLATTEST BRICK ARCH IN THE WORLD, with a span of 128 ft (39 m) that rises by only 24 ft (7.3 m). Few believed it would take the weight of a locomotive, but it proved so strong that an exact copy was built when the bridge was extended westwards. The original is known as the Sounding Arch because of the perfect echo that can be experienced when standing on the pathway beneath. The bridge was the subject of a painting by J.M.W. TURNER.

Basildon

The Father of Mechanised Farming

JETHRO TULL was born in 1674 in the Thames-side village of Basildon, now called Lower Basildon (not to be confused with Basildon in Essex). The son of a Berkshire farmer, Tull studied law, but was forced to help out on his father's farm, HOWBERRY FARM, at Crowmarsh, near Wallingford, because of financial difficulties. Crops were sown by hand in those days, which was slow and inefficient, and Jethro Tull hated doing manual work. He also disliked paying wages, so he set about devising a machine that would do the work instead.

In 1701, using pieces of an old pipe organ that he had dismantled, Tull invented the FIRST KNOWN SEED DRILL, a rotating cylinder with grooves cut into it to allow seed to fall from the hopper into a funnel. This directed the seed into a furrow cut by a plough in front of the machine, which was then covered over with soil by a harrow fixed to the back. The whole thing was pulled by a horse and could sow up to three rows at once. The fields where he experimented with this are unfortunately now built over.

> *The pop group Jethro Tull (the first act on the Chrysalis record label) got their name when their manager, Terry Ellis, spotted a copy of* Horse Hoeing Husbandry *in someone's office.*

In 1709, Jethro Tull moved to PROSPEROUS FARM near Hungerford,

where he continued to perfect his design. He also came up with a horse-drawn hoe for clearing weeds and loosening the roots of the crops, which enabled them to absorb water more efficiently. In 1731, he published his theories on farming and plant nutrition in *The New Horse Hoeing Husbandry* or *An Essay on the Principles of Tillage and Vegetation.*

His ideas formed the basis of modern agriculture, and his inventions pioneered the mechanisation of farming. However, although they have been of immense benefit to the whole world, Jethro Tull's labour-saving devices were such a success that they directly contributed to the mass unemployment problems that plagued England in the 18th century.

Prosperous Farm, where he developed his revolutionary ideas, is still there, just south of Hungerford. Ironically, the farm where mechanised agriculture was born today specialises in dairy products produced on a small scale, using traditional, old-fashioned methods. You can visit the Prosperous Farm shop.

Oakley Court

House of Horror

Oakley Court is an eerie 19th-century Gothic pile built on the banks of the River Thames near Bray, which, during the Second World War, served as the HEADQUARTERS OF THE FRENCH RESISTANCE.

Oakley Court

In 1951, HAMMER FILMS moved into the Bray Studios next door, and Oakley Court became the original HAMMER HOUSE OF HORROR, DRACULA'S CASTLE and even ST TRINIAN'S SCHOOL. It is now a luxury hotel.

In the 18th century, DOWN PLACE, which became Bray Studios, was the home of the KIT-KAT CLUB, a group of Whig politicians and literary folk who got together to uphold the Glorious Revolution and the Protestant succession. They originally met at Christopher Kat's tavern in the City, which was famous for its mutton pies known as Kit-Kats. Influential members included the Dukes of Somerset and Newcastle, Sir Robert Walpole, Joseph Addison and Godfrey Kneller. The club also gave its name to one of the UK's best-selling chocolate bars.

BRAY is famous for the pragmatic VICAR OF BRAY, Simon Alleyn, who was twice a Catholic and twice a Protestant during the reigns of Henry VIII and his three children:

whatsoever King shall reign
I'll remain the Vicar of Bray, Sir!

Newbury

Bluestockings

To the south of Newbury, stands SANDLEFORD PRIORY, home of the BLUESTOCKINGS. The remains of a 13th-century Augustine priory were incorporated into a Gothic country house by James Wyatt in 1780 for the rich hostess ELIZABETH MONTAGU (1720–1800). She held literary evenings here for her more serious-minded lady friends where well-known thinkers and writers were invited to talk and entertain the ladies with discussions on the subjects of the day.

One such gentleman was poet and publisher DR BENJAMIN STILLINGFLEET, who became a favourite, due to his wit and humour. Being too poor to afford formal black silk stockings, he was allowed to attend in his informal day wear – blue worsted stockings. ADMIRAL BOSCAWEN, whose wife was a keen supporter of these evenings, referred to them derisively as 'those blue

Sandleford Priory

stocking sessions', and the term was soon applied to the ladies who attended. Today, the term is used to describe a bookish, intellectual woman. Appropriately enough, Sandleford Priory is now a girls' school.

Well, I never knew this ABOUT BERKSHIRE

In the churchyard of the handsome village of SUTTON COURTENAY, beside the River Thames, is the grave of Liberal Prime Minister HERBERT HENRY ASQUITH (1852–1928), who lived nearby in a house called THE WHARF. His administration was confronted with the suffragettes, Irish Home Rule and the First World War, during which he was ousted by Lloyd George. In 1925, he became Earl of Oxford and Asquith, a grand title which led Lord Salisbury to declare, 'It is like a suburban villa calling itself Versailles.' His wife Margot, who is buried with him, was herself a celebrated wit. When asked what she thought about Lloyd George she remarked, 'He could not see a belt without hitting below it.'

Not far away lies GEORGE ORWELL (1903–50), author of *Animal Farm* and *1984*, who is buried under his real name Eric Arthur Blair.

ABINGDON was the home of MG CARS, the initals standing for MORRIS GARAGES, who were the Oxford distributors for Morris cars. The first MGs were modified sporting versions of the standard Morris Cowley but they proved so popular that the newly formed MG Car Company moved to its own factory at Abingdon in 1929, building up a loyal following until the factory closed in 1980.

In 1927, MG had built a one-off prototype saloon with a fabric body of gold and stippled black which was kept as a run-around when the company moved to Abingdon. The local people nicknamed it 'Old Speckled Un', which over time became 'Old Speckled Hen'. In 1979, when the Abingdon brewery of MORLAND'S were asked to brew a special beer to celebrate the the Golden Jubilee of the MG factory, they named the new ale 'Old Speckled Hen'.

At APPLEFORD, by Didcot, near a big elm in the churchyard, lies JOHN FAULKNER, the WORLD'S OLDEST JOCKEY. He rode his first winner at the age of eight in the year that Queen Victoria came to the throne (1837) and rode in his last race when he was 74. He lived here at Appleford, fathered 32 children and died in 1933, aged 104.

Standing alone, back from the road, on an isolated plateau of the Vale of the White Horse, is the atmospheric old moated LYFORD GRANGE, half hidden behind trees in a hollow. Here, on a fateful night in 1581, the Jesuit martyr EDMUND CAMPION was betrayed and captured.

Buckinghamshire

County Town: Aylesbury

'Now fades the glimmering landscape on the sight,
And all the air a solemn stillness holds'

Thomas Gray, *Elegy written in a Country Church-Yard*

Mayflower Barn, built with the timbers from the Pilgrim Father's ship the Mayflower

Colnbrook

Apples and Ghosts

Colnbrook is a rather overlooked, old-world village squeezed between the M25 and M4, right next to Heathrow Airport. In this unlikely setting, in 1825, Richard Cox, a brewer, grew the first Cox's Orange Pippin. In *The Apples of England*, it is described thus: 'all characters so admirably blended and balanced as to please the palate and nose as no other apple can do . . . the greatest apple of this age.' Today, many experts still regard the Cox's Orange Pippin as the best fresh eating apple.

Colnbrook is also the proud possessor of the Ostrich, the third oldest pub in England, which just happens to be the most haunted

PUB IN ENGLAND, too. King John stayed here on his way to sign *Magna Carta* in 1215, as, later, did Queen Elizabeth I and also, reputedly, Dick Turpin. None of them, however, suffered the awful fate of some 60 guests of the 17th-century landlord THOMAS JARMAN. Jarman designed an ingenious bed – a replica of which can be seen at the Ostrich Inn today – which was nailed to a trap door above the kitchen. He would show prosperous single guests into the comfortable-looking Blue Room where the bed was and, when they were asleep, he and his wife would unbolt the trap door, so that the bed tipped up and the unfortunate fellow was plunged into a vat of boiling water set up on the stove below. The guest's body was then thrown into a nearby river and his horse and belongings sold to unsuspecting passers-by. The Jarmans were finally caught when somebody recognised a horse belonging to one of their victims, Thomas Cole, which had escaped and was found drinking in the brook running through the village. Thereafter the brook was known as Colnbrook – the brook where Thomas Cole's horse was found. The ghosts of the Jarmans' victims still haunt the pub's premises today.

Stoke Poges

Goldfinger and Ploughmans

The Curfew tolls the knell of parting day,
The lowing herd winds slowly o'er the lea,
The ploughman homeward plods his weary way,
And leaves the world to darkness and to me

It was in the country churchyard of Stoke Poges, while sitting in the shade of a yew tree, that THOMAS GRAY (1716–1771) wrote these immortal words. Gray was the only survivor of 12 children. An inheritance from his father enabled him to live at Cambridge, studying law, and to buy his mother a house in Stoke Poges, where he spent his holidays writing poetry. As a result of his Elegy, Gray's fame spread across the world. GENERAL WOLFE took a copy of it with him to Canada and was heard to say before scaling the

Stoke Poges Golf Club

Heights of Abraham, 'I would rather be the author of that poem than take Quebec!'

Despite being sandwiched between two motorways and close to Slough, the atmosphere evoked by Gray's Elegy – 'where melancholy marked him for her own' – can still be experienced in this tranquil spot. Gray is buried beside his mother in a brick tomb outside the east end of the church. A short walk away is a huge sarcophagus erected in Gray's memory by JOHN PENN, the grandson of the founder of Pennsylvania, William Penn, in 1799.

John Penn also built the vast white Palladian country house that can be seen across the wall of the churchyard. It is now the clubhouse of Stoke Poges Golf Club and is familiar to all JAMES BOND fans as the clubhouse where James Bond met Auric GOLDFINGER. It is easy to imagine Goldfinger's yellow Rolls-Royce sitting at the entrance, and you can still see the statues, one of which was beheaded by ODDJOB's bowler hat. Close by is the 18th green where Bond won the match against Goldfinger.

Stoke Poges is a popular location for many Bond film scenes because of its proximity to Pinewood Studios, where the Bond films are still made today. JAMES BOND'S WIFE TRACY, for example, is buried in the churchyard at Stoke Poges and we see Bond visiting her grave at the start of *For Your Eyes Only*.

Pinewood

Biggest Sound Stage in the World

Pinewood Studios is BRITAIN'S FOREMOST FILM AND TELEVISION STUDIOS. At its heart lies a Victorian mansion called HEATHERDEN HALL, once a secret retreat for politicians and businessmen. In 1934, the estate was bought by CHARLES BOOT, who joined with J. ARTHUR RANK to build 'THE BEST STUDIOS IN THE WORLD'. They named it Pinewood (which neatly mirrors Hollywood) after the huge pine trees in the garden. By the end of the 1930s, Pinewood was PRODUCING MORE FILMS THAN ANY OTHER STUDIO IN THE WORLD.

The 007 sound stage, where the Bond films are made, is the BIGGEST SOUND STAGE IN THE WORLD, and Pinewood also boasts the BIGGEST EXTERIOR TANK IN EUROPE.

Film locations

In 2004, Cliveden became Lady Penelope's house in the Thunderbirds *movie.*

The scene from Four Weddings and a Funeral *where Andie MacDowell has to hide from the wedding guest who thinks he's 'in with a chance' with that 'damn fine filly' (described in the credits as 'the bore in the inn') was filmed at the Crown Hotel in Amersham.*

The village of Turville, nestling in the Chilterns, is in fact Dibley, from the TV series The Vicar of Dibley.

The windmill high above on the hill was the home of Caractacus Potts, the dotty inventor in Chitty Chitty Bang Bang.

Beaconsfield

Toytown

There are two Beaconsfields, Old and New. The handsome coaching town of Old Beaconsfield is much the more enticing, although New Beaconsfield is home to Bekonscot, the OLDEST MODEL VILLAGE IN THE WORLD. This was the inspiration for NODDY'S TOYTOWN – ENID BLYTON lived in Beaconsfield, in a house built of red brick with black and white half-timbered gables, called GREEN HEDGES. There is a model of it at Bekonscot.

EDMUND BURKE (1729–97), who is buried inside Beaconsfield church, is regarded as one of the greatest political thinkers of all time. His basic belief was that no one individual or institution should have too much power for, as he put it, 'the greater the power, the more dangerous the abuse'. Many of his principles were adopted in the AMERICAN CONSTITUTION:

Bad laws are the worst sort of tyranny.

All that is neccessary for the forces of evil to win in the world is for enough good men to do nothing.

G.K. CHESTERTON (1874–1936) lived in Beaconsfield and is buried in the Roman Catholic cemetery there. He was a prolific writer, renowned for his sense of humour and distinctive look. Standing 6 ft 4 in (1.93 m) and weighing in at over 20 stone (127 kg), he wore a cape and hat, brandished a swordstick and chewed a cigar. He was notoriously absent-minded and would send telegrams to his wife posing such questions as, 'Am at Market Harborough. Where should I be?' His most famous creation was FATHER BROWN, a shabbily dressed priest with an umbrella who possessed a remarkable insight into the evils of the human mind.

TERRY PRATCHETT, Britain's leading science fiction and fantasy writer, was born in Beaconsfield in 1945.

Newport Pagnell

Now Pay Attention 007

James Bond and Buckinghamshire come together again at Newport Pagnell, near Milton Keynes. Here they build the cars that will forever be associated with James Bond, ASTON MARTINS.

Before *Goldfinger*, Aston Martin was a small specialist company known only to a few wealthy enthusiasts. After *Goldfinger*, the Aston Martin DB5 was the BEST-KNOWN AND MOST SOUGHT-AFTER CAR IN THE WORLD. And yet Aston Martin had at first been reluctant film participants. The film's producer, Cubby Broccoli, wanted a car that epitomised English class, discreetly powerful, unruffled, hand-made, rare and refined, like Bond himself. The DB4 was perfect, but Aston Martin, already struggling to build six cars a week, couldn't spare one. Somewhat hesitantly, they lent Broccoli two DB5s, and the rest is history.

Now owned by Ford, Aston Martin still build cars by hand at Newport Pagnell. In order to visit their factory in Tickford Street, you must cross TICKFORD BRIDGE – built in 1810, it is the OLDEST IRON BRIDGE IN BRITAIN STILL CARRYING HEAVY TRAFFIC.

Hambleden

First Paper Boy and Last Saint

Hambleden is an almost perfect village, nestling in a tree-embowered Chiltern valley, with neat timbered cottages clustered round an old church and a grand manor house. The first lords of the manor were the CLARE family, whose name is the FIRST TO APPEAR ON MAGNA CARTA. The present owner of the manor house, and most of the village, is VISCOUNT HAMBLEDEN, descendant of W. H. SMITH, the newsagent. In 2003, the estate was put up for sale for £16.5 million, but was subsequently taken off the market.

In 1828, WILLIAM HENRY SMITH (1792–1865) took over a small newsagents on the Strand, London, from his father. He then set about creating the best newspaper delivery service in Britain, using fast horses and carts to collect papers from Fleet Street and take them to stage-coach stops. His son, also WILLIAM HENRY SMITH (1825–91), opened the FIRST RAILWAY BOOKSTALL at Euston Station in 1848. Soon W. H. Smith began opening branches in town centres served by railways. They went on to become the BIGGEST AND MOST FAMOUS NEWSAGENT IN THE WORLD. In 1868, William Jnr the second W. H. Smith, who had become an MP and Leader of the Commons, bought the Greenlands estate, which included much of Hambleden, and he is buried in the churchyard. His widow was created Viscountess Hambleden in his honour. His son bought Hambleden Manor in 1923.

Hambleden is the birthplace of two notable characters, Thomas de Cantelupe (1218–82), the last Englishman to be canonised before the Reformation, and Lord Cardigan (1797–1868), who led the Charge of the Light Brigade in 1854 and was born in the present manor house. The knitted woollen sweater he wore against the cold in the Crimea is named after him.

Well, I never knew this ABOUT BUCKINGHAMSHIRE

Standing almost side by side on the A5 Watling Street in Stony-Stratford are the Cock and the Bull, inns of ancient repute. In the 18th century, coaches would stop off here on their way from London to the north west and many a traveller's tale would be embellished as it flew between the two establishments, fuelled by good ale and a good audience. Hence, an unlikely story became a Cock and Bull story.

Off Station Road in Amersham on the Hill is High and Over, a white house of concrete and steel built in 1929. This is the first house in Britain to be designed using the 'functionalist' concept of Swiss architect Le Corbusier.

Ruth Ellis (1926–55), the last woman to be hanged in Britain, lies at St Mary's church, Amersham.

Chesham was home to the Mad Hatter from *Alice in Wonderland.* Roger Crabbe suffered dreadful head injuries during the English Civil War and retired to Chesham to open a hat shop, where he lived on turnips and dressed in sackcloth.

Cliveden

There has been a house at CLIVEDEN, with its unmatched views of the River Thames, since 1666, when the Duke of Buckingham built a hunting lodge here. It was at Cliveden, in 1740, while Frederick, Prince of Wales, was living here, that the *Last Night of the Proms'* favourite, RULE BRITANNIA, was performed for the first time. It was written by a Scottish poet named James Thomson as part of a masque, and put to music by Thomas Arne.

In 1961 Secretary of State for War, John Profumo, met a show girl called Christine Keeler by the swimming pool at Cliveden and started a brief affair with her. It turned out she was also sleeping with an attaché at the Soviet Embassy and, in June 1963, Profumo resigned, having misled the House of Commons by claiming that there was 'no impropriety whatever' in his relationship with her.

DORNEY COURT, a beautiful Tudor manor house near Eton, passed by marriage to the PALMER family in 1537 and has remained in the family ever since. BARBARA VILLIERS, favourite mistress of Charles II, was the wife of Roger Palmer of Dorney. The FIRST PINEAPPLE GROWN IN ENGLAND was produced here in 1665 and given to Charles II.

MARY SHELLEY (1797–1851), wife of the poet Percy Bysshe Shelley, wrote *Frankenstein* while living in West Street, MARLOW. The Gothic-style cottage in which they lived is still there and marked by a plaque. The suspension bridge across the Thames at Marlow was built in 1831 by WILLIAM CLARK as a prototype for his famous bridge over the Danube linking Buda and Pest in Hungary.

Cambridgeshire

County Town: Cambridge

'And Cambridgeshire of all England
The Shire for Men who Understand'

Rupert Brooke

North Brink, Wisbech. Wisbech was home to England's first canning factory.

Cambridge

Let the Bells Ring Out

Hobson Street in Cambridge recalls a 16th-century benefactor and Mayor of Cambridge, Thomas Hobson, who brought the first 'fresh' water to the city along Hobson's Conduit, which still runs alongside Trumpington Street. Hobson was also a 'carrier', and would hire out his horses in strict rotation – a customer could choose from any horse, provided it was the one standing next to the stable door. This became known as Hobson's Choice. (A notable advocate of this principle was Henry Ford, who told his customers that they could have their Model T in any colour, provided it was black.)

The Great Court at Trinity College is the largest enclosed courtyard in Britain, measuring 340 ft (104 m) by 288 ft (88 m). A famous tradition is for the undergraduates to try and run around the Great Court in the time it takes the big clock on the north side to strike twelve. This feat was immortalised in the film *Chariots of Fire*, although the scene was actually filmed at Eton, as the Trinity authorities refused the

producers permission to film on the premises.

England's only non-royal head of state, OLIVER CROMWELL rests in an unmarked grave near the doors to the chapel of SIDNEY SUSSEX COLLEGE. At the Restoration, Cromwell's body was disinterred from Westminster Abbey and his head was stuck on a pole outside Westminster Hall. It stayed there for 20 years until it was blown down in a storm and collected by a passer-by, as a rather freakish souvenir. It then passed through a number of hands until, in 1960, it was left to Sidney Sussex College by Canon Wilkinson, in whose possession it had ended up.

The oldest building in Cambridge is ST BENEDICT'S church. The bells hanging in its Saxon tower were the FIRST IN THE WORLD TO BE USED FOR CHANGE RINGING, invented here in about 1650 by the patron saint of bell ringers, FABIAN STEDMAN. He was both clerk of the parish and a printer, who printed his changes on paper and taught them to the bell ringers of St Benedict's. Change ringing is the playing of a melody or tune by a team of bellringers, each in charge of their own bell, which is free to rotate on a bell wheel. This is as opposed to a carrillon or chime, such as Big Ben, where a number of fixed bells of different note are struck in order.

Grantchester

Honey Still for Tea

I only know that you may lie
day long and watch the Cambridge sky,
and, flower lulled in sleepy grass,
hear the cool lapse of hours pass,
until the centuries blend and blur
in Grantchester

Thanks to these evocative lines, written by RUPERT BROOKE (1887–1915), Grantchester, near Cambridge, has gained immortality as the perfect English village, where gentlefolk take tea on warm, drowsy, summer afternoons and the vicar plays croquet on the lawn. Indeed, it was at the OLD VICARAGE in

Grantchester that Rupert Brooke came to live in 1909, while studying at Cambridge University, and his happy memories of life here inspired his famous poem which concludes

In Grantchester, in Grantchester . . .
. . . stands the Church clock at ten to three?
And is there honey still for tea?

Rupert Brooke also wrote:

If I should die, think only this of me,
That there's some corner of a foreign field
That is forever England.

In fact, he did die abroad, in the Dardanelles in 1915, at the age of 28, defending, like so many other young men of his generation, the idyllic England he portrayed in his poetry, which only goes to make his wistful recollections more poignant.

Grantchester today is by no means idyllic, but is still a tranquil spot and the Old Vicarage has maintained at least some of its literary connections – the novelist JEFFREY ARCHER lives there.

Ely

Island of Adventure

The Isle of Ely is named after the eels found in the waters that once surrounded this small hill rising 68 ft (21 m) high above the Fens. The town of Ely is dominated by the vast cathedral, which was begun in the 11th century, although its history dates back far before that time.

In 673, Etheldreda, wife of King Egfrid, and known as St Awdrey, founded a monastery on the Isle of Ely, which had been left to her by a previous husband. The annual fair held at Ely, called St Awdrey's Fair, was notorious for cheap trinkets and jewellery and items bought there became known as St Awdrey or, as we say today, TAWDRY. The monastery was finally sacked by the Danes in 870.

The crowning glory of Ely Cathedral is the OCTAGON, the ONLY GOTHIC DOME IN THE WORLD. An incomparable feat of medieval engineering, there is nothing else like it anywhere. It was built by ALAN DE WALSINGHAM in the early 14th century, to replace the Norman central tower which had collapsed in 1322. Walsingham wanted to utilise

the whole space that had been opened up, but he realised that the span of 74 ft (23 m) was too wide for a stone vault. So he scoured England until he found, at Chicksands in Bedfordshire, eight oak trees large enough to make the massive pillars necessary to support 200 tons of timber, glass and lead. Light and colourful, the whole edifice seems to float in space.

Foul Anchor

Lost Treasure

On 11 October 1216, King John (1167–1216) set out from (King's) LYNN in Norfolk, at the head of a baggage train containing the Crown Jewels, household treasures and the booty he had plundered from the rich merchants and farming folk of East Anglia. In a hurry to head north, his party attempted to cross the broad estuary known as the WELLSTREAM without a guide. In the days before the Fens were drained, this stretch of water and mudflats, where the river meets the sea, was a maelstrom of whirlpools and strong, shifting currents. The horsecarts, heavy with treasure, sank into the mud, becoming completely stuck. The tide swept in and the waters closed above them. The king himself had to swim, barely escaping with his life, and died a week later, at NEWARK, possibly from the shock of the ordeal and the loss of all his possessions.

John's son, Henry III, was later crowned with a gold circlet, instead of the magnificent bejeweled crown his father had worn – which continues to lie somewhere under the mud at FOUL ANCHOR, along with the rest of the treasure. The area still attracts bounty hunters and has a melancholy air. Just occasionally, the plaintive sobs and whinnies of drowning men and horses can be heard on the chill sea winds, mingling with the cries of the scavenging gulls.

Sawston

Refuge for a Queen

SAWSTON HALL found itself at the centre of royal intrigue in 1553. MARY TUDOR, daughter of Henry VIII, was riding to London to see her

brother, Edward VI, unaware that the king had died and that Lady Jane Grey had been proclaimed Queen by the Duke of Northumberland. A secret message reached Mary that she was riding into a trap set by the Duke, who planned to imprison her, so she changed course and rode hard for Sawston Hall, which was owned by a Catholic supporter named HUDDLESTON. Here she spent the night.

The Duke found out where she was and sent a force to capture her the next morning, but Mary escaped dressed as a kitchen maid. Looking back at Sawston from the GOG MAGOG hills, Mary saw the house in flames, set alight by the enraged soldiers. 'Let it burn,' she said, 'I will build Huddleston a better house.' And she did. When she became Queen, Sawston Hall was rebuilt at Mary's expense, using blocks of clunch (a hard chalk found in East Anglia) from the ruins of Cambridge Castle.

Always a refuge for persecuted Catholics, Sawston Hall contains a priest hole built by NICOLAS OWEN (*see* Priest Holes, Worcestershire) hidden in the stairs of the circular tower. The Huddlestons remained owners until the 1970s. The hall is now a language school.

Well, I never knew this ABOUT CAMBRIDGESHIRE

TRUMPINGTON CHURCH contains the SECOND OLDEST BRASS IN BRITAIN (*see* Stoke D'Abernon, Surrey). It dates from 1289 and is dedicated to Sir Roger de Trumpington, who went on a Crusade with Edward I.

Just east of Parson Drove, near Wisbech, is WOAD MILLS FARM, which stands on the site of the LAST WOAD MILL IN ENGLAND (the remains of which are in Wisbech Museum). It closed down in 1910. Woad was the only source of blue dye for colouring clothes that could be grown in northern climes and was famously used to paint the bodies of ancient Britons to make their appearance more fearsome. The bright yellow flowered plant was grown in abundance here as a field crop. Using a horse-powered mill, the leaves were chopped into a paste, which was then dried into a powder. As it became easier to import indigo, which gives a brighter and stronger blue dye, from southern Asia, the use of woad gradually died out.

The BRIDGE INN at WILBURTON is the LOWEST-LYING PUB IN BRITAIN – it stands just 8 ft (2.4 m) above sea level.

The windmill at BOURN, west of Cambridge, is the OLDEST SURVIVING WINDMILL IN BRITAIN. It was first recorded in 1636, but may be older. It is a post mill, and the whole structure revolves around a central post so that the sails can be faced into the wind (*see* Outwood, Surrey). The mill is currently being restored.

The CAVENDISH LABORATORY in Cambridge is named after the 18th-century scientist HENRY CAVENDISH, who DISCOVERED HYDROGEN and MEASURED THE WEIGHT OF THE EARTH. Here, in 1897, PROFESSOR J.J. THOMPSON DISCOVERED THE ELECTRON – the particle that makes up the atom, which was previously believed to be the smallest structure known. Here also, in 1952, the STRUCTURE OF DNA WAS DISCOVERED by JAMES WATSON and FRANCIS CRICK. This discovery has led to, amongst other things, forensic testing (pioneered at the O.J. Simpson trial in America) and cloning (Dolly the Sheep).

The last private owner of the LARGEST HOUSE IN CAMBRIDGESHIRE, WIMPOLE HALL, was Rudyard Kipling's eccentric daughter Elsie Bambridge. She was fiercely protective of her privacy and when a carload of impertinent sightseers spread their picnic on her lawns by the grand drive, she traced their registration number and gained revenge by having her chauffeur drive her to their suburban home, where she enjoyed her own picnic in their front garden!

CHESHIRE

COUNTY TOWN: CHESTER

'Chester pleases my fancy more than any town I ever saw'

JAMES BOSWELL in a letter to DR JOHNSON

Chester Rows

Chester

Camping on the Dee

Chester's racecourse, THE ROODEE, or 'Rood Island', lies on the site of the old Roman wharves and is BRITAIN'S OLDEST SPORTING VENUE. Horse races have been run here since 1540, making CHESTER RACES the OLDEST SPORTING EVENT IN BRITAIN STILL HELD AT ITS ORIGINAL SITE.

The charming black and white timbered Chester Rows (illustrated above) are UNIQUE IN ENGLAND and make shopping here a delightfully different experience. The Rows, dating from the 14th century, are made up of two tiers of shops, one tier at street level and one above, set back to create a covered walkway reached by steps from below.

When Chester's GROSVENOR BRIDGE across the Dee opened in 1832, the first person to cross it was 13-year-old PRINCESS VICTORIA. At the time, the bridge had the BIGGEST SPAN OF ANY STONE ARCH IN THE WORLD, 200 ft (61 m) across and 60 ft (18 m) high.

In the OVERLEIGH CEMETERY, near

Grosvenor Bridge, across the river from the Castle, lies EDWARD LANGTRY, alone in his grave, as in life. He was the husband of LILLIE LANGTRY – the 'Jersey Lily', favourite mistress of Edward, Prince of Wales, later Edward VII. In 1897, driven mad by separation from his beautiful wife, Edward Langtry died in Chester Lunatic Asylum. Lillie didn't attend his funeral. She is buried in Jersey.

The Channel 4 teen 'soap' *Hollyoaks* is set in Chester.

Birkenhead

Women and Children First

Not much over 150 years ago, Birkenhead was a tiny hamlet. It is now the BIGGEST TOWN IN CHESHIRE. The transformation began in 1824, when WILLIAM LAIRD set up his shipbuilding company here. CAMMELL LAIRD quickly grew into one of the biggest and busiest shipyards in the world. One ship in particular, named, appropriately enough, after the town, became a byword for heroism.

The *HMS Birkenhead*, launched in 1845, was one of the first iron-hulled warships to be commissioned by the Admiralty. In January 1852, she sailed out of Portsmouth carrying reinforcement troops for the Frontier War in South Africa. There were 638 people on board, including 13 children and 7 women.

The weather was perfect as they reached the Cape of Good Hope but, at 2 am, on the morning of 26 February, just off Danger Point, the *Birkenhead* hit a sunken rock at full speed. The hull was ripped open and many of the troops were drowned as they slept. The surviving soldiers helped to pass the women and children into the three working lifeboats and then set about trying to save the ship. It swiftly became clear that the *Birkenhead* was going to sink and CAPTAIN SALMOND, as he prepared to go down with his ship, advised everyone to jump overboard and make for the boats, with the cry 'Every man for himself!' LIEUTENANT-COLONEL SETON, however, in command of the soldiers, ordered his men to stand fast. He realised that if they all tried to clamber into the lifeboats the lives of the women and children would be endangered. Not a soldier or a sailor cried out or broke ranks as the ship disappeared beneath the waves. Four hundred and forty-five men perished with the *Birkenhead*, including Captain Salmond and Colonel Seton, but not a woman or child was lost. This gallant

precedent inspired the naval protocol that now prevails across the world of 'Women and Children First'.

A tablet at the YMCA Hall in Birkenhead commemorates the inauguration of the first Boy Scout movement here, by Baden Powell in 1908.

Actresses Glenda Jackson (b. 1936) and Patricia Routledge (b. 1929) were born in Birkenhead.

Mobberley

A Mountain Mystery

Mobberley, near Knutsford, is a large and prosperous village full of Cheshire charm and is the birthplace of a true English hero, mountaineer George Mallory. He was born here in 1886, and gained a head for heights by clambering up the church tower as a boy. Mallory was of that breed of adventurers who needed to achieve something that no one else has done. Mount Everest, the highest mountain on earth, remained unconquered, and it called to Mallory. When asked why he wanted to climb Everest, Mallory replied, 'Because it's there.'

Everest had never been explored, lying as it did between Tibet and Nepal, both countries closed to travellers. Mallory gained permission to enter Tibet and, in 1921, he and his team surveyed the mountain for any possible route up. On a second trip, they climbed 27,000 ft (8,230 m) – higher than anyone had been before – and realised that to get to the top they would need oxygen, or what their Sherpas called 'English Air'.

The third attempt was made in 1924. Mallory, as the most experienced and capable climber, was to lead the final assault on the summit and he chose, as his companion, a young man from the Wirral called Sandy Irvine, who knew how to look after the crude oxygen bottles they would need for their survival. On the morning of 6 June, departing with a handshake and a prayer, they set off from the North Col at 23,100 ft (7,041 m), hoping to make it to the top within three days. They had with them a camera, loaned by another member of the team, Howard Somervell, with which to take pictures of each other on the roof of the world.

On 8 June, early in the afternoon, they were spotted from far below by one of their support team, Noel Odell. He saw two black dots on the base of the final summit pyramid, tantalisingly close to their goal. Just then a sudden snow squall swept in and Odell lost sight of them. They were never seen again.

Did they reach the summit, 29 years before Sir Edmund Hillary? Odell believes they did, although there is no direct evidence. In 1933, an ice axe with Irvine's trademark three nicks in it was found at 28,000 ft (8,534 m). In 1975, a Chinese climber reported that he had come across an 'English dead', 750 ft (229 m) directly below where the ice axe was found. Was it Irvine? Several expeditions failed to relocate the corpse. Finally, in May 1999, Mallory's remarkably well-preserved body was found at 27,000 ft (8,230 m) on the North Face. Was this the body of the first man to climb to the top of Mount Everest? If the camera that Somervell had lent them could be found, it could reveal the truth. There is a constant search for it, the greatest treasure hidden on Mount Everest, and one day the mystery may be solved.

There is a beautiful memorial window in the church dedicated to Mobberley's heroic son, 'lost to human sight between earth and heaven', as it says on the inscription. And, in a poignant tribute, Mallory's grandson, George Mallory II, reached the summit of Mount Everest in 1995.

Because salt mines are clean, and have a constant temperature of 14°C, they are useful for storage. During the Second World War, it is believed that the Crown Jewels were kept in Winsford Mine. In 2004, the government gave permission for the mine to become a dump for toxic waste – a plan fiercely opposed by the local inhabitants.

Northwich

Old Salt

Much of Cheshire is built, quite literally, on salt. You can tell by the names – Nantwich, Northwich, Middlewich – 'wich' or 'wych' meaning a saltwater spring. The sea retreated from here millions of years ago, depositing the salt, which has been mined since Roman times. Salt has been used to flavour and preserve food since ancient times and was considered precious enough to be genuinely 'worth its weight in gold'. The word 'salary' comes from the Latin 'sal', meaning salt – part of a soldier's pay was measured in salt rations or 'salarium'.

Modern salt mining began in MARBURY, near Northwich, in 1670, and England became the WORLD'S LARGEST PRODUCER OF SALT, most of it coming from the vast Cheshire mines. The OLD MINE at MARSTON, 360 ft (110 m) deep and covering 35 acres, was big enough for the Tsar of Russia to dine inside with members of the Royal Society in 1844.

ICI (Imperial Chemical Industries), one of the world's leading chemical companies, grew out of the Cheshire salt mines. In 1873, SIR JOHN BRUNNER, a politician and businessman, joined with DR LUDWIG MOND, a pioneering chemist, to form Brunner Mond. Together they bought the 18th-century WINNINGTON HALL, on the River Weaver, and built their first chemical works. They produced soda ash, used for making soap powder, and soon became the WORLD'S LARGEST PRODUCER OF ALKALIS. Winnington Hall is now the ICI staff club.

In 1926, ICI was formed when Brunner Mond merged with three other chemical companies, including Nobel Industries, founded in 1870 in Scotland by ALFRED NOBEL, the INVENTOR OF DYNAMITE and CREATOR OF THE NOBEL PRIZE.

Another legacy of salt mining in Northwich is subsidence. The town is built on pillars of salt holding up the abandoned mines 300 ft (91 m) below and over the years holes have appeared in the ground and buildings have toppled over or sunk. Today there is a serious risk that the whole town centre may disappear altogether and the government has had to agree to pump £30 million into stabilising the area.

The ONLY WORKING SALT MINE LEFT IN BRITAIN is at WINSFORD, three miles south of Northwich. It has been worked since 1844, and from here we get the rock salt used to keep our roads free from frost in the winter. The scale of the site at Winsford is immense. The mine covers 5 sq miles (12.9 sq km), is over 500 ft (152 m) deep and contains more than 100 miles (161 km) of underground roads, running through tunnels tall enough for a double-decker bus and lit by street lights. This is just as well, as they have to accommodate the biggest underground digger in the world which gouges out 20 tons of salt in one scoop.

Anderton

Hold the Lift

Across the River Weaver from the ICI works at Winnington stands a magnificent monument to Victorian ingenuity, the ANDERTON BOAT LIFT, the FIRST BOAT LIFT IN THE WORLD and the only one working in Britain today. Known as the 'Cathedral of the Canals', it was built in 1875 to allow passage between the River Weaver and the Trent and Mersey Canal, which runs alongside 50 ft (15 m) higher up. The River Weaver flows down to the docks at RUNCORN, on the Mersey, while the canal feeds into England's extensive inland waterway system.

The lift consists of two watertight tanks, big enough to hold two narrow boats, which are raised and lowered by means of hydraulic rams. It was much in demand by commercial traffic well into the 1950s, but fell into disuse as trade on the waterways declined. Left almost derelict for 20 years, it has recently been completely restored and is once more fully operational, giving rides to pleasure boats and visitors.

Well, I never knew this ABOUT CHESHIRE

'The happy spot where I was born' is how Charles Dodgson, better known as LEWIS CARROLL, remembers DARESBURY, near Runcorn, where he came into the world in 1832. He spent his formative years here, where his father was the vicar, and there is a memorial window to him in the church depicting many of the characters from *Alice in Wonderland.*

HUXLEY, a tiny village south-west of Chester, was the inspiration for ALDOUS HUXLEY'S *Brave New World* – the author was descended from the family who lived here in the beautiful moated Jacobethan Huxley Lower Hall, whose crooked chimneys can be seen from the road rising above the trees beyond a stone bridge. Aldous Huxley's grandfather THOMAS HUXLEY was the man who coined the term 'AGNOSTIC'.

Emma Lyon, better known as LADY HAMILTON, mistress of Lord Nelson, was born in 1765 at Swann Cottage, by the River Dee in NESTON on the Wirral. The cottage is still there, on an S bend in the road from Ness Gardens.

GREAT BUDWORTH, near Northwich, was the model for STACTON TRESSLE, where those 'Dear Ladies', Dr Evadne HINGE and Dame Hilda BRACKET lived.

LYME PARK, a magnificent Elizabethan house in the village of DISLEY, just outside Stockport, became Mr Darcy's home, Pemberley, in the 1995 BBC TV adaptation of Jane Austen's *Pride and Prejudice.*

CORNWALL

COUNTY TOWN: TRURO

'We are so highly sensible of the merits of our County of Cornwall'

CHARLES I

Minack Theatre, built almost single-handedly by Rowena Cade

Redruth

First House Lit by Gas

In the late 17th century, Redruth was the capital of the LARGEST AND RICHEST METAL MINING AREA IN BRITAIN, thanks to the deep mining of copper which was used to make brass, an important material in the Industrial Revolution. In the middle of the 19th century, TWO-THIRDS OF THE WORLD'S COPPER CAME FROM CORNWALL.

The FIRST HOUSE IN THE WORLD TO BE LIT BY GAS is in Redruth. WILLIAM MURDOCK (1754–1839) was an engineer working for Boulton and Watt, who made steam engines in Birmingham. Many of them were put to use in the Cornish mining industry and Murdock came to live in Redruth in 1782, as local manager for the company. He had a brilliant mind and was often years ahead of others in his ideas. In 1794, he built a closed coal fire in his garden and ran a pipe from it into the house, where he lit the gas coming through from the burning coal – the world's first gas lighting system.

In 1784, Murdock devised a method of using steam pressure to drive a piston inside a cylinder and he used this to drive a small model carriage for over 2 miles (3.2 km). He also invented, albeit on a small scale, the locomotive, 20 years before Richard Trevithick's full-scale version. It is possible to follow the route he took, late at night, from his house in Cross Street, past Redruth church, where the terrified vicar thought the hissing, fiery apparition was the Devil! Unfortunately, Murdock failed to persuade his employers of the potential for this invention and turned his talents elsewhere, leaving Trevithick to take the accolades as inventor of the steam engine.

MURDOCK HOUSE, as it is now called, stands in Cross Street, Redruth, and is marked with a plaque.

Gwennap

Hold the Lift

On 5 January 1842, a Cornish engineer, MICHAEL LOAM (1798–1871), gave a successful demonstration of the WORLD'S FIRST LIFT. He called it a MAN ENGINE and it was installed at the Tresavean Mine in Gwennap, near Redruth. It was powered by a waterwheel and reached a depth of 150 ft (46 m). When it proved effective, it was extended to 1,000 ft (305 m).

Loam had invented the Man Engine in a effort to relieve miners of the back-breaking climb to and from the workface. Some mines were over 2,000 ft (610 m) deep. The basic design involved a series of stepped wooden rods which moved up and down between a succession of platforms which were fixed to the mine shaft wall. The miner would step off a platform on to the rod, step off that on to the next platform and wait for the next rod. It was slow, but relatively safe, and much less exhausting than climbing a ladder. The FIRST-EVER LIFT ACCIDENT occurred on 31 September 1843, when a 14-year-old boy miner missed his step and plunged 100 ft (30.5 m) to his death.

Steam engines soon replaced waterwheels, which made the lifts much faster, and cages were provided to protect the men from falling. The last Man Engine was dismantled at the Levant Mine in 1919.

Bude

He built his House on Sand

Down on the beach, amongst the sand dunes of Bude, is BUDE CASTLE, a remarkable building that was the WORLD'S FIRST PERMANENT STRUCTURE TO BE BUILT ON SHIFTING SANDS. It was put up in 1830, by SIR GOLDSWORTHY GURNEY (1793–1875), who overcame the problem of instability by laying a strong concrete platform directly on to the sand for the foundations, thereby inventing a building technique widely used in the modern construction industry. Thanks to this ingenious Cornish inventor, engineers knew how to build the world's tallest buildings, the Petronas Towers, at Kuala Lumpur, Malaysia, on soft, wet limestone.

Gurney had picked up his enthusiasm for engineering from a chance meeting with RICHARD TREVITHICK, a fellow Cornishman and pioneer of steam propulsion. In 1825, Gurney invented a steam carriage that could carry passengers. This wasn't entirely successful as people were reluctant to sit right beside the unstable boiler, so Gurney subsequently designed a separate passenger carriage and this became known as the 'Gurney drag'. In 1829, the steam carriage travelled from London to Bath at an average speed of 15 mph (24 kph) – the FIRST LONG JOURNEY BY A SELF-PROPELLED VEHICLE AT A SUSTAINED SPEED ANYWHERE IN THE WORLD. Gurney also invented the WORLD'S FIRST PRACTICAL ROAD ENGINE, but he was before his time. The government imposed taxes on steam-driven vehicles to protect the owners of horse-drawn carriages, and he went bankrupt.

The high speeds made possible by Gurney's steam engines, and the resulting need for timetables, made necessary the creation of a uniform time, covering the whole of Britain. It was decided to set a standard time from Greenwich and so GREENWICH MEAN TIME, or GMT, came into being, another of Gurney's legacies.

Gurney also INVENTED LIMELIGHT, by forcing a mixture of oxygen and hydrogen through a blowpipe to produce a hot flame and then adding lime to create a bright light. He lit the whole of Bude Castle with one light, using a series of mirrors to reflect the beams into different rooms. This was known as the 'Bude light', and Gurney went on to light the Houses of Parliament using three light sources and an arrangement of prismatic mirrors, saving thousands of candles in the process. He also put it to use in lighthouses, where the single source was placed on a revolving platform to provide a flashing beam. In addition, the light was used in theatres to light the stage, as it was safer and brighter than trational gas lighting, hence the phrase to be 'in the limelight' or centre stage.

Sir Goldsworthy Gurney is buried at LAUNCELLS, just outside Bude, and there is a plaque to him at nearby POUGHILL.

Scilly Isles

Lyonesse

The Scilly Isles, 30 miles (48 km) off Cornwall, are said to be all that is left of the lost kingdom of Lyonesse and the burial place of King Arthur. The first English land to taste the Atlantic breakers, they nonetheless bask in a warm current from the Gulf Stream and grow fruit and flowers earlier and for longer than the rest of Britain. Prime Minister Harold Wilson liked to spend his holidays here.

TRESCO is considered the most beautiful of the Scilly Isles. It was transformed into a garden island by a 19th-century squire called AUGUSTUS SMITH, who leased the island and built a house named the Abbey, in memory of the 10th-century abbey founded there by Athelstan. In 1834, Smith introduced the islanders of Tresco to the FIRST COMPULSORY EDUCATION IN BRITAIN – 30 years before it was introduced on the mainland.

The jagged rocks off the Scilly Isles have lured many a ship to its doom, especially in the days before accurate forms of navigation were known. In 1707, the flagship of ADMIRAL SIR CLOWDISLEY SHOVELL, *The Association*, at the head of a fleet returning, in thick fog, from the seige of Toulon, hit rocks to the west of Scilly and sank swiftly. The Admiral, barely alive, was washed ashore in the bay at PORTH HELLICK on St Mary's, where he was found by a poor island woman. Tempted by the emerald ring on his finger she suffocated him by pushing his face into the sand and then buried the body. On her deathbed, 30 years later, she confessed all, gave up the ring, and revealed where the Admiral's body lay. Sir Clowdisley Shovell was recovered and taken to rest in Westminster Abbey. His temporary tomb on the island of St Mary's is marked by a quartz block.

This disaster, allied to the increasing number of transatlantic voyages, prompted the government to offer a huge prize for anyone who could devise a means of determining longitude. It was won, in 1761, by John Harrison, who invented the marine chronometer.

The Torrey Canyon

First Supertanker Disaster

The invention of John Harrison's marine chronometer did not help in March 1967 when the *Torrey Canyon*, one of the first oil supertankers, hit the Seven Stones Reef between the SCILLY ISLES and LAND'S END, resulting in the FIRST DISASTER IN THE WORLD INVOLVING AN OIL SUPERTANKER.

The *Torrey Canyon* was heading for Milford Haven, carrying 120,000 tons of oil from Kuwait. The captain had a choice of sailing between the Scilly Isles and Land's End along a deep water channel 7 miles (11.3 km) wide, or he could take a safer route to the west of the Scilly Isles, but this was 40 miles (64 km) further and would add two hours to the journey time. The captain decided on the former – he knew the waters well and the channel was quite wide enough, even for a ship as slow to manoeuvre as his supertanker.

Once in the channel, however, the *Torrey Canyon* was forced to steer to port to avoid some fishing nets, leaving them too close to the Seven Stones Reef. When the captain realised they were off course, he switched from autopilot to manual but the lever had been inadvertently knocked into disengage, which, it was later discovered, could too easily happen due to a design flaw. The *Torrey Canyon* did not respond and, driven on by its own momentum, it hit the rocks at 17 knots and began to break up.

Because this was the world's first big oil disaster, no one knew what to do. Initially, they tried to salvage the ship by dragging it off the rocks with tugboats. This merely caused it to break up more quickly. Then they tried to disperse the oil with detergents. Finally, Harold Wilson gave the order to bomb the ship with napalm and to set fire to the remaining oil before his holiday islands were devastated for ever.

The coastlines of the Scilly Isles, southern England and northern France were blighted for two years, marine life was destroyed and beaches ruined, but at least the lessons learned from the *Torrey Canyon* disaster have helped to prevent countless similar catastrophes across the world.

Well, I never knew this
ABOUT
CORNWALL

It's possible, when standing in ST JUST, to believe that the words of the hymn are correct, and that 'those feet, in ancient times, did walk upon England's mountains green' and that 'the Holy lamb of God was at St Just in Roseland seen'. Here is a beautiful 15th-century church, set in a garden churchyard beautiful beyond words, full of palms and roses, hydrangeas and polyanthus, right beside the waters of St Just Creek off the Carrick Roads. It has a drowsy, peaceful air, heavy with colour and scent, the water lapping gently against the mossy church walls. Just the sort of spot where you could imagine Jesus wading ashore and walking upon England's pleasant pastures. It is known that the Phoenicians and the Romans visited Cornwall and legend says that Joseph of Arimathea, a tin merchant, brought the boy Jesus here on one of his voyages to purchase tin from the Cornish mines. It certainly seems possible, indeed probable, when you stand in this blessed place.

SIR HUMPHRY DAVY, inventor of the miners' safety lamp, is buried here.

The FIRST ROYAL MAIL PACKET STATION IN THE WORLD was set up at FALMOUTH in 1698. Mail was sent to Falmouth by coach from London and other parts of the country and then carried over the oceans by the fast, lightly armed 'Falmouth packets'. The port became the communications centre of the growing British Empire and flourished until business was moved to the steam packets of Southampton in 1852.

They shall not grow old, as we that are left grow old:
Age shall not weary them, nor the years condemn.
At the going down of the sun and in the morning
We will remember them.

These powerful lines were written by LAURENCE BINYON in 1914, as he sat on the cliffs above POLZEATH, near Padstow. Binyon was born in Lancaster in 1869, and worked at the British Museum, where he was an expert in Oriental art and literature. In 1908, he wrote the first-ever European treatise on the subject, *Painting in the Far East.* In 1916, he went to the front to work for the Red Cross. He was a successful playwright as well as a poet. Laurence Binyon died in 1943 and is buried at Aldworth in Berkshire.

ROBERT STEPHEN HAWKER was the Vicar of MORWENSTOW, north of Bude. He INVENTED THE MODERN HARVEST FESTIVAL in 1843, when he invited parishioners to a special

Thanksgiving service and encouraged them to decorate the church with their home-grown produce. A well-respected poet, Hawker built himself a driftwood hut halfway down the cliffs where he would retire and write. The hut is still there, protected by the National Trust

The bottomless DOZMARY POOL, in the middle of bleak and barren Bodmin Moor, is where Arthur's knight, following Arthur's instructions, cast away Excalibur and a woman's arm, clad in white, rose out of the water, clasped the sword and sank back beneath the surface. Excalibur lies there still. The cold, black, lifeless water does not entice you to dive in and look for it.

The 6th-century St PIRAN'S ORATORY, south of NEWQUAY, is the OLDEST CHRISTIAN CHURCH IN BRITAIN. St Piran was a monk who sailed to Cornwall from Ireland and became the patron saint of tinners, and of Cornwall. The broken walls of his tiny Oratory, built where he landed, lie hidden in the dunes behind Perran beach. A long walk across the sand brings you to the site which is marked by a cross.

PENZANCE was the birthplace of MARIE BRONTË, mother of the Brontë sisters. The house where she was born is still there in Chapel Street.

LIZARD VILLAGE is the ONLY VILLAGE IN MAINLAND BRITAIN TO LIE SOUTH OF THE 50TH PARALLEL.

CAPE CORNWALL, the headland north of Land's End, is ENGLAND'S ONLY CAPE.

CUMBERLAND

COUNTY TOWN: CARLISLE

The Roof of England

Greystoke Castle sits at the heart of the largest enclosure in England without a road or public right of way running through it.

Cockermouth

Mutiny and Poetry

FLETCHER CHRISTIAN was born in Cockermouth in 1764, at MOORLAND CLOSE, a farmhouse on the road south out of town. He joined the Royal Navy aged 18 and, in 1787, sailed with CAPTAIN BLIGH to the West Indies as a midshipman. Christian impressed his captain with his enthusiasm and leadership qualities, and was chosen by Bligh to be his first mate on *HMS Bounty*. In 1788, the *Bounty* sailed to Tahiti to collect breadfruit saplings for the plantation slaves in Jamaica. After ten months at sea, the *Bounty*'s crew relished the warmth and beauty of the island and were beguiled by the friendliness of the Tahitian women. Fletcher Christian fell in love with a girl called MAIMITI, whom he later married.

Three weeks after leaving the island, the crew of the *Bounty* mutinied, casting Captain Bligh adrift and returning to Tahiti. The cause of the mutiny has always been attributed to Bligh's cruelty, but it seems just as likely that the sailors were reluctant to leave behind the women and idyllic life of Tahiti and return home to dark, dank England.

Christian, with eight others and their womenfolk, searched the ocean for an island where they could live safe from discovery. On 23 January 1790, they settled on PITCAIRN, a volcanic island 1,350 miles (2,172 km) south-east of Tahiti, named after Robert Pitcairn, the midshipman who had first sighted it in 1767.

Life was pretty savage and, within 15 years, all but one of the original mutineers was dead, including Fletcher Christian, whose son, Thursday October Christian, was the first child born on the island. In 1838, the Pitcairn Islands were granted an amnesty and welcomed into the British Empire. Today, all but a handful of the 50 or so inhabitants of Pitcairn are direct descendants of the mutineers.

WILLIAM WORDSWORTH (1770–1850), attended the same school as Fletcher Christian. The smart,

Georgian house in the town centre where Wordsworth was born in 1770 is now owned by the National Trust.

I wandered lonely as a cloud
That floats on high o'er vales and hills,
When all at once I saw a crowd,
A host, of golden daffodils;
Beside the lake, beneath the trees,
Fluttering and dancing in the breeze.

These immortal lines were written in April 1802, after Wordsworth had been walking with his sister Dorothy along the north shore of ULLSWATER, near AIRA FORCE. As they approached Lyulph's Tower, they came across 'a long belt of beautiful daffodils, the breadth of a country turnpike road, under the boughs of the trees', spreading right down to the water's edge. The exact spot is, today, slightly ruined by a main road and car park, but daffodils still flourish, and there is a lovely walk up to Aira Force across a bridge that serves as a memorial to SIR CECIL SPRING-RICE, who wrote the words to the hymn 'I Vow to Thee My Country'.

Keswick

Poets' Corner

The charm of Keswick is its setting, at the foot of Skiddaw and at the gateway to that most beautiful of the lakes, Derwentwater. To this simple grey town came a noble array of poets. SHELLEY brought his bride Mary here for their honeymoon. In 1800, SAMUEL TAYLOR COLERIDGE came to live at GRETA HALL, followed, two years later, by ROBERT SOUTHEY, who was married to Coleridge's wife's sister. Southey later became Poet Laureate and lived here for 40 years. He wrote and published a version of the old tale of the Three Bears, which went on to become *Goldilocks and the Three Bears.* The house, once a girls' school, is now a private residence. He wrote the following lines:

It is not for man to rest in absolute contentment. He is born to hopes and aspirations as the sparks fly upward.

Robert Southey is buried in the churchyard at GREAT CROSTHWAITE, just outside Keswick to the north, alongside a roll call of remarkable men, including SIR JOHN GEORGE WOODFORD, wounded by the last shot fired at Corunna, during the Peninsular War, and SIR EDMUND HENDERSON, FOUNDER OF SCOTLAND YARD'S CID.

A later owner of Greta Hall was CANON HARDWICKE DRUMMOND RAWNSLEY (1851–1920), who was Vicar of St Kentigerns, Great Crosthwaite, and is buried in the churchyard. Whilst Vicar of Wray, near AMBLESIDE, he used to visit the 16-year-old BEATRIX POTTER and her parents, who rented Wray Castle as a holiday home. He took a great interest in Beatrix's drawings and encouraged her to publish her first book, *The Tale of Peter Rabbit,* for which he wrote some verse. Rawnsley

was a great lover of the Lakeland scenery and, in 1896, together with Octavia Hill and Robert Hunter, founded the NATIONAL TRUST. He raised the money for the Trust's first purchase, BRANDLEHOW WOOD, on the west shore of Derwentwater. Beatrix Potter's father was the first life member of the National Trust.

Sellafield

Milk's Off

In 1957, on a quiet, isolated stretch of the Cumberland coast, the WORLD'S FIRST LARGE-SCALE ATOMIC POWER STATION suffered the WORLD'S FIRST LARGE-SCALE ATOMIC ACCIDENT. Because it had never happened before, nobody knew what to do.

Throughout the 1940s, Britain had collaborated with the Americans on the Manhattan Project to produce the atom bomb. In 1945, and despite the fact that British scientists had been largely responsible for the success of the project, the US refused to share the technology. Britain, wanting to remain at the top table, had to embark on its own atomic weapons programme.

To this end, in 1946, an old Ordnance munitions factory at WINDSCALE (since renamed Sellafield) was chosen as the place to build the reactors for producing the necessary plutonium from uranium. There was plenty of cooling water and the site was suitably remote. Constructed with remarkable speed, the reactors, or 'piles', were ready by 1950 and, by March 1952, the first plutonium was ready for transport to the Aldermaston weapons factory near Oxford. It went into making BRITAIN'S FIRST ATOM BOMB, detonated off the coast of Australia in October that year.

The Windscale reactors were built rather more quickly than the scientists' understanding of the processes involved merited. On 8 October 1957, reactor number one was being

heated up to allow the release of energy from the graphite core. The primitive recording instruments showed that the reactor was too cool, when in fact it was too hot, and the technicians boosted the heating further, causing a fire. In those early reactors, the plutonium piles were cooled by fans blowing air through them, which meant that radiation from the fire was blown into the outside atmosphere through the cooling towers. The fallout cloud was blown south-eastwards and, to be on the safe side, all milk production and consumption was banned for a 200-mile (322-km) radius around Windscale, milk being considered most at risk from the contamination.

Back at Windscale, scientists tried to put out the blaze by pumping in carbon dioxide gas to smother the flames, but this merely fed the fire with oxygen. They eventually decided to take a gamble and flood the reactor with cooling water, even though this might create hydrogen gas that could explode. All the while the temperature was increasing by 20°C every minute. Fortunately, the gamble worked.

Today, Sellafield is a bright and cheery seaside visitor attraction with no visible sign that, 50 years ago, Britain was brought to the brink of nuclear catastrophe. On the scale of disasters, Windscale is rivalled only by Three Mile Island and Chernobyl. As it was, nobody died, lessons were learned and the courage and quick thinking of the team at Windscale prevented a calamity.

Caldbeck

D'ye ken John Peel with his coat so gray?
D'ye ken John Peel at the break of day?
D'ye ken John Peel when he's far far away?
With his hounds and his horn in the
morning?

Caldbeck is a tidy granite village nestling amongst the Fells of Northern Lakeland. At first sight, a church, a few houses and a duck pond are all that are left of what was once a thriving industrial centre. In the 17th and 18th centuries, Caldbeck was humming with corn mills, wool mills, paper mills and, indeed, a brewery, all taking advantage of the becks tumbling down off the hillside.

A short walk takes you to the HOWK, a rocky, wooded limestone glen dotted with the remains of these various enterprises. Of particular interest is the ruined bobbin mill (now being restored), which used to possess the LARGEST WATERWHEEL IN ENGLAND, 3 ft (0.9 m) wide and 42 ft (12.8 m) across. An old corn mill, called the Priest's Mill, has been converted into a small arts and crafts centre, and there is a restaurant for visitors, most of whom come here to see the grave of JOHN PEEL in the churchyard.

John Peel was born near Caldbeck in 1776. While still in his teens, he eloped to Gretna Green with a local girl, Mary White. They had 13 children. He was fond of fox hunting and kept a kennel of hounds which he hired out to local hunts. One evening he was sitting with his friend, JOHN WOODCOCK GRAVES, reflecting on the day's hunting over a glass of something jolly, when Granny started singing the children to sleep upstairs. Graves snatched up his pen and began jotting down a ditty about his guest, John Peel, to the tune she was humming, an old air called 'Bonnie Annie'. They spent the rest of the night singing it to each other amidst howls of laughter and, as John Peel was leaving, Graves slapped him on the back and cried 'By Jove, John Peel, you'll be sung when we're both run to earth!'

In 1977, a gang of anti-hunt protesters smashed up John Peel's headstone, dug a hole in the grave and left a fox's head in it. His remains were undisturbed and the tombstone has been carefully watched ever since.

He was right. John Peel died in 1854, at the age of 78, while the song 'D'ye ken John Peel?' is still hugely popular today, particularly in Cumberland.

Well, I never knew this ABOUT CUMBERLAND

In 1880, HER MAJESTY'S THEATRE in CARLISLE was the FIRST THEATRE IN ALL OF ENGLAND TO BE LIT BY ELECTRICITY.

The FIRST PILLAR BOX IN ENGLAND was put up at BOTCHERGATE, CARLISLE, in September 1853.

The RAVENGLASS AND ESKDALE RAILWAY, known as 'Old Ratty', from the Cumbrian for 'little narrow way', was the FIRST NARROW GAUGE RAILWAY IN ENGLAND. It was originally built to transport iron ore from Boot village to Ravenglass.

Standing at 1,000 ft (305 m) above sea level, ALSTON, in the Pennines, is a contender for ENGLAND'S HIGHEST TOWN, along with Buxton. ALSTON STATION (875 ft/267 m) is on ENGLAND'S HIGHEST NARROW GAUGE RAILWAY, the Alston to South Tynedale Railway. This was built along the old track bed of the standard gauge Alston branch of the Newcastle to Carlisle line.

SCALE FORCE WATERFALL, above Buttermere, has, at 148 ft (45 m), the LONGEST UNBROKEN FALL OF WATER ABOVE GROUND IN ENGLAND.

NENTHEAD, in the Pennines near Alston, battles it out with Flash, in Staffordshire, for the honour of being ENGLAND'S HIGHEST VILLAGE. They both hover around 1,500 ft (457 m) above sea level.

BROAD CRAG TARN on SCAFELL PIKE is, at 2,748 ft (837 m), the HIGHEST LAKE IN ENGLAND.

DERBYSHIRE

COUNTY TOWN: DERBY

'There are prospects in Derbyshire as noble as any in Greece or Switzerland'

LORD BYRON

In Midland Road, near Derby Station, is the Midland Hotel, the oldest surviving railway hotel in the world, opened in 1840.

Derby

First Factory

This bustling north Midlands town seems ordinary enough, but Derby has done much to shape our modern world. It stands on the River Derwent and has been a busy market centre since Norman times. The glory of the town is the magnificent 16th-century tower of the Cathedral, which soars 210 ft (64 m) above the town centre and is one of the loveliest examples of Gothic architecture in England. Derby was one of the first English towns to be industrialised in the 18th century, and many of the town centre streets date from this period.

In 1721, JOHN LOMBE opened the FIRST SILK MILL IN ENGLAND – the FIRST TRUE FACTORY IN THE WORLD – on the banks of the River Derwent in Derby. It was built to accommodate 26 new machines for twisting silk into thread. Lombe had worked

Silk Mill

in the silk trade in Italy and had secretly copied the design of the spinning machines in use over there. A water wheel provided the power and Lombe's mill was able to produce enough silk to seriously compete with the Italians. In 1722, Lombe died suddenly from an unknown ailment. It was suspected that he had been poisoned by a girl sent over from Italy in revenge for his industrial espionage. Silk production ended at the mill in 1908, and the building burnt down in 1910. The tower, however, was saved and has been incorporated into a new building which now houses the Derby Industrial Museum.

The world's first arboretum and public park was opened in Derby in 1840. The Arboretum was given to the townsfolk by mill owner Joseph Strutt as an area for public recreation and exercise.

Cromford

Arkwright's Mill

A few miles outside MATLOCK, in a deep rocky dell, beside the ruins of an old bridge chapel, are the remains of the WORLD'S FIRST WATER-POWERED SPINNING MILL. It was built in 1771 by RICHARD ARKWRIGHT, first industrial entrepreneur and ARCHITECT OF THE FACTORY SYSTEM that was to power the Industrial Revolution and make Britain the workshop of the world.

Richard Arkwright was a barber and wig-maker born in 1732. Much of England in the 18th century was involved in the cotton business and, while travelling around the country selling his wigs, Arkwright came across a spinning machine invented by a reed-maker named THOMAS HIGHS, which was the prototype of JAMES HARGREAVE'S SPINNING JENNY. Arkwright realised there was money to be made from a machine that could speed up the spinning process, and he went away to devise a simple roller spinner and then water frame that could be operated by unskilled workers.

Horses could not provide enough power for these machines, so Arkwright searched for a suitable site that offered sufficient water power. This he found at Cromford, where

the Bonsall Brook enters the River Derwent. There was also plenty of cheap labour from the area's declining lead mines. The Bonsall Brook was diverted into channels to work the mill wheels, and mills, workshops, smithies and everything else needed for the mass production of textiles from raw material to finished product was constructed.

There is some debate as to whether Richard Arkwright was responsible for the design of this new machinery or whether he simply copied and improved on the ideas of others, but there is no doubt that he was the first to put this new machinery to good use, and the first to set up an entire factory system. His mill at Cromford was so successful that it was copied all over the world. Arkwright's next mill was MASSON MILL next door, which still operates, but is now mainly given over to shops.

Today, Arkwright's Mill at Cromford is being restored. In the pavement on the main road you can see a bollard made from an old cannon – this was brought in by Arkwright to protect the mill against the 18th-century machine wreckers. Richard Arkwright is buried nearby in the church he had built himself.

Melbourne

Australia's Second City and the First Package Tour

Melbourne is a rather unexpectedly delightful, small, stone town, a few miles south of Derby. Rather overshadowed by its famous Australian namesake, Melbourne in Derbyshire has been quietly going about its business for a thousand years and boasts one of the finest Norman churches in England. Two men from here have served to take the name of Melbourne around the world.

Melbourne Hall, a mainly Georgian house standing next to the church, was the home of William Lamb (1779–1848), the second VISCOUNT MELBOURNE. Melbourne was Queen Victoria's first Prime

Minister, and he gave his name to Australia's second city, which was established during his premiership in 1835. Lord Melbourne was a stalwart support to the young queen, who relied heavily on her Prime Minister's advice and experience before her marriage to Prince Albert. There was even talk that she might marry Melbourne, despite the 40-year age gap, for he had recently lost his wife Caroline and their only child.

Another famous son was THOMAS COOK, the FIRST TOUR OPERATOR, who was born here in 1808. His birthplace at Quick Close is no longer there but, close by, are the Memorial Cottages which he built as accommodation for the poor and elderly of his home town.

Thomas Cook was a strict Baptist and prominent member of the local temperance society and, in 1841, he decided to arrange an excursion to a temperance meeting in Loughborough, taking advantage of the newly opened Midland railway line from Leicester. For one shilling (5 p) his customers got their rail ticket and lunch on the train. This was the FIRST EVER 'PACKAGE TOUR'. He progressed with tours to Liverpool and Scotland and, in 1850, he organised for some 200,000 people to visit the Great Exhibition. His first foreign tour was to Antwerp in 1855, and included visits to Brussels, Waterloo, the Rhine, Cologne and Paris. In 1872, he offered a 212-day Round-the-World trip for 200 guineas.

Thomas Cook was the first person to offer a package deal to include all travel, hotel and food expenses so that the customer knew exactly the cost of his trip. He was hugely pleased that he had managed to bring down costs so that the working man might be tempted to spend his money on educational travel instead of the demon drink. In 1865, he opened an office in London and, for the next 25 years, was pre-eminent in the holiday travel business, so much so that the phrase 'Cook's Tour' became part of the language. Thomas Cook died in 1892, but his sons continued to run the business until 1928. It is now owned by a German tour operator and known as Thomas Cook AG.

Chatsworth

Palace of the Peak

THE EMPEROR FOUNTAIN at Chatsworth is the TALLEST FOUNTAIN IN BRITAIN. It was built by SIR JOSEPH PAXTON to celebrate the Tsar of Russia's visit in 1844. The sixth Duke of Devonshire wanted his fountain to be higher than the Tsar's fountain at the Imperial Palace of Peterhof, which reached a height of 120 ft (37 m). When it was first run, the Emperor Fountain achieved a height of 269 ft (82 m). It is powered by water pressure from a reservoir on the moors above Chatsworth.

Joseph Paxton also built the WORLD'S LARGEST GLASS HOUSE at Chatsworth. It was known as the GREAT CONSERVATORY and was the prototype for his Crystal Palace, which housed the Great Exhibition in Hyde Park, London, in 1850. It was demolished in 1920.

Inside the house at Chatsworth is the LARGEST VASE EVER MADE FROM A SINGLE PIECE OF BLUE JOHN. Blue john, from the French *bleu jaune*, or 'blue yellow', is a unique mineral fluorspar. The only two places in the world Blue John is found are the BLUE JOHN and TREAK CLIFF caverns below Castleton in the Peak District. We know it must have been discovered by the Romans as artefacts made from Blue John have been found in the ruins at Pompeii.

The Great Conservatory

The PEAK CAVERN, right beneath the castle at Castleton, has the LARGEST NATURAL CAVE OPENING IN BRITAIN, and is 33 ft (10 m) high and 100 ft (30.5 m) across. It used to contain a rope factory and a row of cottages.

Kinder Trespass

The PEAK DISTRICT NATIONAL PARK was designated BRITAIN'S FIRST NATIONAL PARK in 1951. The greater part of the park is in Derbyshire, including the PEAK DISTRICT'S HIGHEST POINT, KINDER SCOUT (2,088 ft/636 m).

In 1932, there was a mass trespass on Kinder Scout, which was a major catalyst in the freeing up of the countryside to the public. In the recession of the 1930s, rambling was one of the few pastimes open to the unemployed. Less than 1 per cent of the peak area, the nearest open land to a number of large industrial cities, including Manchester, Sheffield and Leeds, was accessible to the public. Kinder Scout itself was privately owned and kept for grouse shooting for 12 days every year; the rest of the time it was deserted, but walkers were not allowed. For many years, ramblers had tried to get the landowners to open a public path across Kinder Scout when the land was not in use, but this was refused and anyone straying was chased off by gamekeepers with guns and dogs. Times were changing, though, and some began to question whether it was right for great swathes of the most beautiful English countryside to be privately owned.

The BRITISH WORKERS SPORTS FEDERATION was an organisation set up to campaign for, amongst other things, a Sunday football league. In April 1932, they called for a mass trespass in response to a group of their ramblers being assaulted by gamekeepers during an Easter camp at Rowarth in the Peaks. Five hundred, mostly working people, turned up in the village of HAYFIELD on the morning of 24 April. They were met by dozens of police and were forced to move on to a quarry where they reassembled before moving off on to the mountain. Halfway to the top, they were confronted by a team of gamekeepers and there was a scuffle during which a keeper fell over and turned his ankle. The gamekeepers fled and the trespassers went on to the top, where they met with another group who had come from Sheffield.

When the ramblers got back to Hayfield, the ringleaders were arrested and charged with riotous assembly. They were sentenced to six months in jail and the injustice of this caused outrage. During the trial, thousands of protesters marched over Kinder Scout. The RAMBLERS ASSOCIATION began to hold annual demonstrations, attracting up to 10,000 people. The movement became unstoppable and, in 1949, Clement Atlee's Labour government passed the National Parks Access to the Countryside Act, with the result that Kinder Scout was 'nationalised'. There are now a dozen national parks in England and Wales, with part of the New Forest being the most recent in 2004.

In 2002, Environment Secretary Michael Meacher attended the 70th anniversary celebrations of the Kinder Scout Mass Trespass, held in the quarry on the road between Hayfield and the Kinder reservoir. On behalf of Her Majesty's government, he praised those who had taken part for achieving 'far reaching changes to an unjust and oppressive law'.

ARTHUR LOWE (1914–82), Captain Mainwaring in TV's *Dad's Army*, was born in HAYFIELD.

Well, I never knew this ABOUT DERBYSHIRE

Standing at 1,000 ft (305 m) above sea level, BUXTON is the HIGHEST TOWN IN ENGLAND, a title that Alston in Cumberland also claims for itself. There is no dispute that Buxton possesses the LARGEST UNSUPPORTED DOME IN ENGLAND. Built over the courtyard of the stables for the hotel in the Crescent in 1881, it has a diameter of 164 ft (50 m). The stables were later converted and have now become the Royal Devonshire Hospital.

The first two DERWENT VALLEY reservoirs in the High Peak District were created to supply water to Derby, Sheffield, Nottingham and Leicester by the building of two Gothic-style dams in 1912 and 1916. Because the topography of the Derwent Valley was so similar to that of the Ruhr Valley in Germany, the Lancaster bombers of the 617 'DAMBUSTERS' squadron used the reservoirs to practise dropping Barnes Wallis's 'bouncing bomb' for their attack on the Ruhr dams in 1943. *The Dambusters* movie was also filmed here in 1954.

The SMALLEST DETACHED HOUSE IN THE WORLD is THIMBLE HALL, in the Peak District village of YOULGREAVE.

Rutland Arms Hotel

It measures 11 ft 10 in (3.6 m) by 10 ft 3 in (3.1 m) and is 12 ft 2 in (3.7 m) high. In the 19th century, it was lived in by a family of eight . . .

LITTLE JOHN, Robin Hood's best friend and right-hand man, is buried in a huge grave in the churchyard at HATHERSAGE. His cottage, a little to the east of the church, stood until about 100 years ago.

SIR MAURICE OLDFIELD (1915–81), is buried at OVER HADDON, near Bakewell. He was head of MI6 from 1973 until 1978.

The delicious BAKEWELL PUDDING was a mistake. An absent-minded cook at the WHITE HORSE INN (now the RUTLAND ARMS) in Bakewell was making a strawberry tart and she spread the egg mixture meant for the pastry straight on top of the jam. By the time she spotted her mistake it was too late to start again and she sent the puddings through in the hope that no one would notice. They were so popular that Mrs Wilson, the wife of the candle-maker who lived nearby, obtained the recipe and set up in business in her husband's shop, which is now called the Old Original Bakewell Pudding Shop. Bakewell puddings are still made here from the secret recipe and sent all over the world. They should be eaten hot, with cream or custard.

Devon

County Town: Exeter

'When Adam and Eve were dispossessed
Of the garden hard by Heaven
They planted another one down in the West
'Twas Devon, glorious Devon!'

William Blake

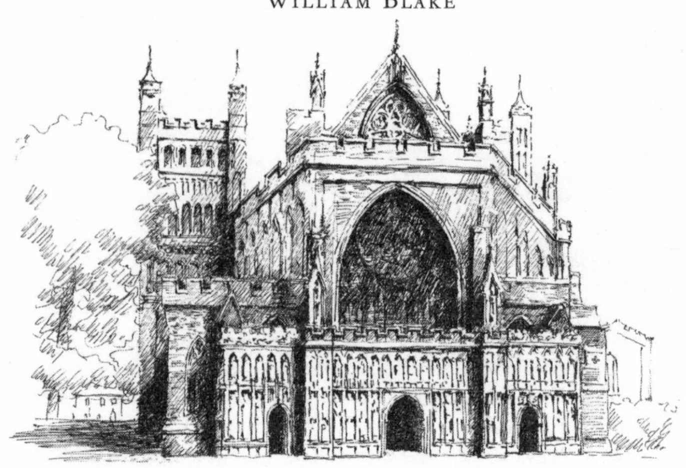

Exeter Cathedral

Plymouth

Bowls, Gin and Pilgrims

In 1439, Plymouth, often voted as the city with the best quality of life, was the first city in England to be incorporated by Parliament rather than by the monarch.

All roads in Plymouth lead to the Hoe, a windswept cliff-top expanse with spectacular views across Plymouth Sound. Sir Francis Drake was playing a game of bowls up here in August 1588 when he was informed of the approach of the Spanish Armada. Testing the wind, he is said to have remarked, 'There is plenty of time to win this game and to thrash the Spanish too.' He did both.

A steep walk down the hill arrives at the BARBICAN, Plymouth's historic heart, which has the LARGEST AREA OF COBBLED STREETS IN BRITAIN. Along one of these streets, a short walk from the harbour, is the BLACK FRIARS DISTILLERY, home of PLYMOUTH GIN since 1793, and the OLDEST WORKING GIN DISTILLERY IN ENGLAND. Plymouth Gin is specified in the first-ever recipe for a dry Martini cocktail.

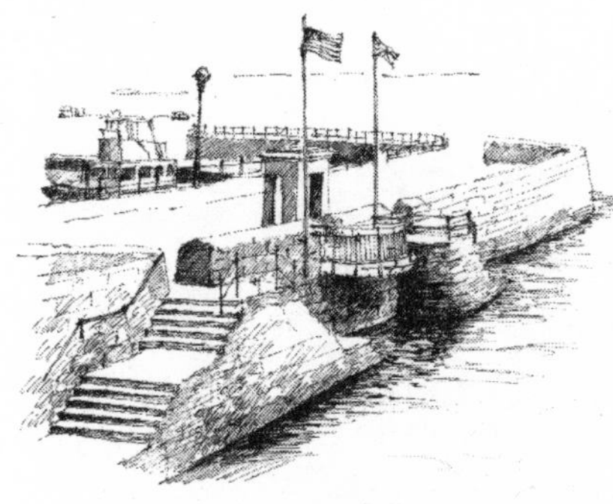

In 1620, the PILGRIM FATHERS stayed here for their last night in England, just two minutes' walk from the MAYFLOWER STEPS. From these steps, they left their homeland forever to sail across the ocean and to found an empire. They named their first landfall in America, Plymouth Rock.

Close by, in Southside Street, is JACKA'S BAKERY, the OLDEST WORKING COMMERCIAL BAKERY IN BRITAIN, where they have been baking bread since the time of the Armada. They baked the ship's biscuits for the Pilgrim Fathers to take with them on the *Mayflower*.

WILLIAM BLIGH (1754-1817), Captain of the *Bounty*, was born in Plymouth. He sailed to the South Seas with James Cook and was, for a time, Governor of New South Wales, but is best known for the part he played in provoking the infamous mutiny on the *Bounty* in 1789.

MICHAEL FOOT, leader of the Labour Party from 1980 to 1983, was born in Plymouth in 1913. As was, ten years later, the actor, DONALD SINDEN. Other famous sons include RON GOODWIN (1925–2003), the musician, best known for his score for the film *Battle of Britain*, DAVID OWEN, Labour Foreign Secretary and founder of the SDP, who was born in 1938, and the ballet dancer WAYNE SLEEP, who was born in 1948.

Dartmouth

The First Steam Engine and Jack Russell

Dartmouth has one of the finest natural harbours on the south coast, and is guarded by the FIRST CASTLE IN BRITAIN TO BE DESIGNED SPECIFICALLY FOR ARTILLERY. On the waterfront, past the tumbling old Butterwalk, is an incongruous shed-like structure that houses the OLDEST WORKING STEAM ENGINE IN THE WORLD, built by a son of Dartmouth, THOMAS NEWCOMEN.

Newcomen was born in Dartmouth in 1663. He became an ironmonger and blacksmith and developed an interest in the Devon

mining industry, which at the time was in decline because the mines were constantly flooding. Several people had attempted to devise ways of pumping water out of the mines, including a Devon neighbour called THOMAS SAVERY, born in Shilstone, and the FIRST MAN TO USE THE TERM 'HORSE POWER', who had patented a very crude steam engine.

Newcomen went into partnership with Savery and improved upon the latter's design, introducing a piston linked by a rocking beam to a pump. As the piston fell, it raised the water. Steam pressure raised the piston, cold water was introduced to cause a vacuum, which pulled the piston down again. The whole contraption looked a bit like the nodding donkey familiar from pictures of old oil fields. The pump proved very inefficient, mainly because the piston was open at the top – James Watt didn't come up with the idea of enclosing the piston until much later. Nevertheless, NEWCOMEN'S BEAM ENGINE saved England's mining industry, pumping out mines all over the country and allowing the retrieval of the raw materials needed to fuel the Industrial Revolution. Many of his engines were still at work 200 years later.

Another son of Dartmouth, born here in 1795, was PARSON JACK RUSSELL, a flamboyant churchman who loved the chase. He developed a new, small strain of terrier especially for hunting, one that was brave, intelligent and could go down fox holes. Jack Russells are now popular all over the world, not just as hunting dogs but as pets. Parson Jack had a favourite white fox terrier called Trump, who is reputed to be the father of all Jack Russell terriers.

Greenway

The Real Miss Marple

GREENWAY HOUSE sits high above the River Dart and, in 1938, it became the home of the MOST POPULAR CRIME WRITER OF ALL TIME, DAME AGATHA CHRISTIE, who was born Agatha Miller, in Barton Road, Torquay, in 1890.

Agatha Christie began writing as a girl, at the suggestion of her mother, when she was confined inside with a cold. In 1914, she married a Royal Flying Corps officer, Archibald

The older she gets, the more interested he is in her.'

She became a Dame in 1971 and died in 1976. Among her best-known novels are *Death on the Nile* and *Murder on the Orient Express,* both of which were made into films. *The Mousetrap* was turned into a play and was first staged in London in 1952. It has since become the LONGEST-RUNNING PLAY IN THE WORLD.

Agatha Christie used many Devon locations in her novels. At Burgh Island, near Salcombe, the setting for *Ten Little Indians*, they throw Agatha Christie mystery weekends in the 1930s Art Deco hotel, which was built in 1929 and frequented by such luminaries as Noel Coward and Edward VIII and Mrs Simpson.

Greenway is now home to Agatha Christie's daughter Rosalind and the gardens, run by the National Trust, are open most days.

Christie, and they honeymooned at the Grand Hotel, Torquay. During the First World War, she worked in Torquay Hospital, where she picked up a useful knowledge of poisons. Her first literary success came in 1920, with the publication of *The Mysterious Affair at Styles*, which introduced the Belgian detective Hercule Poirot. Miss Marple appeared in 1930 in *Murder at the Vicarage.*

In December 1926, Agatha Christie discovered that her husband had been having an affair with a young woman named Nancy Neele. In a mystery worthy of one of her novels, Agatha disappeared. Archibald was suspected of murdering her and various newspapers offered rewards to anyone who could find her. She was found, ten days later, at the Old Swan Hotel in Harrogate, where she had booked in as Teresa Neele.

Agatha divorced Archibald two years later and, in 1930, married an archeologist, Max Mallowan. As she said at the time, 'An archaeologist is the best husband a woman can have.

Paignton

Bright Young Things

Paignton is a holiday town with a zoo, lots of Victorian villas and rock shops, and a tidy stretch of sand. There has been a village here since olden times and the mainly 15th-century church has evidence of an earlier Norman building. The emphasis in Paignton is on fun, though, and this is exemplified by the exuberant OLDWAY MANSION, which

Oldway Mansion

stands above the road to Torquay. In 1871, the house that originally stood here was purchased by the American sewing-machine magnate ISAAC SINGER, who had been forced to leave first New York, and then Paris, because of scandal. The STATUE OF LIBERTY in New York is modelled on one of Isaac Singer's wives, a half-French, half-English actress called ISABELLA, who, in her time, was considered the MOST BEAUTIFUL WOMAN IN EUROPE. Isabella and Isaac had only lived in Paignton for a few short years before Isaac died in 1875 and their son, Paris, moved in. He remodelled the house on the Palace of Versailles and filled it with wonderful trophies, including his mistress, the dancer ISADORA DUNCAN.

The Singers seem to have been one of those families that attract bad luck. Paris and Isadora had a child together, who drowned in the River Seine, then Isadora herself died driving in her Bugatti along the French Riviera when her habitual flowing scarf became entangled in one of the back wheels and she was throttled. Oldway Mansion is now owned by Torquay Council and is open to the public. One of the highlights is a replica of a famous painting of the *Crowning of Josephine by Napoleon*. The original had been purchased by Paris Singer but was sold by Torquay to Versailles, where it now hangs.

SUE BARKER, former tennis player, now TV presenter, was born in Paignton in 1956.

Brixham

Abide with Me

Towering above the harbour at Brixham is the 19th-century church of All Saints, where HENRY FRANCIS LYTE (1793–1847) ministered for 25 years. He lived at Berry Head House, now an hotel, high above the town overlooking Torbay. One night, in 1847, towards the end of his life, he was alone and weary, sitting in his garden watching the darkness creep up from the bay, when the words of 'Abide with Me' came to him. This hymn has brought comfort and solace to people everywhere in moments of fear, drama and loneliness. Soldiers sang the words in the trenches in the Great War, and NURSE EDITH CAVELL recited them as she faced execution by the Germans as a spy (*see* Norfolk).

Hold Thou Thy Cross, before my closing eyes
Shine through the gloom and point me to the skies
Heaven's morning breaks and Earth's vain shadows flee
Help of the helpless, O Abide with Me.

Well, I never knew this ABOUT DEVON

On EXETER'S busy, narrow High Street, thrusting solidly out over the pavement, is the OLDEST GUILDHALL IN ENGLAND. Built in 1468, it is still used by Exeter City Council and contains the OLDEST CIVIC SEAL IN BRITAIN, dating from 1175.

SIR ARTHUR CONAN DOYLE stayed in PRINCETOWN on Dartmoor while researching his book *The Hound of the Baskervilles.* FOX TOR MIRE was the model for GREAT GRIMPEN MIRE, and Holmes's hideout on the moor is at GRIMSPOUND.

The story is said to be based on that of a local 17th-century squire named RICHARD CABELL, from Buckfastleigh, who had an evil reputation. When he died, huge, fire-breathing black dogs with red eyes were reputedly seen galloping across Dartmoor, baying fearsomely. BASKERVILLE HALL is thought to be HAYFORD HALL, near Buckfastleigh.

HENRY WILLIAMSON (1895–1977) who wrote *Tarka the Otter* in 1927, lived much of his life in North Devon and set his story around BIDEFORD and the TORRIDGE and TAW rivers. A 'Tarka Trail' has been created around the countryside described in the book, which has hardly altered since it was written.

Tarka's journey started and ended at CANAL BRIDGE on the River Torridge, near Weare Giffard, a few miles south of Bideford.

CHARLES BABBAGE was born, probably in TEIGNMOUTH, in 1791. He was a prolific inventor and mathematician best remembered for conceiving the idea of an 'analytical engine' which could be programmed by punch cards to make a variety of different calculations. His vision was never realised, mainly due to the limitations of the mechanical devices of the time, but his concept is now recognised as the basis for modern electronic computers. Charles Babbage, the 'Father of Computers', died in 1871 and is buried at Kensal Green Cemetery in London.

SIR RICHARD BURTON (1821–90), explorer, was born in TORQUAY. He is best known for his exploits in Africa, where he discovered Lake Tanganyika. He was an officer of the East India Company and introduced into the English langauge the word PYJAMA, from the Hindu for a loose garment.

The west face of EXETER CATHEDRAL is the LARGEST SURVIVING DISPLAY OF MEDIEVAL SCULPTURE IN BRITAIN, while inside, spanning more than 300 ft (91 m), is the LONGEST STRETCH OF UNBROKEN MEDIEVAL

GOTHIC VAULTING IN THE WORLD. If you stand at the west door and gaze down the length of the cathedral, the wonderful fans look like slender trees waving in the breeze.

ROBERT FALCON SCOTT, the Antarctic explorer, was born in DEVONPORT in 1868. As were, later, LESLIE HORE-BELISHA (1893–1957), Minister of Transport from 1934 to 1937, who gave his name to the BELISHA BEACON, and the Soviet spy, GUY BURGESS (1910–63).

PETER COOK (1937–95), comedian, was born in TORQUAY.

DORSET

COUNTY TOWN: DORCHESTER

'One of those sequestered spots outside the gates of the world where may usually be found more meditation than action'

THOMAS HARDY

Hardy's birthplace, setting for Under the Greenwood Tree

Poole

Robinson Crusoe, the Birth of Wireless and the First Boy Scouts

Poole Harbour is the SECOND LARGEST NATURAL HARBOUR IN THE WORLD, after Sydney, Australia. From here, in 1708, two little ships, the *Duke* and the *Duchess*, captained by WOODES ROGERS, set sail to find treasure and adventures in the South Seas. But better than that, they achieved immortality, for they found ROBINSON CRUSOE. Swept far south by a storm off Cape Horn, they put in for shelter at a small island called Juan Fernandez and were amazed, that night, to see a light blazing ashore. Captain Rogers sent out a boat, which returned with a scruffy, bearded man clad in goatskins, who spoke English. He was ALEXANDER SELKIRK, a sailor whose story was retold as *Robinson Crusoe* by Daniel Defoe.

In October 1898, at the HAVEN HOTEL on SANDBANKS, right by the entrance to Poole Harbour, GUGLIELMO MARCONI established one of the WORLD'S EARLIEST RADIO STATIONS, to receive signals from a small transmitter at the Needles in the Isle of Wight. Many experiments were carried out here, which led to the setting up of the FIRST TRANS-ATLANTIC RADIO STATION at POLDHU in CORNWALL. In 1904, the station at the Haven Hotel was the FIRST IN THE WORLD TO RECEIVE LONG-DISTANCE MESSAGES. The Haven Hotel has now developed into a huge modern edifice, but there is a plaque pointing out the small room that gave birth to the 'Wireless Age'.

BROWNSEA ISLAND, 3 miles (4.8 km) round, lies at the mouth of Poole Harbour. Here, in August 1907, the BOY SCOUT MOVEMENT was born, when 20 boys, mostly from local Boys' Brigades, plus some from Eton and Harrow, pitched their tents and began to learn about practical skills, the concepts of fair play and good manners from LIEUTENANT-GENERAL ROBERT BADEN POWELL.

David Cornwell, better known as the author JOHN LE CARRÉ, was born in Poole in 1931.

Moreton

Death of a Hero

Moreton is a tiny, heathland village grouped beside a manor house and church, somewhat over-shadowed by the nearby Bovingdon Army Camp. Moreton House belonged to JAMES FRAMPTON, the landowner who led the persecution of the TOLPUDDLE MARTYRS, but the real fascination of this otherwise rather ordinary place is the simple stone grave, set in the new cemetery across the road from the churchyard, of T. E. Lawrence, who is better known as LAWRENCE OF ARABIA.

Lawrence was one of those few men who have actually changed the world. An archaeologist and historian of the Middle East, he found himself, during the First World War, thrust into the Arab fight against the Turks. Modest and unassuming, he nevertheless possessed the charisma and personality necessary to forge the disparate Arab tribes into a formidable guerilla force. He made possible the victories of General Allenby in Palestine and the defeat of the Turkish army. Much of his work was undone after the War by political treachery and short-sightedness, but

his lasting legacy was to unite the Arab world.

In 1923, Lawrence bought CLOUDS HILL, a small secluded cottage, hidden by rhododendron bushes, just up the road from Bovingdon Camp and close to his relations, the Framptons of Moreton House. Here he was able to retire from the limelight and concentrate on finishing his book about his Arabian adventures, *The Seven Pillars of Wisdom.* He was also able to indulge his passion for motor bikes, and was often to be seen speeding around the Dorset lanes. In May 1935, he rode his Brough to Bovingdon Camp, to send a telegraph, and then set out on the return journey, along the straight stretch of road to Clouds Hill. He had just crested a slight rise when he collided with two errand boys on bicycles and was knocked unconscious. He remained in a coma for several days and died on 19 May, aged only 46. The King of Iraq attended his burial. A tree was planted to mark the site of the accident and the T. E. Lawrence Society have now added a stone memorial.

Worth Matravers

First Vaccination

Worth Matravers is a remote and windswept village high above the ocean on the Purbeck Hills. The houses are all made from local stone carved out of the patchwork of quarries located round about, and the church is one of the oldest in Dorset, with a Saxon doorway and Norman arches. In the bleak churchyard, under a mossy stone, lie a simple farmer and his wife. With their courage and instinct they did more to improve the life of ordinary people than any world leader or vaunted politician.

In 1774, BENJAMIN JESTY was a farmer living at YETMINSTER, near SHERBORNE. At the time, the area was ravaged by smallpox. With a pregnant wife and three small children to care for, he was naturally worried for the health of his family. He noticed that his two dairymaids, both of whom had suffered from the mild complaint of cowpox, had nursed family members suffering from the more serious and highly contagious smallpox, and yet neither of them had caught the disease themselves. From this he concluded that cowpox gave immunity to smallpox.

He determined to give his wife and children a dose of cowpox, and so he took them to a nearby farm at Chetnole, where there was an outbreak of the infection. In an open field, he took some pus from an

infected cow and, using the point of a stocking needle, scratched his wife's arm and injected the pus, thus performing the WORLD'S FIRST RECORDED VACCINATION. The term vaccination comes from the Latin word for cow, *vacca*. He then repeated the procedure on his two sons. All three of them suffered for a few days from the cowpox and then recovered completely. It was to be another 20 years before Edward Jenner first used vaccination on a boy called James Phipps in 1796.

In 1797, the Jestys moved to Worth Matravers, where Benjamin performed many more vaccinations on the local people. On his gravestone are the words, 'the first person (known) that introduced the Cow Pox by innoculation'.

Monmouth's Ash

A Fallen Prince

On 11 June 1685, the DUKE OF MONMOUTH, the pretender to the throne, landed on the beach at LYME REGIS with about 80 men, including England's FIRST NOVELIST, DANIEL DEFOE. They marched north, picking up support as they went, and met with the forces of James II, led by John Churchill (later Duke of Marlborough) at SEDGEMOOR in Somerset on 6 July.

Monmouth's army was soundly defeated and he fled across country with Lord Grey and three companions. They headed to Dorset, making for Poole, where they hoped to catch a boat to Holland. At WOODYATES, just inside Dorset to the north, was an inn owned by the EARL OF SHAFTESBURY and tenanted by Robert Browning, ancestor of the poet. Here, the group left their horses and split up, Monmouth disguised as a shepherd. He made his way into open country near Horton, and was seen climbing over a hedge by an old woman, AMY FARRANT, living in a nearby cottage. A search was organised at sunrise and a militiaman named PARKIN spotted what looked like a pile of clothes in a ditch beneath an ash tree. He dragged out the Duke of Monmouth, by then haggard and scruffy, with nothing in his pocket except raw peas and a badge of the Order of the Garter, given to him by his father, Charles II. The spot has been known ever since as Monmouth's Ash. Monmouth was beheaded on Tower Hill on 15 July. In the aftermath, at the 'Bloody Assizes' of Judge Jeffreys, over 300 of Monmouth's supporters were executed.

The defeat at Sedgemoor was not entirely unproductive for Daniel Defoe. While hiding in a churchyard during his escape, he saw the name ROBINSON CRUSOE on a gravestone and filed it away for later use.

Well, I never knew this

ABOUT

DORSET

Old Smith's Arms

After the Restoration, CHARLES II returned many times to Dorset to thank all those who had helped him during his escape after the Battle of Worcester in 1651. On one of these trips, he stopped in GODMANSTONE and asked at the blacksmith's forge for a glass of porter. The blacksmith replied that he was unable to oblige as he had no licence to sell alcohol. 'From now on, you have a licence to sell beer and porter,' said the King, and the OLD SMITH'S ARMS at Godmanstone was born. At 20 ft (6 m) by 10 ft (3 m), it is the SMALLEST PUBLIC HOUSE IN THE WORLD.

It was on WEYMOUTH BEACH that GEORGE III became the FIRST MONARCH TO USE A BATHING MACHINE. As he went into the water, a band, hidden in another machine, struck up 'God Save the King'!

Most of the questions for the popular board game TRIVIAL PURSUIT were researched in the public library at WEYMOUTH by John Haney, brother of inventor Chris Haney.

It is believed that a foreign ship putting into port at WEYMOUTH brought the BLACK DEATH to England in 1348.

The famous Hovis advert featuring a small boy pushing his bicycle up a steep hill was filmed on GOLD HILL in SHAFTESBURY.

WIMBORNE ST GILES is a handsome brick village near Cranborne and the ancient seat of the EARLS OF SHAFTESBURY. In the grand church, refashioned in the 18th century, is the imposing tomb of SIR ANTHONY ASHLEY. A strange ball carved on his tomb gives away his guilty secret, for Sir Anthony was the first man to introduce into England that green vegetable despised by schoolboys across the land, the cabbage. He brought it across from Holland and, in 1539, the FIRST CABBAGE GROWN IN ENGLAND was cultivated in the kitchen garden of St Giles House, Wimborne St Giles. The ball on the tomb represents that cabbage.

In 1980, Meryl Streep starred in *The French Lieutenant's Woman*, which was filmed mainly at LYME REGIS. The most enduring image is of Streep dressed in a black cloak standing on the breakwater known as the COBB.

DURHAM

COUNTY TOWN: DURHAM

'Grey towers of Durham
Yet well I love thy mixed and massive piles
Half church of God, half castle 'gainst the Scot.'

SIR WALTER SCOTT

Gateshead

Let There Be Light

Gateshead is an ancient town with a modern skyline. In 1720, DANIEL DEFOE wrote *Robinson Crusoe* here. In 1854, much of the town was destroyed by fire. Not long after that, a Gateshead house became the FIRST HOUSE IN ENGLAND TO BE LIT USING ELECTRIC LIGHT BULBS.

SIR JOSEPH SWAN, born in Sunderland in 1828, had been experimenting with light bulbs using a carbon fibre

filament since 1850 and, in 1878, he was able to unveil the WORLD'S FIRST PRACTICAL, LONG-LASTING LIGHT BULB, which he demonstrated in his own home, UNDERHILL, on Low Fell, Gateshead. The key was to create a vacuum in the bulb so that there was no oxygen to ignite the filament; thus it could glow white hot without catching fire. In 1881, Swan started the SWAN ELECTRIC LIGHT COMPANY, the first foundations of a worldwide industry. Gateshead truly did give light to the world. Swan's demonstration came almost a year before THOMAS EDISON unveiled his light bulb. Edison at first accused Swan of copying his work, but it became clear that they had developed their bulbs coincidentally, at the same time, but on different sides of the Atlantic. Eventually, the two men became partners and formed a company known as the Edison and Swan United Electric Light Company.

The ANGEL OF THE NORTH, by ANTONY GORMLEY, stands above the A1 in Gateshead, marking the southern entry to Tyneside. Assembled in 1998, it is 65 ft (20 m) high and has a wing span of 180 ft (55 m) and is one of THE BIGGEST SCULPTURES IN BRITAIN along with the B of the Bang in Manchester.

Two well-known athletes, STEVE CRAM, the long-distance runner, and PAUL GASCOIGNE, the England footballer, were both born in Gateshead – Steve Cram in 1960 and Paul Gascoigne in 1967.

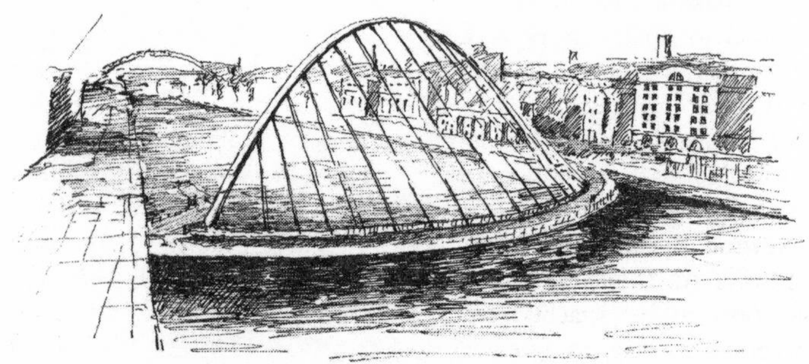

The Gateshead Millennium Bridge, opened in September 2001, is the world's only tilting bridge. The design is so energy efficient it costs just £3.60 each time it opens.

Darlington

Where the Railways Began

The Flying Scotsman, the Union Pacific Railroad, the Trans-Siberian Railway, the French TGV, the Japanese Bullet train. They all owe everything to this little Durham town on the River Skerne where, on 27 September 1825, the FIRST TRAIN MADE THE FIRST TRAIN JOURNEY ON THE FIRST PUBLIC RAILWAY LINE IN THE WORLD. From Darlington, the railways spread across the world, opening up continents, enabling new industries to develop and creating new possibilities and horizons.

'George, you must think of Darlington, remember it was Darlington sent for thee.' So said EDWARD PEASE to GEORGE STEPHENSON when they were discussing the route for a railway line to carry coal to Stockton. A Quaker businessman, Edward Pease had the vision to see how the railway could benefit his home town and the wealth to make it happen. He hired Stephenson to do the work and so began the Railway Age.

On that momentous day, LOCOMOTION NUMBER ONE, brought by road from Newcastle overnight, was placed on the tracks at HEIGHINGTON, near Newton Aycliffe, and taken to the MASONS ARMS LEVEL CROSSING AT SHILDON to be attached to 12 coal wagons, 21 wagons fitted with seats and one passenger coach called 'Experiment'. With George Stephenson himself driving, and preceded by a signalman on horseback, the train drove to Darlington and then on to Stockton, at an average speed of 12 mph (19 kph). Three hundred tickets were sold and nearly 600 passengers made the journey. The world would never be the same again.

Locomotion Number One is now in the Darlington Railway Museum located in the original 1842 North Road Station. A little to the north of the Bank Top Station, on the main line from London to Edinburgh, is a notice indicating where the Darlington to Stockton line crosses the main line.

Stockton

A Match for Anywhere

Stockton-on-Tees is a bustling and airy industrial town near the mouth of the River Tees, famous for its market, which dates back to 1310. THOMAS SHERATON, the furniture maker, was born here in 1751.

Stockton has the WIDEST HIGH STREET IN ENGLAND and, at No. 58, is the shop where chemist JOHN WALKER invented the FRICTION MATCH in 1827. He was born in

Stockton in 1781 and sold his first batch of matches to a Stockton solicitor. He did a roaring trade for two or three years, but then rather lost interest and left others to develop the idea further. His, however, was the initial spark.

At the south end of the High Street is Bridge Road, which leads to the eastern terminus of the WORLD'S FIRST PUBLIC RAILWAY, the Stockton and Darlington Railway (*see* Darlington). A little further on, across the road, there is a small building, once an inn, sporting a plaque that reads:

Here, in 1825, the Stockton and Darlington Company booked the first passenger, thus marking an epoch in the history of mankind.

This was the FIRST RAILWAY BOOKING OFFICE IN THE WORLD.

Washington

Cradle of a Superpower and the Queen of Iraq

From the quiet Durham mining village of Washington springs the family that gave America its first President. The first men to bear the name of Washington came here in 1173 and then spread throughout the country – the President's branch to Sulgrave in Northamptonshire. Their old home, Washington Old Hall, is now owned by the National Trust.

In 1868, there was born in Washington a girl who became known as the QUEEN OF IRAQ. GERTRUDE BELL, daughter of Sir Thomas Bell, the iron master, had a passion for travel. After obtaining a first in history at Oxford before she was 20, she went exploring in the Middle East, through Turkey, Syria and Palestine, riding a camel through the Arabian desert where no western woman had ever ventured.

She made friends of the Arabs, who called her 'daughter of the desert'. She mapped uncharted sands, located water wells and railway lines, and picked up an unsurpassed understanding of the culture and politics of the people. She knew who could be friends to Britain and who might be foes, and her experience made her a vital asset to Britain's Arab Bureau in the First World War. Her knowledge made possible the exploits of LAWRENCE OF ARABIA (*see* Moreton, Dorset) with whom she became great friends.

After the War, she was invited to the Middle East Conference in Egypt convened by Winston Churchill to determine the future of MESOPOTAMIA. She was, at this time, the most powerful woman in the British Empire. It was she who drew up the boundaries of the new Middle East, particularly the borders of Iraq, and she promoted Prince Faisal as Iraq's first ruler. She was his close friend and adviser for many years, which earned her the title the 'Queen of Iraq'. Many people hold her responsible for the troubles in the Middle East today. Lawrence of Arabia, for instance, walked away from the Conference believing that the Arabs were being betrayed by the British. Gertrude Bell thought she could serve them better by staying and helping them develop and coalesce as nations. She died in Baghdad in 1926, and is buried there in the British Cemetery.

BRYAN FERRY, pop singer originally with Roxy Music, was born in Washington in 1945.

Causey Arch

The World's First Railway Bridge

There is something melancholy here. The countryside is bleak, the towns industrial and grim. A grey road strikes north from Stanley. The car park is scruffy. A path leads to dark, dank woods and descends into the gloom. No birds sing, the walls of the canyon close in, the silence is oppressive. Nothing seems to happen here, time hangs heavy. But follow the mossy path along the rocky stream and then, suddenly, stark against the grey sky, there it is: a simple, perfect arch, completely beautiful, suspended above the river, the FIRST RAILWAY BRIDGE THE WORLD HAD EVER SEEN.

Built in 1726, Causey Arch was financed by a group of coal owners called the 'Grand Allies' to carry a waggonway for transporting coal from Tanfield to the River Tyne. At its peak, more than 900 wagons a day

crossed this bridge, drawn by horses along two timber railtracks. For 30 years, it was the LONGEST SINGLE SPAN IN BRITAIN, 105 ft (32 m) across and 80 ft (24 m) high above the Causey Burn. It was the most ambitious feat of enginering anyone had attempted since Roman times. In fact, since no one had any experience of constructing anything like it, the builder, local mason RALPH WOOD, relied on what he knew of Roman technology. His first attempt, in 1725, fell down, and he was so sure that this second effort would collapse too that he hurled himself off the bridge and plunged to his death in the gorge below.

His wondrous creation, however, stands to this day, forerunner of such marvels as the Sounding Arch (*see* Maidenhead, Berkshire) and the Forth Bridge, yet there is something forlorn about it now. The glory days are gone and Causey Arch sits here, forgotten and brooding, a mournful memorial to its tortured creator.

If you follow the track way from the bridge, you come to Causey Station, which is the southern terminus for the Causey to Sunniside section of the Tanfield Railway. This follows the route of the original 1725 waggonway for which Causey Arch was built and is the OLDEST WORKING RAILWAY IN THE WORLD.

Well, I never knew this ABOUT COUNTY DURHAM

The FIRST PURPOSE-BUILT LIFEBOAT IN THE WORLD, the *Original*, was launched at SOUTH SHIELDS on 30 January 1790.

HIGH FORCE on the River Tees, near Middleton, is the BIGGEST WATERFALL IN ENGLAND in terms of water flow, and has a drop of 70 ft (21.4 m).

ST PETER'S CHURCH at MONKWEARMOUTH in Sunderland was the FIRST ENGLISH CHURCH TO HAVE GLASS WINDOWS. It was built in 674 by Benedict Biscop, who went on to build St Paul's Monastery and Church in Jarrow. Of the original structure, only the tower and west wall remain, marooned in the middle of a traffic island.

SUNDERLAND FC was the FIRST FOOTBALL CLUB IN THE WORLD TO GO ON AN OVERSEAS TOUR. They went to the United States of America in 1894.

ALAN PRICE, pop singer, was born in DURHAM in 1942.

The beautiful and simple 7th-century Saxon church at Escomb, outside Bishop Auckland, is the oldest church in its original form in England. On the south wall is a Saxon sundial, the oldest sundial in England.

The first keep-fit class for housewives in England was held in Sunderland in 1929.

In the Napoleonic Wars, a French warship was wrecked offshore of Hartlepool and the only survivor to reach land was the ship's monkey. The citizens of Hartlepool didn't get out much and had never seen a 'Frenchie' before, so they assumed that this poor ape must be one. They manhandled him into the town square and hanged him as a spy.

In 1720, Mrs Clements of Durham produced England's first mustard in paste form.

On 1 October 2002, Durham became the first city in Britain to introduce a congestion charge.

Essex

County Town: Chelmsford

'Low hills, rich fields, calm rivers
In Essex seek them all'

Arthur Shearly Cripps

Tymperley's, in Colchester, home of William Gilbert, physician to Elizabeth I and the first person to coin the word 'electricity'

Chelmsford

Dawn of Radio

There has been a settlement at Chelmsford since Roman times, when it was an important staging post between Colchester and London. Since 1218, it has been the county town of Essex – always a good question for a pub quiz as Colchester seems a much more likely answer. Chelmsford, set in rich farmland, is a busy industrial and market town, with few architectural pleasures and a modest cathedral, but it has always been at the cutting edge of technology, producing, for example, BRITAIN'S FIRST ELECTRIC TOASTER, THE ECLIPSE.

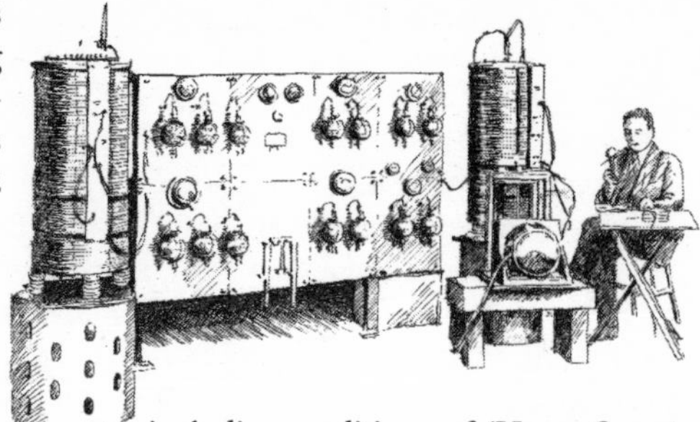

However, Chelmsford truly lives in glory as the HOME OF RADIO. In 1898, MARCONI had already set up a crude, experimental transmitting station at Poole (*see* Dorset) but, in 1899, he opened the WORLD'S FIRST RADIO FACTORY in Hall Street, Chelmsford. The site is marked with a blue plaque. In 1912, Marconi moved into the WORLD'S FIRST PURPOSE-BUILT RADIO FACTORY in New Street, Chelmsford and, in January 1920, inaugrated BRITAIN'S FIRST BROADCASTING SERVICE from here. On 12 February 1920, the WORLD'S FIRST WIRELESS NEWS SERVICE was inaugurated from Chelmsford, read by W.T. DITCHAM. Then, in June 1920, DAME NELLIE MELBA became the FIRST PROFESSIONAL ARTISTE TO BROADCAST IN BRITAIN with a 30-minute show from Chelmsford, commissioned by Lord Northcliffe of the *Daily Mail* and including renditions of 'Home Sweet Home', 'Nymphs and Sylvains' and 'Chant Venitien'. A blue plaque resides on the front door of the New Street factory, which is now a listed building.

Shortly after this, transmissions from Chelmsford were suspended, as they were thought to be interfering with vital communictions to ships and aircraft. Just up the road, however, in the gorgeous old village of WRITTLE, Marconi had set up a small station in a long wooden hut in Lawford Lane. Writtle, much overshadowed by Chelmsford, is one of the loveliest villages in England, with a ravishing variety of ancient

Writtle

cottages surrounding a lush green, complete with duck pond. It already had a place in the history books as the birthplace, in 1274, of ROBERT THE BRUCE, at Montpeliers Farm on Margaretting Road. On 14 February 1922, Writtle became the site of the FIRST REGULAR PUBLIC BROADCAST PROGRAMME IN BRITAIN, written, produced and presented by CAPTAIN P.P. ECKERSLEY, the FIRST RADIO STAR. Since he also played music, he could be described as the FIRST DISC JOCKEY.

During 1922, three other radio stations were set up in Britain, Marconi's, and Western Electric in London and Metropolitan Vickers in Manchester. In November, they all merged into the BRITISH BROADCASTING COMPANY operating out of Marconi's London studios. Writtle remained independent and, for its last two months, was the only alternative to the BBC, until pirate radio in the 1960s. Writtle closed down in January 1923 and Captain Eckersley became the BBC's FIRST CHIEF ENGINEER. The old wooden hut is now at the Chelmsford Science and Industry Museum at Sandford Mill.

In 1927, the BBC was nationalised and became the British Broadcasting Corporation. In 1937, Marconi's in Chelmsford introduced Britain's FIRST FIVE-DAY WORKING WEEK.

Bradwell

The Oldest Church in England

Here, we are on the edge of the world. The land is flat, the wind races over the fields, the marshes echo with the haunting cries of birds. A long stretch of Roman road leads east from the village, becomes a track and then a path. At the end of this path, where the sea meets the sky, is the OLDEST CHURCH IN ENGLAND.

ST PETER'S CHAPEL, BRADWELL-ON-SEA, was built to mark the spot where St Cedd landed in 654, on his mission from Lindisfarne to lighten the Dark Ages of the heathen East Angles. This must have been one of the biggest buildings in the land when it was constructed. Using bricks and stone from the ruined Roman fort of Othona, the Saxons created what was almost a cathedral, 50 ft (15.2 m) long, 22 ft (6.7 m) wide and 25 ft (7.6 m) high. The people of Essex worshipped here for 600 years or more, but, so remote was this spot, that congregations soon

dwindled and the chapel eventually passed out of knowledge, which is probably how it has survived.

In 1920, a passing rambler noticed the noble proportions, the round window high up in the walls, the arches and the gables. He started to excavate and soon realised that what he was looking at was something wondrous. This was sacred ground. The hay bales and the horse carts were tidied away and St Peter's Chapel was restored as a place for peace and reflection. It is still a long way away from the rest of the world, but well worth the pilgrimage.

Dick Turpin

The highwayman Dick Turpin was born in the 17th-century CROWN INN in HEMPSTEAD, near Saffron Walden, in 1706.

The real Dick Turpin was rather different from the legend. Caught stealing meat from the butcher to whom he was apprenticed, he disappeared into the Essex countryside with his friends and survived by robbing isolated farmhouses, torturing the occupants until they gave up their valuables. A bounty of £100 was put on his head, along with his 'Essex Gang'. His fortunes took a turn for the better when he met and teamed up with the swashbuckling TOM KING, a well-known highwayman with a reputation for gallantry and style. They lived rough in a cave in Epping Forest from which they

could watch the road and waylay anyone likely who came past.

Disaster struck when they stole a fine horse which was traced to the Red Lion at Whitechapel, where they were celebrating, and Tom King was arrested. In the ensuing scuffle, King was accidently shot by Turpin, who fled. He realised it was now unsafe for him to remain in Essex and he headed for Yorkshire, where he led the life of a country gentleman, calling himself John Palmer. He financed his way of life with frequent trips into Lincolnshire, where he rustled cattle and committed numerous highway robberies. He was finally caught poaching from his landlord and put in gaol in York where, through an extraordinary concatenation of circumstances, he was recognised as Dick Turpin by his old schoolmaster. He was sentenced to death and was hanged at York Racecourse on 19 April 1739. He faced execution with a certain amount of courage and style, thus augmenting his reputation so that it has survived years after his death.

Well, I never knew this ABOUT ESSEX

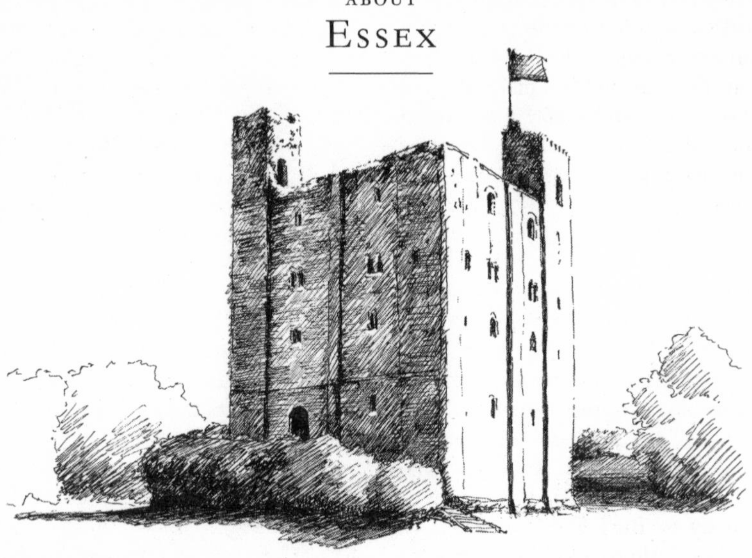

The great keep of CASTLE HEDINGHAM, at over 100 ft (30.5 m) high, is the BEST PRESERVED KEEP OF ITS KIND IN ENGLAND. The roof of the Great Hall on the second floor is held up by the LARGEST NORMAN ARCH IN THE WORLD with a span of 28 ft (8.5 m).

ST BOTOLPH'S CHURCH overlooking the thatched north Essex village of HADSTOCK has the OLDEST DOOR IN ENGLAND. It's possible that this church is the minster built by King Canute to celebrate his victory over Edmund Ironside at Assandun in 1016; the door dates from that time, making it not far short of 1,000 years old. It is the ONLY KNOWN SAXON DOOR IN ENGLAND STILL IN USE.

A plain, inoffensive looking bungalow in the Essex countryside south of Ongar hides a dark and sinister secret from the past. The bungalow, at KELVEDON HATCH, is, in fact, the government's top secret, Cold War NUCLEAR BUNKER. Burrowing into the hillside behind, rather like a Hobbit hole, is a labyrinth of secret passages and rooms where the Prime Minister and his staff would have tried to run whatever was left of a post-nuclear Britain. Stretching 75 ft (23 m) underground and encased in reinforced concrete 10 ft (3 m) thick, the whole complex was constructed without any of the locals knowing what was going on. The government must feel safer today as the bunker is now open to the public.

First presented in 1244, the DUNMOW FLITCH is the OLDEST RECORDED COMPETITION IN ENGLAND. A side of pork is awarded to the couple who can best convince the judge and jury that they 'having been married for at least a year and a day, have never once, sleeping or waking, regretted our marriage or wished ourselves single again'.

GREENSTED CHURCH, hidden in a bower of trees near CHIPPING ONGAR, has the OLDEST WOODEN WALLS IN ENGLAND, is the OLDEST WOODEN BUILDING IN EUROPE and the OLDEST WOODEN CHURCH IN THE WORLD. The oak trees used to build it gave shade to the Romans. King Edmund's body rested here on its journey to Bury St Edmunds from London. Almost within earshot of the M25, it is a little piece of Essex untroubled by modern times.

SOUTHEND-ON-SEA has the LONGEST PIER IN THE WORLD, at 1⅓ miles (2.1 km) in length. It was begun in 1889 and extended in 1898 to accommodate the steamers bringing day trippers from London – when the tide recedes it leaves over 1 mile (1.6 km) of mudflats. In 1929, it reached its present record length. The pier has been hit by a number of fires over the years and, in 1986, the *MV Kings Abbey* sliced through it about two-thirds of the way out. The pier has since been fully repaired and featured in the closing credits of the TV series *Minder*. A small electric train runs along the full distance.

WALTHAM ABBEY is reputed to be the burial place of KING HAROLD. His grave lies outside, beyond the eastern wall of the present building, on the site of the old high altar. The grand Norman nave that remains is second only to that of Durham Cathedral.

In 1903, at the Tudor BRADWELL LODGE, a former rectory, in the village of BRADWELL-ON-SEA, ERSKINE CHILDERS wrote one of the

FIRST SPY STORIES, *The Riddle of the Sands*, about a German invasion of Britain. Childers had Anglo-Irish parentage and became a staunch advocate of Irish Home Rule. A keen yachtsman, he used his boat to smuggle arms into Ireland for the Easter Uprising of 1916. Nonetheless, he served with distinction in the Royal Navy during the First World War, winning a DSC. In 1921, he became a Member of the Irish Parliament for Sinn Fein and, along with Eamon de Valera, was one of the leaders of the IRA rebellion against the Irish Free State under Michael Collins. He was executed by an Irish Free State firing squad on 24 November 1922, for possession of a firearm.

In 1696, an energetic, non-conformist minister arrived in MALDON and built a new chapel on the site where he preached to crowds of 400 people or more. His sermons were fervent, full of gusto, impassioned – and long. His name was JOSEPH BILLIO, and such was his enthusiasm that his name passed into the language, as in the phrase 'to do something like billio'.

Gloucestershire

County Town: Gloucester

'Yes, I remember Adlestrop . . .
. . . because one afternoon
Of heat, the express train drew up there . . .
And for that minute a blackbird sang,
Close by and round him, mistier,
Farther and farther, all the birds of
Oxfordshire and Gloucestershire'

Edward Thomas

Gloucester Cathedral

Gloucester

Ice Cream and Wizards

Gloucestershire's county town is often compared unfavourably to Cheltenham or Tewkesbury, although it is older and more hard working than both. It has been heavily industrialised, and boasts the LARGEST ICE CREAM FACTORY IN EUROPE (Wall's), as well as a huge ICI paintworks. In addition, it is still a working port, and has both a robust jauntiness and a whiff of the sea about it.

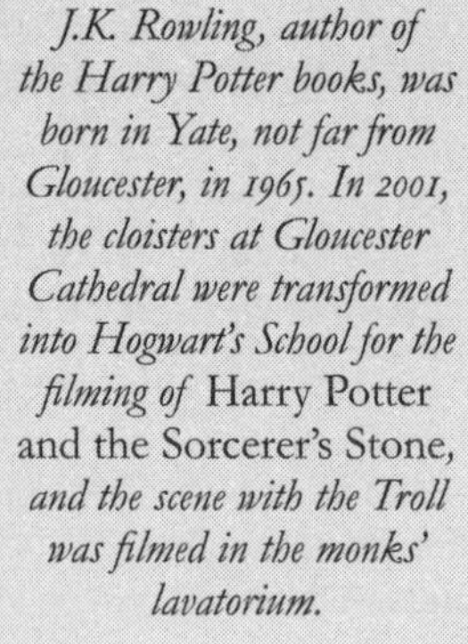

J.K. Rowling, author of the Harry Potter books, was born in Yate, not far from Gloucester, in 1965. In 2001, the cloisters at Gloucester Cathedral were transformed into Hogwart's School for the filming of Harry Potter and the Sorcerer's Stone, *and the scene with the Troll was filmed in the monks' lavatorium.*

The cathedral is one of the most remarkable buildings in Europe. Built round a Norman core, it is the FIRST GREAT EXAMPLE OF THE ENGLISH PERPENDICULAR STYLE. The tower, in particular, is renowned. Two royals are buried within, ROBERT OF NORMANDY, son of William the Conqueror, and EDWARD II. The great east window, known as the Crécy Window, is, at 72 ft (22 m) by 38 ft (11.5 m), the LARGEST STAINED GLASS WINDOW IN BRITAIN. The exquisite fan vaulting in the cloisters, which dates from the 14th century, is the FIRST EXAMPLE OF FAN VAULTING IN BRITAIN.

Crécy Window

Also buried in the cathedral is JOHN STAFFORD-SMITH, the man who composed the tune for the AMERICAN NATIONAL ANTHEM, the 'Star-Spangled Banner'. He was born in Gloucester in 1750, and wrote the music as a constitutional song for the Anachreonic Society, a group of musicians and composers whose members have included J. S. Bach and Henry Purcell. The tune was chosen, in 1814, by FRANCIS SCOTT KEY, to accompany the words he had written to celebrate the defiant flag flying over the beseiged Fort McHenry, outside Baltimore, during the War of American Independence.

The WORLD'S EARLIEST KNOWN BACKGAMMON SET, dating from 1120, was found in Gloucester. It was discovered in 1990, in a cesspit on the site of Gloucester Castle, where it had been disposed of by WALTER OF GLOUCESTER when he renounced all his vices to become a monk.

W. E. HENLEY (1849-1903), poet, was born in Gloucester (*see* Cockayne Hatley, Bedfordshire), as was SIR CHARLES WHEATSTONE (1802–75), inventor of the accordion and the FIRST BRITISH ELECTRIC TELEGRAPH.

Bristol

Cradle of the New World

The mighty city of Bristol, gathered on its hillside above the River Avon, has a long history of adventure, exploration and trade. From here, in 1497, JOHN and SEBASTIAN CABOT set sail in the little ship *Matthew* and found AMERICA. Columbus only discovered islands. It was an English flag from Bristol that was first planted on the American mainland, at LABRADOR. CABOT TOWER commemorates this achievement, and every Bristolian knows that the New World was named in honour of the man who was Sheriff of Bristol at the time, RICHARD AMERYCKE. And it was Bristol men who formed the Society of Merchant Venturers to exploit the new discoveries and underwrite the development of the early American colonies. They sent out ships to every part of the known world, making the name of Bristol a byword for efficiency and enterprise – 'all ship shape and Bristol fashion'.

Towering beside the old harbour area is the church Elizabeth I described as 'the fairest, goodliest and most famous parish church in England', ST MARY REDCLIFFE.

Across the road from here, in 1783, lived a plumber called WILLIAM WATTS. He was sitting inside one day, watching the rain, when he realised that the falling raindrops were not tear shaped but perfectly spherical, pulled into the shape of least

St Mary Redcliffe

resistance by surface tension. If that was so for raindrops, then why not molten lead? He rushed up to the top of St Mary's tower to experiment and found that his theory worked. So he built a tower on to his three-storey

William Watt's Shot Tower

home, doubling the height, knocked holes in each floor and installed a water tank at the bottom. At the top, he poured molten lead into a sieve, to separate it into pellets, and, by the time the droplets had fallen six floors, they were formed into perfect spheres, which solidified as they were immersed in the water at the bottom. William Watts had created PERFECT BUCK SHOT and made a fortune. He lost it all not long afterwards, financing the building of WINDSOR TERRACE, the massive Georgian block of houses, perched on the cliffs beneath the Clifton Suspension Bridge.

Lead was made at Watt's self-built shot tower until the 1960s, when it was knocked down to accommodate the widening of Redcliffe Hill. In 1968, a new shot tower was built by the harbour in Cheese Lane, which produced shot until 1995. A prominent landmark, this has now been converted into offices.

Behind St Mary Redcliffe, at 9 Colston Parade, SAMUEL PLIMSOLL was born in 1824. It was as a result of the book he wrote about the dangers of overloading ships that the Merchant Shipping Act of 1876 came into being, which required a 'PLIMSOLL LINE' to be painted on every ship to mark its maximum load line.

At the quayside in cobbled King Street is the LLANDOGER TROW, a black and white inn built in 1664 and named after a type of Welsh sailing barge. It was here that DANIEL

Llandoger Trow

DEFOE met and listened to the tales of his model for *Robinson Crusoe*, Alexander Selkirk, who had been rescued by a Bristol privateer named WOODES ROGERS (*see* Poole, Dorset). Woodes Rogers died at a house in Queen Square in 1732 and the site is marked with a plaque.

Almost opposite is the Theatre Royal, home of the BRISTOL OLD VIC. Opened in 1766, this is the OLDEST CONTINUOUSLY WORKING THEATRE IN BRITAIN.

A short walk away, on the pavement outside the Corn Exchange, are four bronze pedestals called 'NAILS'. These were used by merchants for transactions and, when a deal had been agreed, the money was placed on top of the nail – hence the expression 'to pay on the nail'.

Archibald Leach, better known as Hollywood actor CARY GRANT (1904–86), was born in Bristol, at 15 Hughenden Road, Horfield.

Little Sodbury

Education for All

The lonely, lovely, gabled manor house at Little Sodbury, hidden away down winding lanes, not far from Bath, is a very special place. Here, nearly 500 years ago, the first tender shoots of England's democracy began to sprout. Alone in a little attic room, one courageous man began his lifetime's work to translate the Bible into the sort of language that every Englishman could understand

In 1520, WILLIAM TYNDALE, a young and fiery chaplain from Slimbridge, arrived at Little Sodbury as tutor to the children of Sir John Walsh. Much influenced by the ideas of John Wycliffe, Tyndale passionately believed that every Englishman, be he ploughman or parson, farmer or fisherman, should be able to study

the Word of God in his own language. Then he would be able to see through the ignorance and false pieties of the corrupt priesthood. In those days, despite the efforts of John Wycliffe in the 14th century, the Bible was written only in Latin and was interpreted by the Church to serve its own interests. If ordinary folk were given access to reading and knowledge, then the power and authority of a self-serving intelligentsia could be broken.

Tyndale was only able to finish a small portion of the New Testament at Little Sodbury before it became unsafe for him to continue and he had to leave for the Continent. For the next ten years he was harried and chased across Europe, while he tried to complete his work. Eventually, he was betrayed, imprisoned in Brussels and burnt at the stake. His translations of the New Testament and much of the Old survived, however, and, when it suited Henry VIII in his fight against the Church, Tyndale's English Bible was put on sale throughout England. About nine-tenths of the *King James Authorised Bible* is William Tyndale's achievement.

Cheltenham

Greenfly and Gold Cups

Cheltenham is an elegant Regency spa town which celebrates MORE FESTIVALS THAN ANY OTHER TOWN IN ENGLAND – amongst them the renowned CHELTENHAM LITERARY FESTIVAL and the premier NATIONAL HUNT festival, which culminates in the CHELTENHAM GOLD CUP, the blue riband of steeplechasing.

The tree-lined PROMENADE is one of England's loveliest shopping streets. Cheltenham also boasts two famous public schools: CHELTENHAM BOYS' COLLEGE and CHELTENHAM LADIES' COLLEGE. The girls from the Ladies' College wear a pale green uniform and are known locally as 'greenfly'. In 1968, the Boys' College was the location for the anarchic film *If*, starring Malcolm McDowell as a pupil who leads a violent revolt on Speech Day. The film's director, Lindsay Anderson, had been a pupil at the school and there was a terrible furore when the film was released – Anderson had assured the Headmaster that it was going to be a respectable picture, similar to *Tom Brown's Schooldays*!

In 1831, Cheltenham inaugurated ENGLAND'S FIRST REGULAR PASSENGER SERVICE USING SELF-PROPELLED ROAD VEHICLES. Three Gurney steam coaches, designed by Sir Goldsworth Gurney (*see* Bude, Cornwall), travelled between Cheltenham and Gloucester, a distance of 9 miles (14.5 km), from February to June.

In 1838, Cheltenham was the scene of the FIRST SUCCESSFUL PARACHUTE JUMP BY AN ENGLISHMAN. JOHN HAMPTON took off in a balloon from Montpelier Gardens at the top of the Promenade and jumped out at a height of several thousand feet. He landed safely after a descent lasting 13 minutes.

SIR ARTHUR 'BOMBER' HARRIS (1892–1984), Head of Bomber Command during the Second World War, was born in Cheltenham, as was the composer GUSTAV HOLST (1874–1934), the aircraft designer SIR FREDERICK HANDLEY PAGE (1885–1962), the actor SIR RALPH RICHARDSON (1902–83), and the polar explorer EDWARD WILSON (1872–1912), who died in the Antarctic with Captain Scott.

Well, I never knew this ABOUT GLOUCESTERSHIRE

Badminton House

The Olympic game of BADMINTON was 'invented' at BADMINTON HOUSE, not far from Bristol, in 1863, by the children of the eighth Duke of Beaufort, who were seeking something to do inside during a bleak midwinter. It was, in fact, an English adaptation of an old Indian game, but it proved so popular with the Duke's house guests that it became known as 'that Badminton game'. It is the WORLD'S FASTEST RACQUET SPORT with the shuttlecock reaching speeds of up to 200 mph (322 kph). The magnificent façade of Badminton House is also famous as the backdrop to the BADMINTON HORSE TRIALS, introduced in 1949 by the tenth Duke, a fearsome foxhunter known simply as 'Master'.

DODINGTON, a beautiful 18th-century house outside Bristol, is the home of JAMES DYSON, inventor and manufacturer of the bagless vacuum cleaner.

STROUD is an old Cotswold wool town of steep, narrow streets, set where five deep valleys meet. THE REVD W. AWDRY, author of *Thomas the Tank Engine*, lived just outside, at RODBOROUGH, from 1965 until his death in 1997. Stroud's present-day celebrity is the romantic novelist KATIE FFORDE, who has lived here for 20 years.

In the museum at STROUD you can see the WORLD'S FIRST LAWNMOWER, a FERRABEE, invented in 1830 by Stroud engineer EDWIN BUDDING and made at the PHOENIX IRON WORKS at THRUPP, just down the road. His first customer was Mr Curtis, the Head Gardener at Regent's Park Zoo in London.

In the churchyard of ST LAURENCE CHURCH, STROUD, is the grave of LIEUTENANT JOSEPH DELMONT, who died in 1807, the unfortunate victim of the LAST FATAL DUEL IN BRITAIN.

ANNA FORD, newscaster, was born in TEWKESBURY in 1943.

Author LAURIE LEE (1914–97), best known for his novel *Cider with Rosie*, was born in SLAD, near Stroud, the setting for his novel.

CATHERINE PARR, sixth wife of Henry VIII, and the only one of his wives to outlive him, is buried at SUDELEY CASTLE in Winchcombe. Sudeley was the home of her fourth husband, Sir Thomas Seymour, and she died there in 1548 from complications in childbirth. She was born at Kendal Castle, Westmorland, in 1512. Sudeley is thought to be the model for P.G. WODEHOUSE'S BLANDINGS CASTLE, home of Lord Emsworth.

SIR JIMMY YOUNG, veteran radio broadcaster, was born in CINDERFORD, in the Forest of Dean, in 1921.

Composer RALPH VAUGHAN WILLIAMS (1872–1958) was born in DOWN AMPNEY, near Cirencester.

Hampshire

County Town: Winchester

'the most charming plains that can anywhere be seen, far (in my opinion) excelling the plains of Mecca'

Daniel Defoe

Winchester Cathedral, the longest medieval cathedral in Europe

Basingstoke

Classic Waterproofs

Basingstoke is best known today as the headquarters of the AA. It is one of England's fastest-growing towns, and there is not much left that is ancient. As modern industrial centres go, it is bright and breezy with nicely laid out squares and plenty of green spaces.

In the 19th century, a Basingstoke draper found inspiration from a regular customer who was a local shepherd. He noticed that the shepherd's smock appeared to be waterproof, a quality that the shepherd attributed to an oily substance, absorbed into the smock from wool while he was dipping his sheep. Building on this concept, the draper devised a method of waterproofing his yarn before weaving, as well as on to the finished cloth. He set up a factory in New Street, in the middle of Basingstoke, and never looked back. In 1892, he built a bigger factory in London Street to manufacture the cloth and moved his shop to larger premises in Winchester Street. Eventually he opened a flagship store in the Haymarket in London. He called his product 'GABARDINE' and his name was THOMAS BURBERRY. The Burberry shop in Winchester Street, Basingstoke is still there today, having been rebuilt by Thomas Burberry after a fire in 1905. He died in 1926 at the age of 91.

THE VYNE, a 16th-century country house near Basingstoke, built for Lord Sandys, Henry VIII's Lord Chamberlain, has ENGLAND'S FIRST CLASSICAL PORTICO, which was added in the 17th century. It now belongs to the National Trust.

Alresford

A Heroine

In the little Norman church at BISHOP'S SUTTON, near New Alresford, is a tablet to one of England's unsung heroines, ETHEL RHODA MCNEILE. She gave up her seat in the last lifeboat launched on the *Egypt* and was drowned when the ship sank off Ushant in 1922.

On 20 May, the P&O ship *Eygpt*, with 335 passengers and crew on board, was bound for Bombay, carrying over a million pounds in gold and silver bullion in her hold. In dense fog, 25 miles (40 km) south-west of Ushant, she was struck amidships by the French icebreaker *Seine* and almost sliced in half. The ship keeled over so fast that the women and children had to lie along the rail while the lifeboats were launched, to avoid sliding down the deck and into the sea.

As the last lifeboat was being boarded, the Chief Purser called, 'Three more!' Ethel McNeile was number three but, as she was about to clamber in, she heard a distraught woman cry out, 'Oh my children! What will they do without a Mother?' Ethel picked the woman up and passed her into the waiting boat saying, 'If you don't mind, we will change places.' The lifeboat barely had time to stand off before the

Eygpt rolled over and disappeared beneath the waves. It had taken just 20 minutes to sink.

Old Alresford Rectory

In the Rectory at OLD ALRESFORD, in 1876, the Rector's wife, MARY SUMNER, hosted the FIRST-EVER MEETING OF THE MOTHERS' UNION.

New Forest

Death of a King

The New Forest, ENGLAND'S NEWEST NATIONAL PARK, is the OLDEST AREA OF MAN-MADE WOODLAND IN ENGLAND. It was created in 1079 by William the Conqueror as a hunting ground for deer and wild boar. Hunting was only for the king and his companions, so William established the Ancient Verderers Court to administer the Forest and protect the animals and their habitat. This court still exists and is now one of BRITAIN'S OLDEST JUDICIAL COURTS.

The 'capital' of the New Forest, and site of the Verderers Hall, is LYNDHURST. In the churchyard at Lyndhurst lies Mrs Reginald Hargreaves (1852–1934), who is better known as ALICE LIDDELL, the inspiration for Lewis Carroll's *Alice in Wonderland*.

In a leafy glade near MINSTEAD, just off the A31, is the RUFUS STONE, which marks where William Rufus, King William II, was shot through the heart with an arrow. William Rufus, so known because of his ruddy complexion, was not loved by his people. On 2 August 1100, he was hunting in the New Forest when a deer broke cover, suprising the king and his party. A Norman knight, SIR WALTER TIREL, loosed off an arrow, which missed the deer and glanced off an oaktree, hitting William in the chest. Tirel escaped to safety, crossing the River Avon at a spot still called TYRREL'S FORD. The rest of the king's companions rode off to find William's brother Henry who, fortuitously, was also in the forest, hunting.

The dead king's body was left where it fell, until a charcoal burner named PURKIS found it and took it to Winchester on the back of his cart.

Henry had already been and gone, secured the treasury and ridden on to Westminster to be crowned Henry I. William was buried without a single mourner present, his body interred under the central tower of the cathedral. The next year the tower fell down.

Beneath an oak tree at the east end of the churchyard in Minstead lies the creator of Sherlock Holmes, SIR ARTHUR CONAN DOYLE (1859–1930).

Southampton

Home of the Spitfire

Southampton is the home of the SPITFIRE, the fast and beautiful little plane that, along with the Hawker Hurricane, won the BATTLE OF BRITAIN and so saved the country from invasion. The Spitfire was the brainchild of R.J. MITCHELL, the chief designer at Supermarine, a small outfit based in Southampton. Between 1927 and 1931, he won the SCHNEIDER TROPHY three times with his racing seaplanes. The Spitfire amply demonstrated this racing pedigree, proving faster and more manoeuvrable than its rival the German Messerschmitt 109. Perhaps its most innovative feature was its elliptical wings.

The Spitfire was produced mainly in Southampton, in the Supermarine factory at WOOLSTON, although it was also manufactured at Castle Bromwich in the Midlands. Mitchell died of cancer in 1937, just a year after his masterpiece took to the skies over EASTLEIGH on 5 March 1936.

In 1930, the world's first television interview came from the Ideal Home Exhibition in Southampton, where actress Peggy O'Neil was interviewed by a journalist from the Southern Daily Echo.
Her first words were reported to be, 'This is the first time I have been interviewed by television and it's a rather jolly experience.'

The Queen Mary, *docking at Southampton after her maiden voyage to America on 31 August 1936, was filmed by the BBC for the world's first televised news presentation.*

Southampton was the FIRST TOWN IN BRITAIN TO SAMPLE FISH FINGERS (1955) and the VEGEBURGER (1982).

BORN IN SOUTHAMPTON

CHARLES DIBDIN (1745–1814), composer of rousing sea shanties. In 1803, he was paid by the government to write songs to 'keep alive the national feelings against the French'. He wrote the lines 'In every mess I find a friend, in every port a wife', which gave rise to the notion of sailors having 'a girl in every port'.

SIR JOHN EVERETT MILLAIS, Bt (1829–96), Pre-Raphaelite painter. There is an art gallery named after him in Southampton.

ADMIRAL EARL JELLICOE (1859–1935), Commander of the Grand Fleet at the Battle of Jutland in 1916.

BENNY HILL (1925–92), comedian.

KEN RUSSELL, film director, born 1927.

HOWARD JONES, singer/songwriter, born 1955.

CHARLIE DIMMOCK, TV gardener, born 1966.

JOHN STONEHOUSE (1925–88), MP and Postmaster General under Harold Wilson. John Stonehouse lost the confidence of his party when he was suspected of spying for Czechoslovakia. Unable to progress further up the greasy pole, and with a wife and daughter to support, he turned to business, but was soon under investigation for fraud. In 1974, he disappeared leaving a pile of clothes on a beach in Miami and was thought to have drowned. However, one month later, he was discovered living in Melbourne, Australia, with his secretary and mistress, SHEILA BUCKLEY. Someone in their hotel told the police he had spotted Lord Lucan. Stonehouse was arrested and extradited back to Britain, where he was sent down for seven years. He married Sheila Buckley in 1981 and died of a heart attack on live television in March 1988. His story mirrored that of a television programme being shown on the BBC at that time called *The Fall and Rise of Reginald Perrin*, starring Leonard Rossiter, about a man under pressure who faked his own death.

Portsmouth

Pompey

Just inland from the docks at Portsmouth is the site of No. 1 BRITAIN STREET, where the Second Greatest Briton, according to a BBC poll, engineer ISAMBARD KINGDOM BRUNEL, was born on 9 April 1806. A plaque marks the spot.

Dickens's birthplace

A modest Georgian house at 393 OLD COMMERCIAL ROAD, north of the new city centre shopping centre, was the birthplace, in 1812, of CHARLES DICKENS. It is now a museum in his memory.

Portsmouth can boast of many other distinguished natives, including the Victorian novelist GEORGE MEREDITH (1828–1909), who wrote *Diana of the Crossways*, as well as former Labour Prime Minister

JAMES CALLAGHAN, who was born here in 1912.

In 1712, JONAS HANWAY, a philanthropist who founded the MARINE SOCIETY, was born in Portsmouth. He was the FIRST MAN IN ENGLAND TO USE THAT BADGE OF THE ENGLISH GENTLEMAN, THE UMBRELLA. Hanway travelled widely in the East as a representative of the Russia Company and bought back the prototype of the umbrella from Persia, where they were used to provide shelter from the sun. (*Umbra* is Latin for shade or shadow.) The first English umbrellas were made of wood covered with oiled canvas and were often known as a 'Hanway'.

Portsmouth's neighbouring resort town of SOUTHSEA is the birthplace both of PETER SELLERS, born there on 8 September 1925, and of SHERLOCK HOLMES – SIR ARTHUR CONAN DOYLE practised as a doctor in Southsea at Bush Villas in Elm Grove and wrote his first Holmes novel, *A Study in Scarlet*, there.

Isle of Wight

Royal Retreat

The Isle of Wight, almost an England in miniature, has for a long time been a retreat for troubled royals trying to get away from their cares and problems on the mainland.

In the 11th century, ODO, half brother to WILLIAM THE CONQUEROR, having been accused of treasonable acts, sought sanctuary at CARISBROOKE CASTLE, but was caught and arrested by William himself.

In 1647, CHARLES I fled to the Isle of Wight, hoping that the Governor, COLONEL ROBERT HAMMOND, would assist him in getting away to France. Instead, Hammond imprisoned the king in Carisbrooke Castle. Charles tried to escape by climbing out of a window and sliding down a silk cord, but was caught after becoming wedged in the window bars. He was kept there until 1648, when he was taken away to await his execution at Whitehall on 30 January 1649.

Charles I's daughter, PRINCESS ELIZABETH, born in 1635, was sent to Carisbrooke Castle by Parliament after her father's execution. She died there, of a fever, aged just 14, and was buried by the altar in the church at NEWPORT, where her grave was marked by a simple ES. In 1856, QUEEN VICTORIA restored the grave from obscurity and erected a monument in her ancestor's memory.

Queen Victoria herself retired to OSBORNE HOUSE on the Isle of Wight after the death of Prince Albert and spent much of her time there. She died at Osborne House in 1901.

Well, I never knew this
ABOUT
HAMPSHIRE

The handsome brick village of GREYWELL, near Odiham, stands at the mouth of the 1 mile- (1.6 km-) long tunnel on the Basingstoke Canal. About ¼ mile (400 m) in, the tunnel has collapsed and now provides a home for the LARGEST BAT ROOST IN EUROPE.

Crowning a high hill overlooking Farnborough is ST MICHAEL'S ABBEY, resting place of the LAST OF THE BONAPARTES. After being deposed at the end of the Franco–Prussian War in 1870, NAPOLEON III, nephew of the first Napoleon, was exiled to Chislehurst in Kent, where he died in 1873. His wife EUGENIE moved, in 1880, to a huge rambling Victorian mansion, built by THOMAS LONGMAN of publishing fame, called FARNBOROUGH HILL. There she founded the Abbey and, in the crypt, she laid to rest her husband and son, Leopold, who died fighting with the British against the Zulus in 1879. She died in 1920 and is buried next to them.

A fine viewpoint on the Hampshire hills near Kingsclere, overlooking Lord Andrew Lloyd-Webber's country seat at Sydmonton, is WATERSHIP DOWN. Here, Hazel the rabbit and his friends come to live after their adventures in RICHARD ADAMS's novel of the same name. Adams was born near here, at NEWBURY in BERKSHIRE, and set his best-selling novel in the beautiful countryside he remembered exploring as a boy.

Within the fortifications of the old iron-age fort on BEACON HILL, high point of the north Hampshire Downs, is the grave of the fifth Earl of Carnarvon. He paid for the expedition that discovered the TOMB OF TUTANKHAMEN in the River Nile's Valley of the Kings in 1922. The Earl died in Cairo shortly afterwards, some believe as a result of the Curse of Tutankhamen: 'Death will slay with his wings whoever disturbs the peace of the Pharaoh.' Beacon Hill overlooks the Earl's seat, Highclere Castle, which stands in one of England's loveliest parks. The 7th Earl was the Queen's racing manager.

On 12 July, 1910, at a tournament in BOURNEMOUTH, the HON. C. S. ROLLS, co-founder of Rolls-Royce, became the FIRST BRITISH MAN KILLED IN AN AIR ACCIDENT when his Wright Flyer crashed.

HEREFORDSHIRE

COUNTY TOWN: HEREFORD

'Oh pastoral heart of England!'

SIR ARTHUR QUILLER-COUCH

Hereford

Cider and Oranges

Hereford, heart of England's quietest county, sits on the peaceful banks of the River Wye, clustered round its great red sandstone Norman cathedral. The cathedral possesses the LARGEST CHAINED LIBRARY IN THE WORLD, with 1,444 books, some of them dating back more than 1,000 years, locked and chained to their bookcases. In medieval times, books were so precious that they had to be secured, so that they could be read but not taken away. The library's first book was the *Anglo Saxon Gospel*, written around AD 800.

Also here is the MAPPA MUNDI, drawn in 1289 by RICHARD DI BELLO, Prebend of Hereford, at a time when

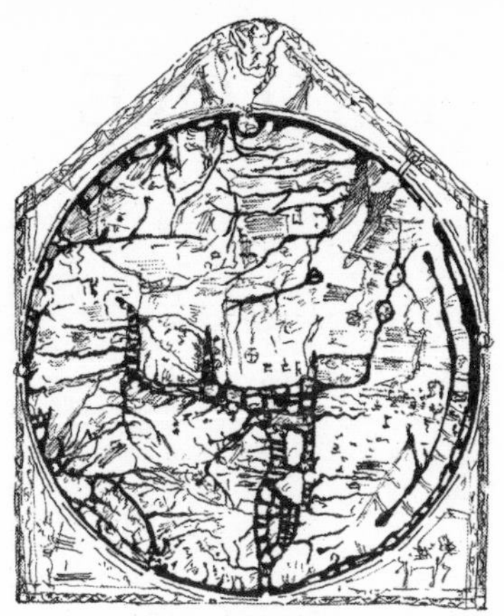

the world was thought to be flat. The map is circular, with Jerusalem, God's city, at the centre, Europe below on the left and Africa to the right. Along the top is Asia. The central sea is the Mediterranean, while the oceans circle the land around the rim. England is situated at the edge of the world. In the 1980s, the cathedral tried to sell the *Mappa Mundi* to raise funds. There was an understandable outcry, which was only quietened when Sir Paul Getty came to the rescue with a sizeable donation, saving the treasure for Hereford and the nation.

A few hundred metres away, at All Saints church, is the SECOND LARGEST CHAINED LIBRARY IN THE WORLD, which contains 300 books donated by WILLIAM BREWSTER in about 1735. The legendary actor and theatre manager, DAVID GARRICK, born in Hereford on 19 February 1717, was christened at All Saints.

Another theatrical icon from Hereford was Charles II's favourite mistress, NELL GWYN. A plaque on the wall of the Bishop's Garden on Gwynne Street, leading down to the river, marks where she was born in 1650. Attracted by the bright lights, Nell Gwyn took herself up to London as a young girl and got a job selling oranges at the King's Theatre. Her quick wit and repartee caught the eye of the theatre company and she was taken on as a comic actress. Dryden wrote several plays specifically for her. She soon became a mistress of Charles II, who adored her boisterous humour and the fact that she had no desire to dabble in politics, unlike his other mistresses, notably Barbara Villiers. She also managed to endear herself to ordinary people because she never took on airs and graces, plus she was also a Protestant. Once, when an angry crowd was jostling her carriage, thinking that the haughty Catholic Duchess of Portsmouth was inside, Nell leaned out of the window and cried, 'Pray good people be civil. I am the Protestant whore!' She had two sons by Charles, one who died and one who was made the Duke of St Albans. His son became Bishop of Hereford. The King loved her to the end and his last words were, 'do not let poor Nellie starve'.

The BULMERS factory in the town is the LARGEST CIDER FACTORY IN THE WORLD. Inside is the Strongbow vat, which has a capacity of 1.63 million gallons (7.4 million litres) and, at 65 ft (20 m) high and 75 ft (23 m) in diameter, is the WORLD'S LARGEST VAT.

Ledbury

Of Poets and Publishers

Ledbury is set on a hilly ridge in the lee of the Malverns. In the words of Poet Laureate JOHN MASEFIELD, who was born here in 1878, in a house still standing called the KNAPP, it is a place 'pleasant to the sight, fair and half timbered houses, black and white'. Masefield is best remembered for his nautical poems.

I must go down to the sea again
To the vagrant gypsy's life

and

Quinquireme of Nineveh from distant ophir
Rowing home to Haven in sunny Palestine
With a cargo of ivory and apes and peacocks
Sandalwood, cedarwood and sweet white wine

An earlier poet born in Ledbury in 1332, before the town was made beautiful in black and white, was WILLIAM LANGLAND, author of *Piers Plowman*. Considered one of the greatest Middle English poems, *Piers Plowman* describes the life and times of an English peasant in the 14th century.

Inside the church is a marble memorial to EDWARD BARRETT, father of the poet ELIZABETH BARRETT BROWNING. Elizabeth knew Ledbury well for, in 1809, when she was three, her family came to live at HOPE END in Colwall, a few miles up the road on the edge of the Malvern Hills. Her father, who became High Sheriff of Herefordshire, had received a tidy inheritance from a Jamaican sugar plantation and built a flamboyant house, complete with turrets, in the middle of 475 acres of park and woodland.

Elizabeth had a happy childhood but her health was never robust and she spent much of her time inside, writing poetry. At the age of 15, on her way to Ledbury, a loose saddle caused her to fall from her horse, inflicting the back injury that was to make her an invalid for the rest of her life. Her mother died when she was 20 and a reversal of the family fortunes meant that Hope End had to be sold and the family moved first to Sidmouth and then to Wimpole Street in London.

Hope End was sold to Thomas Heywood, a banker from Manchester, whose daughter, MARY SUMNER, went on to found the MOTHERS' UNION.

Leintwardine

A Tarnished Hero

Leintwardine is remote and quiet, built on the foundations of the Roman city of Bravinium. At the bottom of the steep main street is a stone bridge, at the top a 12th-century church, gathering in old houses around its skirts. On a wall inside the church is a monument showing a cavalry officer sporting his plumed helmet and sword, SIR BANASTRE TARLETON.

Tarleton was born in Liverpool in 1754, son of a slave merchant. He squandered his inheritance and was forced to buy himself the least expensive commission in the Army, that of a cavalry coronet. Strong, brave, arrogant and a born leader, he was well suited to the cavalry and volunteered for service in America. By 1778, a lieutenant-colonel at the age of 24, Tarleton was leading the British Legion, or TARLETON'S LEGION as it became known, which he had formed out of several dragoon companies. The Legion had a series of astonishing successes at Charleston and at Waxhaws, although here Tarleton gained himself the name 'BLOODY BAN' when many of the American soldiers trying to surrender were killed. At Charlottesville, in 1781, the Legion almost captured Thomas Jefferson, who later became the third President of the United States. At Yorktown, Tarleton put forward a plan that he believed would give the British victory, but this was not put into action and he was forced to join Cornwallis's humiliating surrender of the British forces in 1781. He returned to England, became an MP for Liverpool and was knighted. He died childless in 1833 at the age of 78 and was buried at Leintwardine.

In Mel Gibson's controversial film, *The Patriot*, the villain, Colonel William Tavington, is allegedly based on Banastre Tarleton. Although undoubtedly cruel and vainglorious, Tarleton was by no means the monster depicted by Gibson. If Tarleton had perpetrated the atrocities shown in the film he would have been recalled to England and court martialled, as would his commanding officer, Cornwallis.

Whitbourne

Man in the Moon

On Hereford's far eastern border slumbers tiny Whitbourne village, dozing in a green hollow by a stream, with a moated house and a mossy stone church. The church should be a place of wonder for all devotees of *Dr Who* and *Star Trek*, for here lies the FIRST ENGLISHMAN TO TAKE US TO THE MOON.

Brilliant, eccentric, far-seeing, FRANCIS GODWIN, Bishop of Hereford, was all these things. Some time around 1600 he wrote *The Man in the Moon*, the FIRST SCIENCE FICTION STORY IN THE ENGLISH LANGUAGE. It tells the tale of a Spaniard, Domingo Gonsales, marooned on an island with his black companion (inspiration for Robinson Crusoe and Man Friday?), who is transported to the Moon by a flock of wild swans. On his voyage he is able to observe the truth of Copernicus's theory that the earth is not the centre of the universe but revolves around the sun. He also perceives that the earth possesses a secret property that pulls things towards it but gets weaker with distance and has no power in space – in other words he describes gravity 70 years before Isaac Newton. On the moon, he meets a race of super beings he calls Lunarians, who have no illness or doctors, no arguments or lawyers, no poverty and no crime; they do, however, smoke! If the Lunarians perceive evil in one of their kind, they exile him to Earth. Gonsales, realising that he can never attain their state of perfection, returns himself to Earth. *The Man in the Moon* was not published until after Godwin had died in 1633, but quickly became hugely popular. Hard to believe, but here, in deepest Herefordshire, a gentle bishop first made men dream of travelling to the stars.

Well, I never knew this ABOUT HEREFORDSHIRE

SYMONDS YAT rock is a wooded limestone outcrop, 400 ft (122 m) above where the River Wye meanders around in a lazy 5-mile (8-km) loop. It is a well-known beauty spot, with magnificent views, the summer home to peregrine falcons and romantic couples. In 1993, Symonds Yat provided the picturesque backdrop to the film *Shadowlands*, a tender love story directed by Richard Attenborough and starring Anthony Hopkins and Debra Winger as the writer C.S. LEWIS and his dying wife, JOY GRESHAM. Also prominent in the film is BICKNOR COURT FARM, 1 mile (1.5 km) down the road.

The little church in the fields at KILPECK, south of Hereford, is regarded as the MOST PERFECT NORMAN CHURCH IN ENGLAND. It rests on a gentle mound with views to the distant Malverns and the Black Mountains of Wales. Sole survivor among the ruins of castle and priory, Kilpeck sports a remarkable gallery of amazingly well-preserved Norman carvings, both inside and out. Animals, dragons, dancing figures, birds, monsters, people doing all manner of things, lovers entangled, priests a praying, all life is here, shown in joyous, uninhibited detail. There are gaps in the outside ring of corbels where the Victorians removed some of the more boisterous exhibits, otherwise Kilpeck is virtually untouched since it was built, no doubt thanks to its remote location. A gem in quietest Herefordshire.

In the far west of Herefordshire, on the Welsh border, the ruins of CLIFFORD CASTLE tower above the River Wye, birthplace, in around 1140, of JANE CLIFFORD. She was FAIR ROSAMUND, beloved mistress of Henry II, poisoned by the Queen in her bower at Woodstock and buried at Godstow (*see* Oxfordshire).

HERTFORDSHIRE

COUNTY TOWN: HERTFORD

'Hearty, homely, loving Hertfordshire'

CHARLES LAMB

St Albans Abbey, shrine to England's first Christian martyr

Hertford

The First Paper Mill

In 1494, JOHN TATE established the FIRST PAPER MILL IN BRITAIN at SELE MILL, on a site opposite the Hertford County Hospital. The EARLIEST KNOWN WATERMARK IN BRITAIN is John Tate's star and circle mark, found on a Papal Bull recognising Henry Tudor's right to the English throne as Henry VII. Henry VII visited the mill on two occasions, no doubt to examine and purchase the paper for the Bull. This paper mill began Hertfordshire's long association with the paper industry.

On 18 July 1602, SAMUEL STONE was born in Fore Street, Hertford. In 1633, he emigrated to America and, in 1636, Stone and his fellow Puritan, THOMAS HOOKER, formed a colony in a Dutch trading fort at the end of the navigable section of the Connecticut River. They called the new town Hartford and it is now the state capital of Connecticut, as well as the headquarters of America's insurance industry. The Dutch in the area called the English 'Jon Quese' or 'John Cheese', a joke on the name John Bull. It sounded to the English like 'Yankee', and that is how the Connecticut English became known.

WILLIAM EARL JOHNS (1893–68), creator of 'Biggles', was born in Hertford.

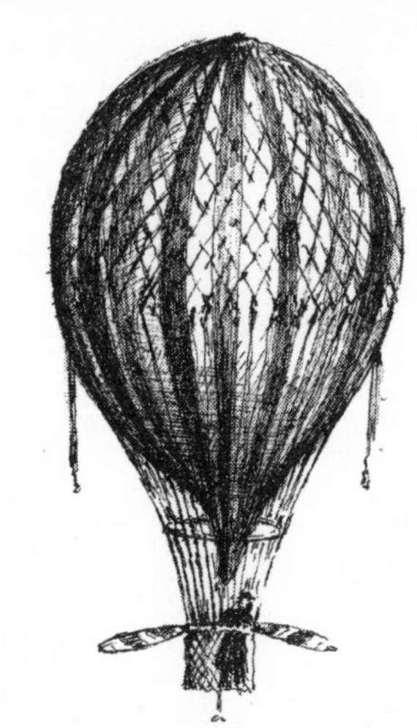

Standon

Balloon Over Britain

One September afternoon in 1784, the good people of STANDON GREEN END, a well mannered village just north of Ware, were going about their business, when an excitable voice hailed them from aloft with strange and unusual cries. Strong men quailed, women gathered up their children and ran, dogs howled. The sky darkened, there was the sound of rushing wind, the rustle of silk and then, with a delicate thud, the great hydrogen balloon of VINCENZO LUNARDI, Secretary to His Excellency the Neopolitan Ambassador to the Court of St James, landed amongst them. He had just completed the FIRST EVER BALLOON FLIGHT OVER BRITAIN. After a brief pause to regain his composure, Lunardi clambered out of the basket with his dog and gave a flamboyant bow to the crowd of red-faced farmers who were encircling him with pitch forks.

Lunardi had taken off, around two and a half hours earlier, from the grounds of the Honourable Artillery Company at Moorfields in London, 30 miles (48 km) away. With him were his dog, his cat, a pigeon and some chicken and white wine. Also on board were a pair of oars, with which he intended to propel the balloon through the air by 'rowing', a stylish refinement that didn't really come off. Only the dog made it all the way with him. At North Mimms, about 10 miles (16 km) to the south-east, noticing that the cat was cold, he had descended and, while hovering just off the ground, handed the animal to a dumbstruck passing gentlewoman. Then, doffing his hat, he wafted back into the sky to continue on his way.

There is a stone set in the ground at Standon Green End, recording this 'wondrous enterprise, successfully achieved by the powers of chemistry and the fortitude of man'.

Rothamsted

Fertile Imaginations

HARPENDEN is one of Hertfordshire's loveliest towns, with a wide, airy common, bordered by handsome houses. All looks peaceful and timeless. Just off the common, is an old, gabled brick house, that looks as if it should belong to the National Trust or maybe to a girls' school. In fact, this is ROTHAMSTED PARK, the OLDEST AGRICULTURAL RESEARCH STATION IN THE WORLD.

Born here, in 1814, was JOHN BENNET LAWES, whose family had owned the Rothamsted estate since the days of Charles II. He had a scientific mind and, after graduating from Oxford, he set up a laboratory in his bedroom here, where he experimented with fertilisers, especially bone meal. In 1842, he was granted a patent to develop his fertilisers, and built a factory to manufacture them. A year later, he established the Rothamsted Research Centre, and began field experiments, dividing the estate into plots where he could examine the effects of various chemicals and nutrients on crops and animal feeds. Scientists came from all over the world to study and learn. Knowledge gathered here has been used to enrich and improve agriculture across the globe.

The PARK GRASS EXPERIMENT, set up by Lawes in 1856 and still ongoing, is now the LONGEST RUNNING ECOLOGICAL EXPERIMENT IN THE WORLD. It basically consists of a hay meadow, to which different fertiliser treatments are applied every year, with the aim of comparing the different effects of organic manure and inorganic fertilisers.

John Bennet Lawes founded the ROTHAMSTED TRUST, to include the laboratory and 40 acres, and endowed it with £100,000. From this has developed ROTHAMSTED RESEARCH, the WORLD'S PREMIER AGRICULTURAL RESEARCH ESTABLISHMENT, which is now financed both by public funds and private contributions. Today, it is at the forefront of the controversial research on GM crops.

Markyate

A Wicked Lady

Beside the A5 north of St Albans, sits an impressive Jacobean house set above a little river valley in fine parkland. This is MARKYATE CELL, home of the notorious 17th-century highwayman known as the WICKED LADY.

LADY KATHERINE FERRARS, born 4 May 1634 and heiress to the estate, was married at the age of 14 to Thomas Fanshawe, an unemotional, older man who spent much of his time away on business. Katherine was a spirited, fun-loving girl and she quickly became bored with living alone in the big house. One evening, she retired early upstairs but, instead of going to bed, she made her way to a secret room built into the chimney above the kitchen, put on men's clothing, a mask and a black cape, and slipped out of the house down a hidden stairway. So began her double life – elegant lady of the house by day, audacious 'lady of the road' by night. Travellers on the road from London to Holyhead soon learned to fear the slight, silent stranger mounted on a tall, black horse with vivid white blazes, unaware that she was just a girl.

Then, one dark night, her victim fought back and Katherine was fatally wounded. She crawled back across the park and fell dead at the bottom of the secret stairway, where she was found the next morning by a servant. She was 26. Her body was carried across Hertfordshire to be buried in the church at Ware, but she is still said to haunt the area, riding across the common on her black horse, her head thrown back in laughter.

In 1840, the house caught fire. Those fighting the blaze heard wicked chuckles and reportedly saw the Wicked Lady swinging from the branch of a sycamore tree growing close to the house. Legend has it that her ill-gotten treasure lies beneath it:

Near the Cell, there is a well,
Near the well there is a tree
And under the tree the treasure be

Nobody has ever dared to look for it.

St Albans

Genesis of the British Film Industry

St Albans is the unlikely BIRTHPLACE OF THE BRITISH FILM INDUSTRY. In 1874, ARTHUR MELBOURNE-COOPER was born in St Albans, son of the city's first professional photographer, Thomas Melbourne-Cooper, who had premises in Osbourne Terrace on the London Road. Arthur learned about photography from his father and, at the age of 18, became assistant to BIRT ACRES, a photographic innovater who had just patented a camera that could take a series of photographs in rapid succession. In 1894, the two of them filmed the opening of the Manchester Ship Canal and the Henley Regatta. The following year, they filmed the Derby and the Oxford and Cambridge Boat Race.

In that same year, 1895, Melbourne-Cooper made a series of short films of local scenes and comedy sketches featuring local people, mainly at SHENLEY. At Christmas, he gave the films a showing at the WELHAM GREEN BOYS' SCHOOL in North Mimms – the FIRST PUBLIC FILM SCREENING IN BRITAIN.

In 1897, he made BRITAIN'S FIRST FILM ADVERTISEMENT for Bird's Custard Powder, which showed an old man falling down stairs with a tray of eggs – not a major disaster, since he was equipped with Bird's Custard Powder! He followed this, in 1899, with a filmed appeal on behalf of Bryant & May for donations to supply matches to the troops fighting in the Boer War. This included what is possibly the WORLD'S FIRST KNOWN USE OF ANIMATION – matchstick men climbing on to a wall and forming themselves into the words: 'Send £1 and enough matches will be sent to supply a regiment of our fighting soldiers.'

With *Grandma's Reading Glass*, made in 1900, Melbourne-Cooper became the FIRST DIRECTOR IN THE WORLD TO USE CLOSE-UPS, INTERCUT WITH MEDIUM SHOTS. In 1901, he founded the ALPHA TRADING COMPANY, and opened studios in Alma Road, St Albans, filming, producing and distributing a new film almost every day, for a variety of clients. In 1908, he achieved a long-held ambition to open a cinema, the ALPHA PICTURE PALACE on London Road, St Albans. This was the FIRST CINEMA IN BRITAIN WITH A SLOPING FLOOR AND PROJECTION BOOTH and the FIRST CINEMA TO CHARGE MORE FOR SITTING AT THE BACK RATHER THAN AT THE FRONT. This innovation was suggested to Melbourne-Cooper by the usherette who soon became his wife. The adjacent studio site covered two acres and included shops, a restaurant, a hairdresser and a swimming pool – Britain's first multiplex. Appropriately enough, the site of the Alpha picture palace is now an Odeon cinema; his studio in Alma Road is now a block of flats called Telford Court. On the wall by the entrance is a plaque which reads:

On this site stood the Alpha Cinematographic works, studios of the local film pioneer Arthur Melbourne-Cooper 1874–1961.

Walkern

Last Witch

A mile or so away, to the east of STEVENAGE, is the village of Walkern, one long, lovely street of assorted houses ending in a Norman church of Saxon origins. In a hovel by the church, in 1711, lived a middle-aged woman named JANE WENHAM, the LAST PERSON IN ENGLAND TO BE SENTENCED TO DEATH FOR BEING A WITCH. A local farmer claimed that she had bewitched him to obtain money; the Rector's servant was convinced that she turned into a cat at night; while several honest fellows said that she flew past them on a broomstick as they were walking back from the pub. They seized her and ducked her in the village pond, and the fact that she floated proved to these simple folk that she must be a witch.

She was taken to Hertford Assizes, where an enlightened judge was reluctant to charge her, saying that he liked cats and there was no law against flying, provided due care was taken. The jury, however, were implacable, pronounced her guilty and she was condemned to death. When the fuss died down, the judge obtained a pardon for her from Queen Anne, and Jane was smuggled away to live out her life in Hertingfordbury, looked after by the local squire. There was a happy outcome, eventually, when the case led to the law against witchcraft being repealed in 1736.

Well, I never knew this ABOUT HERTFORDSHIRE

On the morning of Sunday, 2 September 1916, the FIRST GERMAN AIRSHIP TO BE BROUGHT DOWN OVER BRITAIN was shot down by LT WILLIAM LEEFE ROBINSON of the Royal Flying Corps, flying a BE2 aircraft. It crashed at CUFFLEY and burned for three hours. An obelisk marks the spot. This success was an important morale booster and demonstrated that the Zeppelins were not invincible. Robinson won the Victoria Cross and survived the war but died of influenza on the last day of 1918.

The village of ALDBURY lies under a ridge of hills clad with beech trees, in the shadow of a 200-ft (61-m) tall monument to the 'Father of Canals', the DUKE OF BRIDGEWATER, original owner of nearby Ashridge House. There are thatched cottages, almshouses, a pond, whipping post and stocks. These two last items have a particular resonance here for, just up the road is STOCKS, once the ENGLISH HEADQUARTERS OF THE PLAYBOY CLUB. From here, in the 1970s, Victor Lownes ran his gambling businesses and nightclubs, trained his Bunny Girls and entertained showbiz celebrities and rock stars. The quiet Hertfordshire countryside echoed to the shrieks of party girls, the purr of Rolls-Royces and the clatter of helicopters. Today it is cries of 'fore!' and the clinking of wine glasses that disturbs the peace, for Stocks has become a smart country club. In the early 20th century, the writer MRS HUMPHRY WARD lived at Stocks and wrote about Aldbury in her novel *Bessie Costrell.* Mrs Ward was the granddaughter of Thomas Arnold, legendary headmaster of Rugby School, and the niece of the Gypsy Scholar, Matthew Arnold. The Huxleys were regular visitors.

BORN IN HERTFORDSHIRE

ERIC MORECAMBE (1926–84), comedian, is buried at HARPENDEN.

FRANCES DE LA TOUR, actress, was born in BOVINGDON, near Hemel Hempstead, in 1944.

GEORGE MICHAEL, pop singer, was born in BUSHEY in 1963.

NICK FALDO, golfer, was born in WELWYN GARDEN CITY in 1957.

VICTORIA BECKHAM, pop singer, was born in GOFF'S OAK in 1974.

MID HERTS GOLF CLUB, celebrated on BBC Radio 2 as the home club of Terry Wogan's radio producer, Paul Walters, is at WHEATHAMPSTEAD.

The reception for the first wedding in *Four Weddings and a Funeral* was filmed in a marquee in the grounds of GOLDINGTONS, a Georgian manor house near SARRATT.

HUNTINGDONSHIRE

COUNTY TOWN: HUNTINGDON

'All that I have seen of Huntingdon I like exceedingly'

WILLIAM COBBETT

The Bell, Stilton

Huntingdon

Birthplace of the Lord Protector

Huntingdon is the proud county town of this tiny shire and sits on the River Ouse surrounded by what Daniel Defoe described as 'the most beautiful meadows that I think are to be seen in England'. Since the draining of the Fens and the retreat of the Wash, Huntingdon's use as a port has declined. As a result the town has been spared too much industrialisation, leaving it quiet, unchanged and full of interesting old buildings.

The main street leads down to the lovely 14th-century bridge across the Ouse that links Huntingdon to GODMANCHESTER. The medieval builders started from both sides of the river simultaneously, apparently without consulting each other, for there is a definite kink at the meeting point in the middle.

The first EARL OF HUNTINGDON was Waltheof of Northumberland, who was the last of the Anglo-Saxon earls. His daughter married King David of Scotland so, for a time, the kings of Scotland, including ROBERT THE BRUCE, were also earls of Huntingdon. The great-grandson of King David, Robert, Earl of Huntingdon, was dispossessed of his lands by King John while Richard I was absent at the Crusades and it is thought he could have been the legendary ROBIN HOOD.

Huntingdon was the birthplace, in 1599, of OLIVER CROMWELL, who led the Parliamentary forces in the English Civil War and became Lord Protector after the execution of Charles I. The house he was born in, at the end of the main street, was part of the old Austin Friary and was called 'The Friars'. It is no longer there, but the new building, called CROMWELL HOUSE, incorporates some bricks from the old and there is a plaque above the portico.

Further up the street is All Saints, where Cromwell was baptised and where his father is buried. Opposite is the little Norman schoolroom where both Cromwell and, later, SAMUEL PEPYS (*see* Brampton) studied. It is now the CROMWELL MUSEUM.

A little to the west is HINCHINGBROOKE, a Cromwell seat at the time of Oliver's birth. During the Dissolution of the Monasteries, Henry VIII's right-hand man, Thomas Cromwell, gave the abbeys of Hinchingbrooke and Ramsey to his own nephew, Richard. Richard's son, Sir Henry, rebuilt Hinchingbrooke as a magnificent Tudor mansion and played host to Elizabeth I. Henry's son, Sir Oliver, uncle of the parliamentarian, was renowned for his hospitality, particularly to James I, who stayed many times and declared that he had enjoyed 'such entertainment as was not like in any place before'. It was at Hinchingbrooke, during one of these visits, that Sir Oliver's nephew, the young Oliver Cromwell, first met the man he would send to the scaffold, the future Charles I. By tradition, the meeting was not a success; they scuffled even then – with Oliver drawing royal blood – and had to be separated by Oliver's uncle.

JOHN MAJOR, Conservative Prime Minister from 1990 until 1997, is MP for Huntingdon.

Alwalton

The Best Begins Here

Alwalton, in the far north of Huntingdonshire, is a pretty village, despite being squeezed between Peterborough and the A1 (M), with a fine Elizabethan manor house. It is the home of the East of England Show, but its best claim to fame is as the birthplace, in 1863, of HENRY ROYCE, who grew up to make the 'BEST CARS IN THE WORLD'. His family was not well-off and Henry had to go to London to make his way in the world. His first job was as a newspaper delivery boy for W.H. Smith. He attended nightschool, where he studied electrics, and, in 1894, he formed F.H. Royce and Co. in Manchester, making electrical goods. The firm was a success and enabled Henry to buy a car, a second-hand French Decauville. He soon decided that he could make a better car and, in April 1904, he drove his own two-cylinder Royce on its first journey from Manchester to Knutsford. He made two more Royces, improving on the design each time, and their reputation for innovation and quality was such that a rich enthusiast from London, C.S. ROLLS, came to Manchester to have a look. Henry Royce wanted to make the best car in the world and Charles Rolls wanted to sell the best car in the world, so they got together and, in 1906, ROLLS-ROYCE was formed.

The first Rolls-Royce SILVER GHOST appeared in November 1906. At the beginning of the First World War, Royce started to design and build aero engines. Rolls was killed in an aircraft accident in 1910 (*see* Bournemouth, Hampshire), but Royce remained head of the company until 1930, and continued to design every part of every Rolls-Royce car made, demonstrating an attention to detail and drive for perfection unparalleled in car production before or since. At the factories, the cars are referred to as 'Royces' rather than 'Rolls'. Seventy per cent of Rolls-Royce cars ever built are still road worthy.

Sir Henry Royce died in 1933 and is buried in the church at Alwalton. The Rolls-Royce badge was changed from red to black to mark his passing. Rolls-Royce Cars are now owned by BMW and are made in Sussex.

Conington

A Remarkable Library

Buried in the 15th-century church at Conington, hard by Peterborough airport, is SIR ROBERT COTTON (1570–1631), who amassed the RICHEST AND MOST IMPORTANT COLLECTION OF MANUSCRIPTS EVER ASSEMBLED BY A PRIVATE INDIVIDUAL. He studied at Westminster School under William of Camden and, at the age of 17, began collecting papers about the history of Huntingdon.

After the Dissolution of the Monasteries in the 1530s, many monastic libraries were broken up and books and manuscripts became available for purchase. Cotton took advantage of this and, for the next 30 years, never stopped collecting historical and government records. His library contained the LINDISFARNE GOSPELS, two of the four extant copies of MAGNA CARTA and the sole surviving manuscript of BEOWULF. Cotton wanted his collection to form the basis of a national library and all the great scholars of the day, FRANCIS BACON and BEN JONSON among them, availed themselves of his hospitality.

Cotton also revived the feudal rank of Baronet as a means by which James I could raise revenue by selling titles and was widely consulted by royal advisers on matters of state etiquette and precedent.

Eventually, the powers that be began to get nervous at the concentration of so much official documentation in private hands and, in 1630, a year before his death, Cotton's collection was confiscated. After his death, it was returned to his heirs, but was donated to the nation by his grandson, as Sir Robert had always desired. The COTTON LIBRARY now resides in the BRITISH MUSEUM.

Sir Robert Cotton is recognised as one of the founders of public record and open government by rule of precedence and common law. CONINGTON CASTLE, which he built using materials from the ruined FOTHERINGAY CASTLE, where Mary Queen of Scots was beheaded, no longer stands, knocked down to make way for an airport.

The WOOLPACK INN, now a farmhouse on the Great North Road at Conington, was a favourite haunt of the notorious highwayman Dick Turpin (*see* Essex). It was here that he put his horse's shoes on the wrong way round to confuse his pursuers.

Hemingford Grey

Oldest Inhabited House in England?

Hemingford Grey, beside the River Ouse, is one of Huntingdonshire's most picturesque villages. Set just back from the river, in attractive gardens, is HEMINGFORD MANOR, a Norman house built around 1130 with claims to be the OLDEST CONTINUOUSLY INHABITED HOUSE IN BRITAIN.

In the early 18th century, Hemingford Manor was the home of the 'BEAUTIFUL MISS GUNNINGS', sisters Mary and Elizabeth, who were considered to be the handsomest women in Europe. The poet WILLIAM COWPER saw them one day as he was out walking his dog along the river and described them as 'two nymphs adorned with every grace'. Mary married the Earl of Coventry and Elizabeth the Duke of Hamilton, by whom she had two sons, and then the Duke of Argyll, by whom she had two more sons. She ended up the mother of four dukes.

In 1939, the house was bought by the writer LUCY BOSTON, who spent two years restoring it and laying out the garden. She wrote about Hemingford, and the various inhabitants ofhe house, which she called GREENE KNOWE, in a classic series of stories for children. During the Second World War, she gave gramophone recitals for the British and American airmen stationed nearby and the room she used is left as it was then, with the EMG gramophone still working.

Lucy Boston died in 1990, aged 98, and Hemingford Manor is looked after by her family and kept much as she had it, almost as a shrine to her. The house is open for visits.

Other Contenders for the Title of England's Oldest Inhabited House

England is full of houses that claim to be the oldest in the country. In 2003, a magazine survey declared that SALTFORD MANOR at KEYNSHAM, near Bristol, was the oldest. Here are some other contenders:

EASTRY COURT stands beside the church in the village of EASTRY in KENT, just outside Sandwich. The house is built on the site of a Saxon palace, where two young princes, ETHELBERT and ETHELRED, were murdered on the order of their cousin, KING EGBERT, in 664. Their bodies were buried beneath the Great Hall, but were discovered and moved to Ramsay Abbey. In recompense for his crimes, Egbert gave the Isle of Thanet to the boy's sister, Aebbe, and she founded the monastry of Minster in Thanet in their honour. Eastry Court retains some walls of the old palace from the 10th century and it is these walls that are the basis for its claim.

CHARLESTON MANOR is hidden in its own fold in the South Downs, near LITLINGTON, by the River Cuckmere, in SUSSEX. Charleston's claim rests on its Norman wing, once a great hall with an exquisite Norman window, dating from about

1170. The manor house, now extended, with a mellow Tudor front, is surrounded by lovely gardens showing the influence of Gertrude Jekyll and Vita Sackville-West. From 1928 until 1980, Charleston was the home of the painter SIR OSWALD BIRLEY (1880–1952), and his wife RHODA (1900–80). They held concerts and performances by the Russian Ballet in the long rambling barn beside the house and inaugurated the Charleston Festival. They are both buried in the church at nearby West Dean. Sir Oswald's son, MARK, founded ANNABEL'S nightclub in Berkeley Square, London. Mark named it after his wife Annabel, who later married Sir James Goldsmith, founder, in 1997, of the Referendum Party.

LUDDESDOWN COURT, lost in the hills near ROCHESTER, KENT, is perhaps the least known of the contenders and remains a very private place. The house stands among farm buildings next to a small church and is hidden behind high walls at the end of a track. It is often overlooked because it is so remote and there is an atmosphere of great solitude here, despite Rochester being just a few miles away. It is a mainly Norman building that incorporates brickwork from a previous Saxon house, which itself was built on the site of an Iron-Age wattle and daub hut.

EAST MEON COURT in HAMPSHIRE was built around a Norman hall where the bishops of Winchester used to hold their memorial courts. The house sits next to East Meon church, one of the most magnificent Norman churches in England, and was used as a farm building during the Middle Ages. The Great Hall was restored in the 1920s and, although the house is private, it is sometimes used for concerts or plays.

East Meon Court

Well, I never knew this ABOUT HUNTINGDONSHIRE

HOLME FEN, about 6 miles (10 km) south of Peterborough, and 9 ft (2.7 m) below sea level, is the LOWEST POINT IN BRITAIN.

The village of STILTON gives its name to England's most distinctive blue cheese, excellent with port or melted in a baked potato. But the cheese that made the name of Stilton famous across the world has never been made here at all. It was first produced early in the 18th century, in the area around Melton Mowbray in Leicestershire. One lady in particular, FRANCES PAWLETT, who came from Wymondham, was supremely skilled at making it, and she sold much of her output to Cooper Thornhill, landlord of the Bell Inn at Stilton, a popular coaching stop on the Great North Road. Travellers would tell of 'that delicious cheese we tasted at Stilton', hence it became known as Stilton cheese. Today, over one million Stilton cheeses are made every year, with 10 per cent being exported to more than 40 countries. Made under licence, to the original recipe, by only six dairies, it is produced exclusively in the three counties of Leicestershire, Derbyshire and Nottinghamshire. It takes 136 pints (77 litres) of milk to make one 17-lb (7.7-kg) Stilton cheese.

GRAFHAM WATER is the LARGEST RESERVOIR IN ENGLAND.

By the church at BRAMPTON, near Huntingdon, there is a charming 16th-century farmhouse known as PEPYS FARM. This is where the uncle, and then the parents, of SAMUEL

PEPYS lived, and where the diarist himself spent much of his childhood. He attended the grammar school in Huntingdon and would often walk over to see his cousin, Edward Montagu, at nearby Hinchingbrooke House. In later life, when he could get away from London, Pepys enjoyed visiting Brampton, and felt very lucky that he had 'such a pretty place to retire to'. After the Fire of London in 1666, Pepys sent all his money to Brampton to be buried in the garden for safekeeping, in case of a Dutch invasion. When he came to collect it in 1667, he had to scour the garden, sieving the soil 'just as they do for diamonds in other parts of the world'.

The FERRY BOAT INN at HOLYWELL, on the River Ouse, is a contender for the OLDEST INN IN ENGLAND. There are records showing that liqour has been served here since 560. The inn is also haunted. Inside, on the floor of one of the bars, is a flat black tombstone. Every year on St Patrick's Day (17 March), the ghost of a young girl named Juliet rises from this tomb and floats away towards the river. In 1050, Juliet, daughter of the innkeeper, fell in love with a woodcutter named Tom. He promised to visit her on her birthday, 17 March. She waited down by the river for him all day, but he never showed up and the distraught Juliet drowned herself in the river. She was buried by the ferry crossing and eventually the inn was built above her grave.

ST IVES has ONE OF ONLY FOUR REMAINING BRIDGE CHAPELS IN BRITAIN. The others are at Wakefield and Rotherham in Yorkshire and Bradford-on-Avon in Somerset. Bridge chapels were fairly common in medieval times and were used by travellers to pray for a safe crossing or to give thanks for a safe arrival.

KENT

COUNTY TOWN: MAIDSTONE

'Kent, Sir – everybody knows Kent – apples, cherries, hops and women.'

CHARLES DICKENS, from *Pickwick Papers*

Canterbury Cathedral, Mother Church of the worldwide Anglican Communion

Dover

Gateway to England

Dover is ENGLAND'S BUSIEST PASSENGER PORT and, at 21 miles (34 km) from France, is the NEAREST PLACE IN ENGLAND TO CONTINENTAL EUROPE. The WHITE CLIFFS of Dover are a potent symbol of England. Shakespeare Cliff, to the west, so called because it is a setting in *King Lear* (Act IV, Scene vi), marks the spot where the CHANNEL TUNNEL leaves the English coast. At 31 miles (50 km), it is the SECOND LONGEST RAILWAY TUNNEL IN THE WORLD, after the SEIKEN RAILWAY TUNNEL linking the Japanese islands of Hokkaido and Honshu which is 33.4 miles (54 km) long.

The present Dover Castle, built in 1180 by Henry II, was the first concentric castle in Britain. Standing inside the walls is the Pharos, a Roman lighthouse, once 80 ft (24 m) high. The remains, at 40 ft (12 m) high, are the highest Roman remains in Britain. In the cliffs below the castle, an extensive series of passages and rooms have been carved out of the chalk and it was from here, in 1940, that Operation Dynamo, the evacuation from Dunkirk, was masterminded.

Down in the town of Dover is the Roman Painted House. On the walls are the oldest wall paintings in Britain, dating from the 2nd century. Nearby is St Edmund's Chapel, the smallest church in England still in regular use.

At the eastern end of the Promenade is a bust of Captain Matthew Webb, first person to swim the English Channel. He took 21 hours 45 minutes to swim from Dover to Calais in 1875.

In 1909, Louis Bleriot was the first man to fly an aeroplane across the Channel and across open sea. The spot where he landed, up on the cliffs near the Castle, is

Dover is the chief Cinque Port. The others are Sandwich, Hythe, Romney and Hastings. First mentioned in 1155, these ports were given certain privileges by the monarch in return for providing ships to defend the coastline. In the late 12th century, the ancient towns of Rye and Winchelsea were added. The Cinque Ports are under the jurisdiction of a Lord Warden, whose official residence is at Walmer Castle. Distinguished Lord Wardens have included William Pitt, the Duke of Wellington, Sir Winston Churchill and Queen Elizabeth the Queen Mother. The present Lord Warden is Admiral the Lord Boyce.

marked with a memorial in the shape of his plane. In 1910, CHARLES ROLLS, of Rolls-Royce fame, left Dover to become the FIRST MAN TO FLY BOTH WAYS OVER THE CHANNEL. However, the FIRST MAN TO FLY ACROSS THE CHANNEL was FRANÇOIS BLANCHARD, who flew from Dover to Guines in a balloon in 1785.

Wye

First Woman Author . . . and Spy

APHRA BEHN, ENGLAND'S FIRST FEMALE PROFESSIONAL NOVELIST AND PLAYWRIGHT, was born in Wye in 1640.

As a child, she was taken to Surinam, in South America, then an English possession, which was eventually ceded to the Dutch. On her return, her natural wit and intelligence brought her to the court of Charles II. Because of her knowledge of the Dutch, she was sent by the king to Antwerp, as a spy, where she uncovered a plan by Admiral de Ruyter to sail up the Thames and burn the English ships at harbour. Her information was ignored but, sure enough, in June 1667, the Dutch fleet attacked Sheerness and then sailed up the Medway into Chatham, where they sank three ships and captured the flagship *Royal Charles*, towing it back to Holland.

Disillusioned, Aphra Behn then returned to England and began writing plays and novels laced with themes of sex, power and politics. Her best-known work is *Oroonoko*, the story of an African prince, taken to South America as a slave, whom she had met in Surinam. She died in 1689 and is buried in Westminster Abbey. Virginia Woolf wrote of her:

> *All women together ought to let flowers fall upon the tomb of Aphra Behn, for it was she who earned them the right to speak their minds.*

Eastwell

The Last Plantagenet

Among the ruins of ST MARY'S church, Eastwell, near Ashford, is the rough marble tomb of RICHARD, LAST OF THE PLANTAGENETS.

In 1485, there was growing up in

Eastwell, in the care of the schoolmaster, a young boy named Richard. One August day, a knight rode into the village and told Richard to prepare for a long journey. They rode halfway across England until they came to a huge camp full of soldiers and bowmen preparing for battle. Richard was brought before a noble knight dressed in fine armour, drinking at a stone well. The knight laid hands upon him and said, 'Richard, I am the King of England and I am your father. Tomorrow I go into battle and, if I am defeated, you will be in mortal danger, for the Earl of Richmond will surely seek you out and put you to death. Unless I am victorious tell no one who you are.'

The next day, Richard III was slain at the Battle of Bosworth Field and the reign of the Plantagenets was over. It was the beginning of the House of Tudor. Young Richard made his way back to Eastwell and lived out his life as a labourer, never telling anyone of his royal blood until his last days. He finally told his story to Sir Thomas Moyle of Eastwell House and Sir Thomas built him a tiny cottage in the park where he died in 1550.

Gillingham

Eastern Promise

On the north side of the A2, at Gillingham, stands a smart stone clock tower raised in memory of WILL ADAMS, FIRST ENGLISHMAN TO REACH JAPAN and inspiration for

Osaka Castle

James Clavell's novel *Shogun*. He was born in Gillingham in 1564 and christened at St Mary Magdelene's church.

Adams served in the Royal Navy, under Sir Francis Drake, and became an accomplished pilot and navigator. In 1598, he was chosen as chief pilot for a Dutch expedition of five ships sent to explore the Far East. On the journey across the Atlantic, through the Magellan Straits and up the west coast of South America, four of the five ships were sunk by strong winds and heavy seas, leaving Adams's ship as the only survivor. In 1600, nearly two years after leaving Holland, Adams and 23 crew landed on the western Japanese island of Kyushu. At first, they were suspected of being pirates and imprisoned in Osaka Castle, but the sailor from Kent soon gained the confidence of the Shogun Tokugawa Ieyasu and became a friend and adviser. He built ships for the Shogun, becoming his master navigator, and was rewarded with lands and titles, the FIRST WESTERNER TO BE MADE A SAMURAI.

Adams was not allowed to leave Japan and return to his wife and children in England, so he took a Japanese wife, the daughter of a Samurai, by whom he had two children, and changed his name to Miura Anjin. He set up the FIRST ENGLISH TRADING STATION IN JAPAN, near Nagasaki, and if the East India Company had followed his advice and established trading links with Japan instead of China, then the English would have won the lucrative Japanese trade eventually taken by the Dutch.

Kentish Will Adams, Miura Anjin the Samurai, died at Hirado, north of Nagasaki, in 1620, at the age of 56. He is buried there beneath a fine tombstone and there is a statue and memorial to him in Yokohama, where they hold the annual Anzin festival, in April, to celebrate the anniversary of his arrival in Japan.

The Isle of Sheppey

Pioneers of Flight

The Isle of Sheppey is the Birthplace of British Aviation.

In 1908, the three SHORTS BROTHERS, HORACE, EUSTACE and OSWALD, formed a partnership to build six Wright flyer aircraft, under licence from the Wright Brothers. They already made balloons at premises in Battersea, but these were not big enough for aircraft, so, in 1909, they moved to Sheppey. The land here was perfect for flying, being flat, windy and close to London. It had been leased by a flying friend of theirs, Griffin Brewer. At SHELLNESS BEACH, adjacent to 16th-century MUSSEL MANOR, near LEYSDOWN, they built the WORLD'S FIRST AIRCRAFT FACTORY.

On 2 May 1909, JOHN BRABAZON, who housed his Voisin aircraft in one of Shorts's hangars, flew it 500 yards (457 m) at a height of 35 ft (10.7 m) over the Leysdown fields, thus completing the FIRST FLIGHT IN BRITAIN and becoming the FIRST ENGLISHMAN TO FLY. He was awarded Pilot's Licence No. 1.

Two days later, ORVILLE and WILBUR WRIGHT came to visit the Shorts factory at Mussel Manor and were driven down from London by C.S. Rolls in the first Rolls-Royce Silver Ghost. The first aircraft made by Shorts, Shorts No. 1, was made for C.S. Rolls. Shorts No. 2 was made for Brabazon and it was in this aircraft, on 30 October 1909, that he flew the FIRST CIRCULAR MILE IN BRITAIN, in fact nearly 2 miles (3 km) at a height of 20 ft (6 m) circling over Mussel Manor.

In November 1909, Shorts moved their factory to bigger premises at Eastchurch, just up the road. These buildings have since become Eastchurch Prison. Shorts Brothers went on to design and build sea planes for the Royal Navy and, in 1912, at SHEERNESS, a SHORTS 538 became the FIRST PLANE IN THE WORLD TO TAKE

OFF FROM A WARSHIP. In 1915, a SHORTS ADMIRALTY TYPE 184 became the FIRST AIRCRAFT IN THE WORLD TO SINK AN ENEMY SHIP AT SEA WITH A TORPEDO. Shorts also built the ill-fated R101 at their vast hangars in Cardington, Bedfordshire (*see* Bedfordshire).

C.S. Rolls was killed in a flying accident in 1910. Brabazon gave up flying for a while after Rolls's death, but eventually took to the air again and was the FIRST MAN TO FLY UNDER TOWER BRIDGE. He was given a peerage by Winston Churchill and became Lord Brabazon of Tara. He died in 1964.

Mussel Manor, now Muswell Manor, is still there, hidden behind a collection of holiday caravans, but well worth a visit. Inside there is a fascinating photograph of the 'Founding Fathers of Aviation'. Sitting together in the front row are C.S. Rolls, Orville and Wilbur Wright and John Brabazon, while standing behind are all three Shorts brothers.

Paddock Wood

First Speeding Fine

On 28 January 1896, WALTER ARNOLD of EAST PECKHAM, near Tonbridge, became the FIRST MOTORIST EVER TO BE CONVICTED OF SPEEDING. On 20 January, he was spotted by the local police constable doing 8 mph (13 kph) in a built-up area of Paddock Wood, where the speed limit was 2 mph (3.2 kph). The police constable, who was having his dinner at the time, selflessly abandoned his pork chop, grabbed his helmet, mounted his bicycle and gave chase. He eventually managed to overtake and flag down the felon after a breathless pursuit of some 5 miles (8 km).

Arnold appeared before magistrates at Tonbridge Police Court, and was charged one shilling (5 p), plus costs, for the outrage. Undeterred, he went on to become the FIRST MAN IN BRITAIN TO MANUFACTURE PETROL-ENGINED MOTOR CARS. The Arnold Motor Carriage Company of East Peckham, Kent, salesmen for Benz cars since 1894, manufactured an Arnold motor, based on the Benz design, but with many innovations, in August 1896, the first petrol-driven car ever manufactured for sale in England. Called an ADAM, it was also the FIRST CAR IN THE WORLD TO HAVE AN ELECTRIC SELF-STARTER. The first customer was H.J. Dowsing of Ealing.

In 1914 at ASHFORD, ENGLAND'S FIRST WHITE LINES were painted on to the London to Folkestone road at a series of dangerous bends. In 1928, Kent was the first county in England to try out Tarmacadam on its roads.

Well, I never knew this ABOUT KENT

HENRY VIII and ANNE BOLEYN, mother of the future Elizabeth I, spent their honeymoon at SHURLAND HALL in EASTCHURCH. The magnificent ruins of the gatehouse can be seen on the edge of the village.

The walled garden at GREAT MAYTHAM HALL, near Rolvenden, was the inspiration for FRANCES HODGSON BURNETT'S children's novel, *The Secret Garden*. She leased the house from 1898 until 1907, and would sit writing in the 'beautiful old walled kitchen garden'.

RUSSELL THORNDIKE lived in DYMCHURCH, and used Romney Marsh as the setting for his adventure series *Dr Syn*. Dr Syn was the Vicar of Dymchurch by day and the 'Scarecrow' by night, leader of a gang of smugglers. In one story, they launch a raid on LYMPNE CASTLE. Patrick McGoohan starred as Dr Syn in the 1964 TV series.

EDITH NESBIT (1858–1924), author of *The Railway Children*, lived in DYMCHURCH and is buried just inland at St Mary-in-the-Marsh.

SIR DAVID FROST, TV presenter and journalist, was born in TENTERDEN in 1939.

DEREK JARMAN (1942–94), film director, is buried at OLD ROMNEY.

RUPERT BEAR was born in CANTERBURY, or rather his creator, MARY TOURTEL, was, in 1874. Rupert first appeared in the *Daily Express* in 1920. Mary's husband was night editor on the paper and he asked Mary to invent a cartoon character to rival those in other newspapers. The little bear called Rupert became an instant hit, and has appeared in the *Daily Express* ever since. Mary Tourtel retired in 1935. There have been several writers and illustrators since then, the present illustrator being JOHN HARROLD and writer IAN ROBINSON.

SOMERSET MAUGHAM (1874–1965), the author, had his ashes scattered near the library he had donated to his alma mater, THE KING'S SCHOOL, CANTERBURY, even though he hated the place as a schoolboy.

BRENDA BLETHYN, actress, was born in RAMSGATE in 1946.

HATTIE JACQUES (1924–80), actress, was born in SANDGATE.

WILLIAM CAXTON (1422–91), who was ENGLAND'S FIRST PRINTER, was born in TENTERDEN.

LANCASHIRE

COUNTY TOWN: LANCASTER

Red Rose County

Liverpool Anglican Cathedral, largest cathedral in Britain

Preston

England's Newest City

Although Lancaster is the county town of Lancashire, Preston is the administrative centre. It is also ENGLAND'S NEWEST CITY, having been granted that status by the Queen in 2002 as part of her Golden Jubilee celebrations.

SIR RICHARD ARKWRIGHT, founder of the world's first factory system at Cromford (*see* Derbyshire), was born in Preston in 1732. ARKWRIGHT HOUSE, where he developed his water frame in 1768, still stands in STONEYGATE.

The TEMPERANCE MOVEMENT was founded in 1834 in the BLACK BULL HOTEL in Preston, by JOSEPH LIVESEY.

Preston has the BIGGEST BUS STATION IN EUROPE, and, in 1958, an 8-mile (13-km) stretch of the Preston bypass was opened by Prime Minister Harold Macmillan as BRITAIN'S FIRST STRETCH OF MOTORWAY.

In 1888, PRESTON NORTH END FOOTBALL CLUB WAS ONE OF THE 12 FOUNDER MEMBERS OF THE FOOTBALL LEAGUE, and became the FIRST WINNER OF THE LEAGUE, remaining undefeated during the 1888–89 season. The club also won the FA Cup that season and so became the FIRST CLUB TO WIN THE DOUBLE. It had moved to Deepdale in 1875 and has been playing at the same ground for longer than any other English league football club. In 1887, Preston North End recorded the BIGGEST EVER VICTORY IN FA CUP history with a 26–0 triumph over Hyde United. Perhaps the club's most famous player was Tom Finney.

Other famous sportsmen to hail from Preston are England rugby captain BILL BEAUMONT, and cricketer ANDREW 'FREDDIE' FLINTOFF.

NICK PARK, creator of the Oscar-winning cartoon characters Wallace and Gromit, was born in WALMER BRIDGE, just to the south of Preston, in 1958.

Manchester

Rolls and Rails

Next to the G Mex centre, in the heart of Manchester, is the MIDLAND HOTEL, where, in May 1904, a meeting took place that resulted in the creation of the 'BEST CAR IN THE WORLD'. THE HON. CHARLES ROLLS, car salesman, journeyed up from London to meet electrical engineer and car maker HENRY ROYCE. Rolls liked what he saw of the new hand-made car Royce had both designed and built, and the two agreed to go into partnership as ROLLS-ROYCE. The first Rolls-Royce cars were made at COOKE STREET in HULME, just south of Manchester city centre.

The beautiful 'SPIRIT OF ECSTASY' badge which has adorned every Rolls-Royce car since 1911 was sculpted by CHARLES SYKES and modelled on a young lady named ELEANOR THORNTON. Eleanor was secretary to the second LORD MONTAGU OF BEAULIEU in his capacity as editor of the motoring magazine *The Car*. She was also his mistress. On 30 December 1915, Lord Montagu and Eleanor were sailing for India aboard the *SS Persia* when the ship was torpedoed and sunk by a German submarine off Crete. Eleanor perished, while Lord Montagu somehow survived and was rescued by another ship, several days later.

A short walk away, in Liverpool Road, is the WORLD'S OLDEST PASSENGER RAILWAY STATION, opened in 1830. A terminus of the Manchester to Liverpool Railway, it was built by

GEORGE STEPHENSON and was the WORLD'S FIRST COMMERCIAL PASSENGER LINE. The building is now home to the MANCHESTER MUSEUM OF SCIENCE AND INDUSTRY.

Part of a conservation area, ST JOHN STREET, lined with beautiful Georgian houses, is known as Manchester's 'Harley Street'. CHARLOTTE BRONTË accompanied her father when he came here for treatment on his cataracts and, while she was waiting for him, began writing *Jane Eyre.*

Aviation pioneer JOHN ALCOCK was born in OLD TRAFFORD in 1892. In 1919, with Manchester resident Arthur Brown as his navigator, he became the FIRST PERSON TO FLY ACROSS THE ATLANTIC. They left St John's, Newfoundland, in a Vickers aeroplane on 14 June and landed at Clifden, in Ireland, 16 hours later, having travelled a distance of 1,960 miles (3,155 km) at times reaching a speed of 90 mph (145 kph).

Rainhill

First Railway Passenger Fatality

In 1829, at Rainhill, just south of St Helens, trials were held to determine which locomotive should be chosen to work the world's first regular passenger railway service between Manchester and Liverpool. George Stephenson's *Rocket* won, beating Timothy Hackworth's *Sans Pareil* and Braithwaite and Ericsson's *Novelty*. *Rocket* reached a world record speed of 30 mph (48 kph).

Next to the station at Rainhill is the original SKEW BRIDGE, the FIRST BRIDGE IN THE WORLD TO BE BUILT AT A SKEW. It carries the railway at an oblique angle across the Liverpool to Warrington road.

A little way down the track, there is a memorial stone at the spot where, on 15 September 1830, Liverpool's MP, WILLIAM HUSKISSON, became the FIRST RAILWAY PASSENGER FATALITY. He had alighted from a carriage attached to the *Northumbrian* engine, right into the path of the *Rocket*, which was coming down the other line. He was taken to Eccles on the *Northumbrian*, which covered the 15 miles (24 km) in a record 25 minutes, but died that night, and is buried in Liverpool Cathedral.

Morecambe Bay

Eric and Stan

ERIC MORECAMBE, one half of Britain's best-loved comedy duo, MORECAMBE AND WISE, was born in Morecambe in 1926. His real name was John Eric Bartholomew, but he changed it in honour of his home town. There is a statue of him on the Promenade. Another Lancashire-born comedian, who had no need to change his name to honour his home town, was JIMMY CLITHEROE. Known as the 'Clitheroe Kid', he had a long-running BBC Radio comedy series in the 1950s and 1960s and was born in Clitheroe in 1921. Also born in Morecambe was the actress DAME THORA HIRD (1911–2003).

Just across the sands of Morecambe Bay, the little Lakeland town of ULVERSTON was the birthplace of another comic genius – STAN LAUREL. Stan, the thin half of the fabulous LAUREL AND HARDY duo, was born in a small house in ARGYLE STREET in 1890. Like Eric Morecambe, he changed his name, in his case from Arthur Stanley Jefferson. Unlike Eric, Stan did not adopt the name of his home town, which was probably a blessing – Ulverston and Hardy doesn't have quite the same ring to it.

Connecting Ulverston with Morecambe Bay, just over 1 mile (1.5 km) away, is England's SHORTEST, WIDEST AND DEEPEST CANAL, built by JOHN RENNIE.

Ulverston claims to have INVENTED POLE VAULTING AS A COMPETITIVE SPORT at the Flan Games in 1879; the town certainly produced a world champion pole vaulter, TOM RAY, in 1887.

BORN IN LIVERPOOL

FRANK HORNBY (1863–1936), model train maker.

TOMMY HANDLEY (1892–1949), radio entertainer.

ARTHUR ASKEY (1900–82), comedian.

SIR REX HARRISON (1908–90), actor.

NICHOLAS MONSARRAT (1910–79), author of *The Cruel Sea.*

JEAN ALEXANDER, 'Hilda Ogden' from *Coronation Street*, in 1925.

Twins PETER and ANTHONY SHAFFER, both playwrights, the authors of *Amadeus* and *Sleuth* respectively, in 1926. Anthony died in 2001.

FRANKIE VAUGHAN (1928–99), singer.

KEN DODD, comedian, in 1929.

DAME BERYL BAINBRIDGE, novelist, in 1934.

CILLA BLACK, singer and entertainer, in 1943.

LORD BIRT, former Director General of the BBC, in 1944.

ALAN BLEASDALE, author and playwright, in 1946.

LYNDA LA PLANTE, writer, in 1946.

ELVIS COSTELLO, singer, in 1955.

SIR SIMON RATTLE, conductor, in 1955.

Well, I never knew this ABOUT LANCASHIRE

Hoghton Tower

JAMES I stayed at HOGHTON TOWER, a few miles west of Blackburn, for three days in 1617 as a guest of SIR RICHARD HOGHTON. He so enjoyed the hospitality that he felt compelled to unsheath his sword and graciously knight the sumptuous loin of beef he was about to consume. With the words, 'Arise Sir Loin', James introduced to the world that most succulent steak, the SIRLOIN.

JAMES HARGREAVES, inventor of the SPINNING JENNY, was born in OSWALDTWISTLE in 1720. John Kay's flying shuttle (1733) had so accelerated the process of weaving that the hand-spinners could not produce enough yarn to keep the looms supplied. Hargreaves's Spinning Jenny could spin several threads at once and went some way to solving the problem. The building where he constructed the Spinning Jenny, at STANHILL, in 1764, is now a post office.

The distinctive mass of PENDLE HILL rises to 1,831 ft (558 m) and forms a brooding backdrop to the story of *The Lancashire Witches*. Written by Manchester-born author HARRISON AINSWORTH, this is a romanticised account of the trial, in 1612, of a group of local women known as the Pendle Witches.

In 1652, GEORGE FOX climbed PENDLE HILL and, gazing out over Lancashire, he had a vision of 'a great multitude waiting to be gathered in by God'. This vision inspired him to found the SOCIETY OF FRIENDS, more popularly known as QUAKERS (*see* Leicestershire).

The tiny village of WYCOLLER was abandoned during the Industrial Revolution when the hand weavers of the village moved into the nearby towns to find work in the mills. They left behind three picturesque bridges, an Iron-Age clam bridge, a clapper bridge and a packhorse bridge, all unused for 200 years or more. Also the remnants of a rambling hall with noble rooms and mullioned windows. This is an eerie place and the BRONTË SISTERS would often walk over from Haworth and wander through the ruins soaking up the atmosphere. Charlotte based FERNDEAN MANOR, from *Jane Eyre*, on WYCOLLER HALL.

In an attic of the glorious black and white Tudor 'HALL I' TH' WOOD', on the outskirts of Bolton, SAMUEL CROMPTON invented the SPINNING MULE. Taking Arkwright's water frame and Hargreaves's Spinning Jenny as a base, he improved on them both and came up with a machine that could not only keep up with the demand for yarn, but could also create a material of finer quality than any yet produced. Crompton's Spinning Mule made by far the most important contribution to the success of the cotton industry of any of the new machines, but he was cheated out of any profits by unscrupulous manufacturers. He appealed to Parliament for a grant, which was about to be approved by the Prime Minister, SPENCER PERCEVAL, when the latter was murdered by an enraged bankrupt in the Houses of Parliament, leaving Crompton penniless. The man who had done more than any other to enrich Lancashire died a pauper.

The CHADDERTON aircraft factory, on the outskirts of Manchester, near Oldham, was opened in 1939 and produced BRITAIN'S MOST FAMOUS BOMBER, the AVRO LANCASTER. Another famous plane to emanate from the factory was the AVRO VULCAN bomber, which was designed to carry nuclear bombs. AVRO was founded in 1910 by ALLIOT VERDON ROE, who was born in PATRICROFT, Manchester, in 1877. Unofficially, he was the FIRST ENGLISHMAN TO FLY IN

Hall i' th' Wood

A BRITISH-BUILT PLANE when he took off and flew a distance of 75 ft (23 m) above the Brooklands circuit in Surrey on 8 June 1908 (*see* Surrey). Unfortunately, the achievement was unrecorded and the official honour was accorded to JOHN BRABAZON, who flew above the Isle of Sheppey a year later in May 1909 (*see* Kent). Alliot Verdon Roe went on to invent the FLYING BOAT in 1928.

SIR THOMAS BEECHAM Bt, the conductor who founded the ROYAL PHILHARMONIC ORCHESTRA, was born in ST HELEN'S in 1879. His father was the famous 'pill millionaire', whose family gave us the BEECHAM'S PILLS laxative and BEECHAM'S POWDERS for flu. In 1859, Beecham's opened the WORLD'S FIRST FACTORY FOR MAKING MEDICINES in St Helen's, and, by 1913, they were making one million Beecham's Pills per day. Over time, the Beecham's company acquired MACLEANS toothpaste, LUCOZADE and BRYLCREEM. In 1989, Beecham's merged with SmithKline to become SmithKline Beecham, and are now Glaxo SmithKline.

CARNFORTH STATION was used, in 1945, for the filming of *Brief Encounter*, which was directed by David Lean and starred Celia Johnson and Trevor Howard. There is now a museum at the station devoted to the film.

Singer GRACIE FIELDS (1898–1979) was born in ROCHDALE. Singer LISA STANSFIELD was born in Manchester in 1966, but was brought up in Rochdale.

LES DAWSON (1932–93), comedian, was born in MANCHESTER.

Leicestershire

County Town: Leicester

The Heart of England

Leicester Cathedral, sitting on Norman foundations in the heart of the county town

Leicester

Home of England's Fattest Man

In August 1485, RICHARD III spent the night before the BATTLE OF BOSWORTH FIELD at the BLUE BOAR INN in Highcross Street. A plaque marks the site. As he rode out to battle across BOW BRIDGE, over the River Soar, his spur caught a stone on the parapet, and a watching crone predicted that his lifeless head would soon be dashed against the same stone. After the battle, his dead body was indeed dragged back over the bridge, where it was hung from the parapet for two days before being buried at GREYFRIARS CHURCH. At the Dissolution of the Monasteries, Richard's body was dug up and flung into the river, but his bones were later recovered and buried somewhere near Bow Bridge. There is a memorial to the him in Leicester Cathedral.

In 1530, CARDINAL WOLSEY, Lord Chancellor to Henry VIII, was buried beneath the lady chapel in the ruins of LEICESTER ABBEY. He came here, sick and broken, while on his way to face treason charges in London. He fell from his mule at the doors of the Abbey and died a few days later. He was found to be wearing a hair-shirt next to his skin. There is a simple memorial stone marking his grave in Abbey Park.

Genetic fingerprinting was first discovered at Leicester University in 1985. Leicestershire Constabulary was the first police force in the world to use genetic fingerprinting for criminal detection in the case of Colin Pitchfork, who appeared at Leicester Crown Court in 1987 charged with the murder of two schoolgirls. Pitchfork became the first murderer in the world to be convicted on the evidence of genetic fingerprinting.

In 1770, DANIEL LAMBERT, ENGLAND'S FATTEST MAN, was born in Leicester. When he died, aged 36, he weighed 52 stone (330 kg) and had a waist measurement of 9 ft 4 in (2.8 m). He was so fat he was unsinkable and he used to float along the River Soar carrying local children on his stomach.

In 1841, THOMAS COOK (*see* Melbourne, Derbyshire), organised the WORLD'S FIRST PACKAGE TOUR from Leicester to a Temperance Meeting in Loughborough.

JOSEPH MERRICK, the ELEPHANT MAN, was born in Leicester in 1862. He was paraded as a freak at a theatre on the corner of Wharf Street, which is now a shop but retains the stage. For a while, he worked for his uncle at No. 6 Churchgate, but frightened away all the customers. He died in 1890.

RADIO LEICESTER, opened in 1967, was BRITAIN'S FIRST LOCAL RADIO STATION.

Melton Mowbray

Pies and Red Paint

Melton Mowbray has long been associated with FOX HUNTING, meeting place for three of England's most famous hunts, the Quorn, the Belvoir and the Cottesmore.

In 1837, after a successful day's hunting and a jolly evening of drinking, the THIRD MARQUESS OF WATERFORD and his companions rode through the narrow streets of the town daubing the dignified stone buildings with red paint. This gave rise to the expression 'PAINTING THE TOWN RED'.

The bakery where the famous Melton Mowbray pork pies were first baked in 1831 is now a café and stands next to the Fox Inn. Ye Olde Pork Pie Shoppe near the Market Place has been making pork pies since 1850 and you can watch them being hand raised there still.

Melton Mowbray is also famed for its crumbly Red Leicester cheese.

Loughborough

The Bells, The Bells

The John Taylor Bell Foundry in Loughborough is the biggest in the world. The Taylor family have been making bells since 1784, when they took over the business of Johannes of Stafford, bell maker since the 14th century. In 1839, John Taylor came here from Oxford and set up what is now regarded as the finest bell foundry in the world. The foundry made Great Paul, the biggest bell in Britain, which hangs in St Paul's Cathedral. It stands 9 ft (2.7 m) high and weighs 17 tons.

Loughborough boasts the first carillon in England. The set of bells is contained in the War Memorial Tower in Queen's Park and was opened in 1923 in memory of those who died in the First World War. The first-ever broadcast of bell music came from here.

Quakers

George Fox, dissident preacher and founder of the Society of Friends, was born in Fenny Drayton in 1624. On one of the many occasions he was arrested, Fox bid the judge 'quake at the word of God', and from then on his followers were known as Quakers. Members have never used the term themselves, preferring to be known as 'Friends'.

Quakers reject the religious authority of the established church, believing that The Bible is the word of God and that He can be found in every individual, so no mediation is needed from priests or doctrine. At Quaker services, no minister leads the congregation but, instead, the silence is broken when someone feels 'moved' by the Holy Spirit to speak.

Many Quakers have been conscientious objectors and Quakers were amongst the first to speak out against slavery. Well-known Quakers include:

ABRAHAM DARBY (1678–1717), who kick-started the Industrial Revolution when he discovered how to smelt iron using coke.

EDWARD PEASE (1767–1858), founder of the WORLD'S FIRST PASSENGER RAILWAY, the Stockton to Darlington, and the FIRST QUAKER MP.

JOHN DALTON (1766–1844), FATHER OF ATOMIC THEORY.

THOMAS HODGKIN (1798–1866), pathologist who gave his name to HODGKIN'S DISEASE.

JOSEPH LISTER (1827–1912), who pioneered the use of antiseptics in surgery (LISTERINE mouthwash was named after him).

WILLIAM PENN (1644–1718) who founded PENNSYLVANIA as a Quaker state.

US Presidents HERBERT HOOVER (1874–1964) and RICHARD NIXON (1913–94).

Actors JIM BROADBENT, JAMES DEAN, DAME JUDI DENCH, PAUL EDDINGTON, SHEILA HANCOCK, SIR BEN KINGSLEY and VICTORIA WOOD.

Entertainers DONALD SWANN, JOAN BAEZ and BONNIE RAITT.

Writers MARGARET DRABBLE, A.S. BYATT, JAMES A. MICHENER and OLIVER POSTGATE (*Noggin the Nog*, *Ivor the Engine*, *The Clangers* and *Bagpuss*).

Household names founded by Quaker families include WEDGWOOD POTTERY, LLOYDS BANK, BARCLAYS BANK, HUNTLEY & PALMERS, FRY'S, CADBURY'S and ROWNTREE'S, CLARK'S shoes, BRYANT & MAY matches.

Well, I never knew this ABOUT LEICESTERSHIRE

ANSTEY, near Leicester, was the birthplace, in 1811, of the LUDDITE movement. NED LUDD, the village idiot, was apprenticed to a small Leicestershire weaver and, one night, he broke two stocking frames at which he was working. This incident was seized upon by organised groups of angry workers who, inspired by the French Revolution and the writings of Thomas Paine, went round smashing up new machines such as Arkwright's frame and Joseph Heathcoat's lace maker, which were causing much hardship and unemployment among weavers. They claimed they had been sent by General Ned Ludd, and so gained the name Luddites, a word that has passed into the language to describe anyone resistant to modern technology.

THOMAS BABINGTON MACAULAY (1800–59), author and politician, was born in ROTHLEY. As a politician, he was instrumental in the passing of the Reform Act of 1832, which gave the vote to almost all members of the middle classes. He is best known for his work *History of England*, which included the following opinions:

> *The Puritan hated bear baiting, not because it gave pain to the bear, but because it gave pleasure to the spectators.*
>
> *We know of no spectacle so ridiculous as the British public in one of its periodical fits of morality.*
>
> (Written of public disapproval at Lord Byron's behaviour)

LITTLE DALBY is the birthplace of STILTON cheese (*see* Stilton, Huntingdonshire). It was first made by MRS ORTON in 1730, using the milk from cows in her small close of lush grass, now known as ORTON'S CLOSE. It was originally thought that Stilton could only be made with milk from Mrs Orton's cows.

ASHBY-DE-LA-ZOUCHE comes into Walter Scott's *Ivanhoe* as the setting for the tournament where Richard the Lionheart, disguised as the Black Knight, jousts with Ivanhoe, and Robin Hood wins the archery competition.

JOSEPH HANSOM invented the HANSOM CAB at his workshop in Regent Street, HINCKLEY, in 1835, and drove the prototype along Watling Street.

JOHN WYCLIFFE (1329–84), the FIRST MAN TO TRANSLATE THE BIBLE INTO ENGLISH, was Rector of LUTTERWORTH, in the south of the county, and was buried there. A friend of John of Gaunt, Wycliffe spoke out against the corruption of the Roman Catholic church and the payment of taxes and indulgences to the Pope. He believed that education should be available to all, and to this purpose he began his translation of The Bible. His supporters became known as LOLLARDS, from the Dutch 'to speak softly or mumble'. After his death, the Roman Catholic church ordered Wycliffe's body to be dug up and thrown into the RIVER SWIFT, which runs through Lutterworth. Most of Wycliffe's English Bibles were destroyed by the Church and The Bible continued to be written in Latin until the time of William Tyndale (*see* Little Sodbury, Gloucestershire).

MARKET HARBOROUGH is the home of TUNGSTONE batteries, established in 1898, and the LARGEST BATTERY MAKERS IN THE WORLD.

GEORGE FREDERICK HANDEL often stayed at the GOPSALL ESTATE near MARKET BOSWORTH and composed the music for the *Messiah* in a temple in the grounds. His friend CHARLES JENNENS, whose grandfather owned the estate, wrote the words.

Lincolnshire

County Town: Lincoln

'This Haunt of Ancient Peace'

Lord Tennyson on Gunby Hall,
which stands at the foot of the Lincolnshire Wolds

Boston Stump, England's tallest medieval tower

Woolsthorpe

Father of Science

One warm evening in 1662, 20-year-old ISAAC NEWTON was sitting in the orchard of his family home at Woolsthorpe, near Grantham, drinking tea, his back up against an apple tree. His thoughts were interrupted by the thud of an apple falling to the ground in front of him. 'Why should that apple always descend perpendicularly to the ground?' he ruminated. 'Why should it not go sideways or upwards, but constantly to the earth's centre?' He was on his way to discovering the theory of gravity.

Isaac Newton was born in WOOLSTHORPE MANOR on Christmas Day 1642, a weak and sickly baby 'so tiny you might have put me in a quart pot!' Bright and inventive, he was put to work on his mother's farm, but his mind was elsewhere and he was often found reading a book or thinking great thoughts while the cattle wandered off and the fields remained untended. He was finally sent off to Cambridge by his uncle and there his remarkable imagination was given free rein.

Most of his important experiments were carried out in a small upstairs room at Woolsthorpe. Here he LAID THE FOUNDATION OF CALCULUS, INCREASED OUR UNDERSTANDING OF LIGHT AND COLOUR, constructed the WORLD'S FIRST REFLECTING TELESCOPE, and came up with the principle that stated 'for every action there is an equal and opposite reaction'. Later in life, he wrote the 'Bible' of science, *Principia Mathematica*, in which he lays out the basic rules of scientific theory which are still applied today.

Sir Isaac Newton died in 1727 and is buried in Westminster Abbey. Alexander Pope wrote in his epitaph:

Nature and Nature's laws lay hid in night
God said 'Let Newton be!' and all was light

Newton wrote of himself:

If I have seen farther than others, it is because I was standing on the shoulders of giants.

It is still possible today to sit against a descendant of that apple tree in the orchard at Woolsthorpe, where the modern world began and science was conceived. Woolsthorpe lies in a shallow valley and the view of the attractive grey-stone manor house and the rising fields beyond is almost unchanged since Newton's time, even though the busy A1 and the 21st century are just over the hill top. The manor house now belongs to the National Trust.

Grantham

Spires and Self-Reliance

Grantham, a once fine medieval town standing on the Great North Road, was badly served by the 1960s, when the heart was ripped out and replaced with car parks and office blocks. Nonetheless, some ancient corners remain and something of the spirit that gave us the FIRST SPIRE TO TOP 250 FT (76 M), the OLDEST ENGLISH INN, the WORLD'S FIRST COMPRESSION-IGNITION (DIESEL) ENGINE, the FIRST POLICE WOMEN IN ENGLAND and BRITAIN'S FIRST WOMAN PRIME MINISTER.

The spire, soaring 281 ft (85.6 m) into the sky above the church of ST WULFRAM, was built in the latter half of the 13th century and was for a time the highest spire in England. It is still a prominent landmark for miles around and a memorable sight from the train.

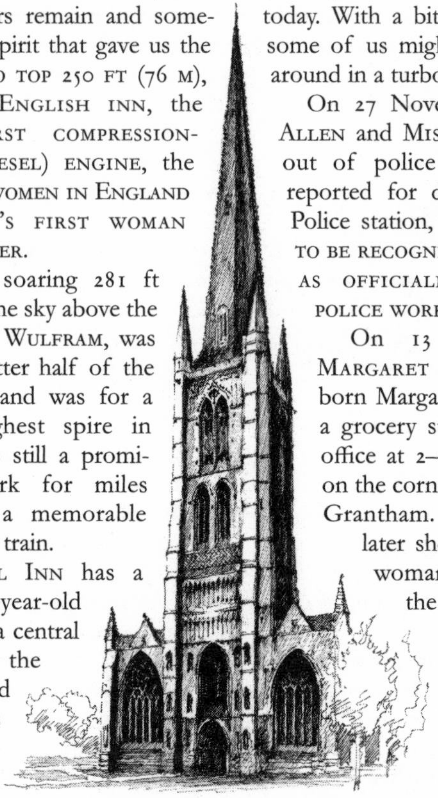

The ANGEL INN has a splendid 600-year-old stone façade, a central archway into the coachyard and projecting bays flanking an exquisite oriel window. The original hostelry was built for the Knights Templar in the 12th century and was visited by KING JOHN and later by RICHARD III, who sentenced the Duke of Buckingham to death here.

In 1892, RICHARD HORNSBY & SONS of Grantham produced the WORLD'S FIRST COMPRESSION IGNITION ENGINE to a design by HERBERT AKROYD STUART. This was essentially a less sophisticated prototype of the kind of engine developed rather later, but more commercially, by RUDOLPH DIESEL, and which bears his name today. With a bit better marketing, some of us might now be driving around in a turbo Akroyd Stuart.

On 27 November 1914, MISS ALLEN and MISS HARBURN, fresh out of police training college, reported for duty at Grantham Police station, the FIRST WOMEN TO BE RECOGNISED, IN ENGLAND, AS OFFICIALLY ENGAGED ON POLICE WORK.

On 13 October 1925, MARGARET THATCHER was born Margaret Roberts, above a grocery store and sub post office at 2–6 NORTH PARADE, on the corner of Broad Street, Grantham. Fifty-four years later she became the first woman ever to cross the threshold of 10 Downing Street as British Prime Minister, and she remained in office for an unbroken 11

Margaret Thatcher's birthplace

years, the LONGEST REIGNING PRIME MINISTER OF THE 20TH CENTURY. The shop is now a natural therapies centre.

Bourne

Wellspring of the English language, Statesmanship, Fashion and Motor Racing

The Burghley Arms, Bourne

The little town of Bourne, birthplace of HEREWARD THE WAKE, has had influence way beyond its size. It is a self-contained place of neat and sturdy houses teetering on the edge of the lonely Fens, gathered about a lovely Norman church – all that is left of the small abbey founded in 1138 by Arrosian Canons.

Robert Manning, known as ROBERT OF BOURNE, was a teacher at Bourne Abbey in the early 14th century and was the FIRST MAN TO WRITE IN ENGLISH. Until then, the church used Latin, and the Royal Court spoke and wrote in French. Robert wanted to enlighten and empower ordinary Englishmen by communicating in their own language. As he puts it in the preface to his first major work, *The Handling of Synne*:

For men unlearned I undertook
In English speech to write this book.

The Handling of Synne is a translation from the French of William de Waddington's *Manuel des Peschiez*, and uses storytelling to illustrate the Ten Commandments and the Seven Deadly Sins, rather in the fashion that Chaucer employed later in *The Canterbury Tales*. Manning used the everyday speech of ordinary Lincolnshire people, and the effect was to standardise the Lincolnshire dialect into a form of national English that is still recognisable today. Manning laid the foundatons and shaped the English language as we know it now, more than anyone else – even Chaucer.

For a few brief years in the 1950s and 1960s, Bourne was at the centre of British motor racing. BRM, or BRITISH RACING MOTORS, were the leading British motor racing team of the time, and the factory where their cars were built was in premises behind EASTGATE HOUSE, birthplace, in 1899, of RAYMOND MAYS. Mays was a successful racing driver between the wars, who founded BRM in 1949, in an effort to break the foreign domination of Grand Prix racing. In

1962, with GRAHAM HILL at the wheel, a BRM became the FIRST ALL-BRITISH CAR TO WIN A WORLD CHAMPIONSHIP. BRM finally closed in 1981, a year after Raymond Mays died at Eastgate House, and the factory has now become an auction house.

Bourne is also the unlikely BIRTHPLACE OF HAUTE COUTURE. Here, in 1825, CHARLES FREDERICK WORTH was born, the FIRST COUTURIER AND FOUNDER OF THE HOUSE OF WORTH, the WORLD'S LONGEST-RUNNING FASHION DYNASTY.

Worth began as an apprentice with the London fabric shop SWAN & EDGAR. He moved to Paris in 1845, and joined MAISON GAGELIN, where he met Marie Vernet, who became his wife. Dress-making was a female occupation in those days, but Worth, versed in the English ways of high quality design for men's clothing, brought these qualities to the designing of women's dresses and proved so successful that he was made Gagelin's head designer. He was the FIRST MALE PROFESSIONAL DESIGNER FOR WOMEN – the word 'couturier' had to be invented for him – and eventually the FIRST DESIGNER TO BECOME INTERNATIONALLY KNOWN. He was also the FIRST DESIGNER TO SIGN HIS WORK and to USE LIVE MODELS to exhibit his designs.

In 1858, Worth opened his own fashion store, the House of Worth, and was soon designing for the wealthiest and smartest women in Europe, including the EMPRESS EUGENIE, wife of Napoleon III (*see* Farnborough, Hampshire). His fame spread to America and, by the time he died in 1895, a Worth-designed dress had become the ultimate symbol of luxury and status, and the House of Worth, on the Rue de la Paix, the centre of world fashion.

The House of Worth was continued by his sons and grandsons until being sold to Paquin in 1956. Parfums Worth are still available, and the name House of Worth has recently been revived in London. There are frequent exhibitions of Worth designs at museums in all the major fashion centres.

BORN IN LINCOLNSHIRE

CHAD VARAH, founder of the SAMARITANS and Rector of St Stephen's, Walbrook, in the City of London until 2003, was born in BARTON-ON-HUMBER in 1911.

JOAN PLOWRIGHT, actress and second wife of Lord Olivier, was born in BRIGG in 1929.

DAME SYBIL THORNDIKE (1882–1976), actress, was born in GAINSBOROUGH.

JOHN ALDERTON, actor, was born in GAINSBOROUGH in 1940.

TONY JACKLIN, golfer, and the FIRST ENGLISHMAN OF THE MODERN PROFESSIONAL ERA TO WIN THE US OPEN, was born in SCUNTHORPE in 1944.

JENNIFER SAUNDERS, comedienne, was born in SLEAFORD in 1958.

Well, I never knew this ABOUT LINCOLNSHIRE

At BOWTHORPE PARK FARM, MANTHORPE, 3 miles (5 km) south of Bourne, stands an oak tree with the LARGEST GIRTH OF ANY LIVING OAK IN BRITAIN. It is 40 ft (12.2 m) in circumference and its leaves were fluttering in the Fenland wind when Hereward the Wake was a child playing in the fields around Bourne.

LOUTH is the MOST NORTHERLY TOWN IN THE WORLD SITED ON THE GREENWICH OR PRIME MERIDIAN. Louth also possesses the HIGHEST CHURCH STEEPLE IN ENGLAND. At 295 ft (90 m), it is 3 ft (0.9 m) taller than St Mary Redcliffe in Bristol and 14 ft (4.3 m) higher than St Wulfram, Grantham.

The church tower at CONINGSBY boasts the LARGEST SINGLE-HAND CLOCK IN THE WORLD.

As well as the splendid remnants of a Saxon abbey, the remote little Fenland town of CROWLAND possesses a remarkable TRIANGULAR BRIDGE, UNIQUE IN ENGLAND. It was built in 1360, at a crossroads, when the town was an island and the streets were waterways. The stone bridge has three 'halves' that meet in the middle, with each 'half' being reached by a flight of steps. There was a wooden bridge recorded on this spot in 716.

PETWOOD HOTEL, at WOODHALL SPA, flies the RAF flag as a special privilege to celebrate its role as OFFICERS' MESS for 617 'DAMBUSTERS' SQUADRON at the time of the bombing raids on the Ruhr dams. The squadron was based at nearby RAF SCAMPTON. There are many photographs of the crews and their commander, Guy Gibson, on the walls of the hotel and, in a flower bed by the front door, rests one of the ONLY REMAINING PROTOTYPES OF THE FAMOUS BARNES WALLIS 'BOUNCING BOMB'. Guy Gibson's beloved dog, NIGGER, was run over and killed on the day before the raids took place on 16 May 1943. Gibson asked that Nigger be buried at RAF Scampton at the exact time of the raids, and this was duly done.

HARRINGTON HALL, near SPILSBY, is where LORD TENNYSON was inspired to propose the invitation 'Come into the garden, Maud'. A splendid suggestion, for the gardens are quite beautiful with mellow red-brick walls and some very rare 17th-century terraces. The grounds are open on some days in summer. The Hall, originally Elizabethan, was gutted by fire in 1991, but has been restored by the present owners. Tennyson was born in nearby SOMERSBY, where his father was the Rector, in 1809.

In the grounds of BOOTHBY PAGNELL HALL stands the MOST COMPLETE AND BEST PRESERVED NORMAN MANOR HOUSE IN ENGLAND. Dating from 1200, it is one of the OLDEST DOMESTIC BUILDINGS IN THE COUNTRY. It can be visited by appointment.

SCRIVELSBY COURT, hidden behind its lion-guarded gate, has been the home of the KING'S CHAMPION since the Norman Conquest. This hereditary office was conferred on ROBERT MARMION by William the Conqueror, along with the Manor of Scrivelsby. In 1350, SIR JOHN DYMOKE married a great-granddaughter of Philip Marmion, and came into the office which has remained with the Dymokes ever since.

It was the duty of the King's Champion, at the Coronation, to don full armour, ride his charger into Westminster Hall and throw down his gauntlet as a challenge to anyone who denied the new monarch's right to the throne. His reward was a gold cup with which monarch and champion drank each other's health, and a number of these cups can be seen at Scrivelsby today. After rowdy scenes at George IV's coronation, this practice has been discontinued and now the Champion merely carries one of the standards at the Coronation. Scrivelsby Court was pulled down after the Second World War and the gatehouse has been converted into a residence by the present Champion, Lieutenant-Colonel John Dymoke.

Middlesex

County Town: Brentford

'those meads for ever crowned with flowers,
Where Thames with pride surveys his rising towers.'

Alexander Pope

Hendon Hall

Harrow-on-the-Hill

Prime Ministers and Poets

When Charles II, staying at Windsor, was asked what he understood by the phrase the 'Visible Church', he pointed to the distant spire of St Mary's church at Harrow-on-the-Hill. It is a still a notable landmark for miles around, 200 ft (61 m) high and standing on the crown of a hill that is also 200 ft (61 m) high.

Byron lay, lazily lay,
Hid from lessons and game away,
Dreaming poetry all alone
Up a top of the Peachey Stone.
Lines from a Harrow School song

In the churchyard of St Mary's is the flat stone of John Peachey's tomb, where the schoolboy Byron sat dreaming instead of attending to his

On Grove Hill, a steep, narrow lane that winds down from the hill towards Harrow town, the first recorded, fatal motor car accident in Britain happened on 25 February 1899. A Daimler, being driven on a demonstration run by E.R. Sewell of the Daimler Motor Car Co., went out of control while going down the hill and hit the kerb at the bottom, pitching the driver and his passenger, 63-year-old Major James Richer, on to the road. Mr Sewell died instantly, the Major four days later of a fractured skull.

studies. It still commands a panoramic view of 13 counties, but is now caged in for protection. In an unmarked grave nearby lies Byron's daughter ALLEGRA, who was born in Switzerland of an unknown English mother. She grew up in Venice with Byron, 'a pretty little girl and reckoned like papa'. Perhaps too much like papa, for he found her headstrong and sent her off to a convent in Ravenna. She died there aged just five. Byron had her body embalmed and sent to Harrow, requesting that she should be buried beneath the elm tree that had sheltered him as a boy.

Six Prime Ministers were educated at Harrow: SPENCER PERCEVAL, SIR ROBERT PEEL, LORD ABERDEEN, LORD PALMERSTON, STANLEY BALDWIN and WINSTON CHURCHILL. Also PANDIT NEHRU, the first Indian Prime Minister, and King Hussein of Jordan. And RICHARD CURTIS, who wrote *Four Weddings and a Funeral.*

While a schoolboy at Harrow, LORD SHAFTESBURY, the great Victorian philanthropist, was standing on the steps of the school when a pauper's funeral procession went past. The rickety coffin dropped on to the road and broke open, spilling the putrid body of a young boy in front of his horrified gaze. That moment determined him to devote his life to reforming the welfare of working children and the poor.

Hendon

A Statesman, an Actor and an Aerodrome

In 1929, a 5-mile (8-km) area around Hendon became the FIRST STRETCH OF GREEN BELT IN ENGLAND.

SIR STAMFORD RAFFLES (1781–1826), lies in St Mary's parish church at Hendon. He founded Singapore in 1819, where the luxurious Raffles Hotel is named in his honour. He also founded LONDON ZOO, the WORLD'S FIRST PUBLIC ZOO, in 1828.

Less than ½ mile (1 km) away is HENDON HALL, built in 1754 by DAVID GARRICK (1717–79), the actor-manager in whose honour the Garrick Club and the Garrick Theatre in London are named. In 1756, he bought the title of 'The Lord of Hendon Manor' for £13,000. The columns of the massive portico over the entrance are said to come from CANONS, the great house at EDGWARE built by the Duke of Chandos and demolished after he lost his fortune in the South Sea Bubble. In the gardens of Hendon Hall, now an hotel, are a memorial to William Shakespeare created by Garrick and one to Garrick himself.

GORDON SELFRIDGE, founder of Selfridge's department store on Oxford Street in London's West End, made the WORLD'S FIRST BUSINESS CHARTER FLIGHT when he hired a biplane to fly from HENDON AERODROME to Dublin on 25 June 1919. There has been an aerodrome at Hendon since 1909 and, from 1911, it was LONDON'S PREMIER AIRFIELD. The FIRST MILITARY AIR DISPLAYS were held there and, in 1920, the FIRST RAF AIR DISPLAY. The aerodrome closed in the 1980s and is now home to the RAF Museum.

Bruce Castle

A Ghost in the Post

There has been a castle at TOTTENHAM since Saxon days, when the manor was owned by WALTHEOF, LAST OF THE SAXON EARLS. Through marriage, it passed to the family of ROBERT THE BRUCE, who spent some of his childhood here, hence the name Bruce Castle. The present building dates from the days of Henry VIII, as does the detached red-brick round tower,

which was used to house birds of prey for falconry.

At the end of the 17th century, Bruce Castle was owned by a cruel tyrant named LORD COLERAINE, who drove his young wife Lucy to suicide. He locked her away in the tiny room under the clock until one day she escaped and jumped off the balcony holding her baby. Every November, on the anniversary of her death, she reputedly appears in the top window.

In 1827, Bruce Castle was bought by SIR ROWLAND HILL and run as a progressive school with no corporal punishment, unique in those times. Sir Rowland Hill went on to found the PENNY POST, and to invent the PENNY BLACK stamp. Today, the Castle is run as a museum of local history, with a special section on the development of the postal service.

The Castle stands in a small park beside the old church of ALL HALLOWS. Alongside is a fine 17th-century house called the Priory, now the vicarage, with a wonderful 18th-century wrought-iron gateway. Altogether they make an unexpected and delightful village picture in an otherwise grim North London landscape.

Stanmore

The Very Model of a Gentleman

GRIMSDYKE is an ancient Saxon defensive earthwork running between Pinner and BENTLEY PRIORY. Bentley Priory, built in the late 18th century for the First Marquess of Abercorn, on the site of a 12th-century priory, was sold to the Air Ministry in 1925. It was AIR CHIEF MARSHAL SIR HUGH DOWDING'S headquarters during the Battle of Britain in 1940.

Some 2 miles (3 km) west along Grimsdyke is GRIMS DYKE, a Victorian pile where SIR WILLIAM S. GILBERT (1836–1911), of Gilbert and Sullivan fame, lived from 1890 until his death. The house, which was built in 1872 for the artist Frederick Goodall, was designed by NORMAN SHAW, who was responsible for New Scotland Yard. Gilbert laid out the extensive gardens and was particularly proud of the lake, complete with an island in the middle, which he had excavated. In the summer, he would bathe in the lake every day and, on 29 May 1911, he invited two local girls to join him. One appeared to get into difficulties and Gilbert dived in to rescue her. He managed to drag her to the shore but the strenuous effort proved too much. He had a heart attack and died. He is buried in St John's church at Stanmore.

Twickenham

Strawberries and Popes

In 1715, the poet ALEXANDER POPE (1688–1744) moved to a house by the river at Twickenham where he laid out a fine garden of 5 acres and put together a notable GROTTO that became famous in its day. The house is no longer there, and the site is occupied by a school, but there is a road called POPE'S GROVE, which follows the line of an avenue of trees he had planted in his garden running down to the river, where there is now a small park. In his garden, Pope planted the FIRST WEEPING WILLOW TREE IN ENGLAND. He had received a gift of figs from Turkey, contained in a willow basket, and planted a sprig from the basket on the river bank. It relished the constant water supply and flourished, and from that tree came all the weeping willows in England today. Pope's grotto survives and is open by appointment. Alexander Pope is buried in St Mary's church. Several of his sayings have passed into common lexicon:

Damn with faint praise.
A little learning is a dangerous thing.
To err is human, to forgive divine.
For fools rush in where angels fear to tread.
Hope springs eternal in the human breast.

In 1747, HORACE WALPOLE (1717–97), son of Britain's first Prime Minister, bought a cottage called Chopped Straw Hall, near the river at Twickenham, which he extended and renamed STRAWBERRY HILL. (Curiously, 59 years later, in 1806, down the road at ISLEWORTH, ENGLAND'S FIRST CULTIVATED STRAWBERRY was unveiled.) Walpole travelled the country seeking ideas for his new home, which took 30 years to complete, and the result is an extraordinary confection that spawned its own style of architecture, Strawberry Hill Gothick. Although quite small, the house was almost a miniature castle, truly exotic and full of atmosphere. In June 1764, Walpole fell asleep while alone in the eerie gloom of Strawberry Hill and experienced a nightmare which inspired him to write *The Castle of Otranto* – the FIRST GOTHIC NOVEL. The house is now part of St Mary's training college and can be visited by appointment.

Well, I never knew this
ABOUT
MIDDLESEX

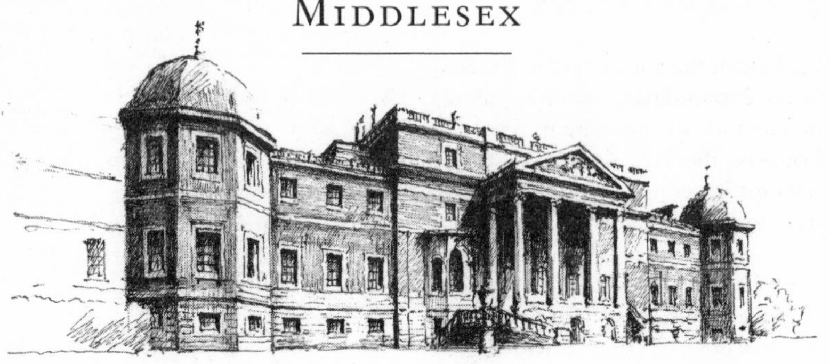

WROTHAM PARK, near POTTERS BAR, was built by ADMIRAL BYNG, who was court-martialled and shot in 1757 for neglect of duty. His death, according to Voltaire, was intended to *'encourager les autres'*. The house stands hidden behind huge gates in its own park of 300 acres. Because of its proximity to London and the nearby studios at Elstree and Borehamwood, Wrotham Park is often used for filming. *Peter's Friends* (1992), directed by Kenneth Branagh and starring Stephen Fry, was filmed there, and it became GOSFORD PARK for the Oscar-winning film of the same name in 2000. Other films that have used Wrotham Park as a location include *The Madness of King George* (1994), *The Wings of the Dove* (1997), *Bridget Jones's Diary* (2001) and *Vanity Fair* (2004).

In the cemetery in Chestnut Avenue, NORTHWOOD, lies EDWARD HONEY, an Australian reporter who thought up the idea of the Armistice Day 2-MINUTE SILENCE. It came to him in a Fleet Street tea shop and when he wrote about it the concept was taken up by the South African government, who were the first country to put the Silence into operation. This inspired King George V to do the same in Britain in 1935.

DEREK JARMAN (1942–94), film director, was born in NORTHWOOD.

Inside the church at the top of the lovely High Street at PINNER lies ZEPHANIAH HOLWELL, who survived the Black Hole of Calcutta. When the Nawab of Bengal attacked the settlement in 1756, the Governor and many of his officers fled, leaving Holwell to control those left behind. The 146 men and women who were captured were packed into a tiny cell 14 ft (4.3 m) by 18 ft (5.5 m) and, according to a disputed account written by Holwell himself, only 23 survived the night. Holwell went on to become Governor of Bengal and set up a monument over the common grave of all those who died.

Outside in the churchyard at PINNER is an extraordinary obelisk put up in memory of his parents by J. C. LOUDON, the Victorian horticulturist who instigated the planting of plane trees in London.

Under a stone tablet in the cemetery in Paines Lane, Pinner, lies HORATIA NELSON (1801–81), daughter of Lord Nelson and Emma Hamilton.

BORN IN MIDDLESEX

SIR ELTON JOHN (real name Reginald Dwight), singer, was born in PINNER in 1947.

JANE MARCH, actress, known as the 'Sinner from Pinner', was born in PINNER in 1973.

SIR NOEL COWARD (1899–1973), playwright, was born in TEDDINGTON.

DAME CLEO LAINE, jazz singer, was born in SOUTHALL in 1927.

Norfolk

County Town: Norwich

'Very flat, Norfolk.'

Sir Noel Coward, *Hay Fever*

Norwich Cathedral

Norwich

Hot Stuff

The 315-ft (96-m) high spire of NORWICH CATHEDRAL, second in height only to Salisbury, has found new fame as the logo for NORWICH UNION, BRITAIN'S BIGGEST INSURANCE COMPANY. The highest point in Norfolk, Roman Camp, near Sheringham, is, at 336 ft (102 m), only 21 ft (6.4 m) higher.

COLMAN'S ENGLISH MUSTARD has been made in Norwich since the early 19th century. Founder JEREMIAH COLMAN, when asked the secret of his success, replied, 'I have made my fortune from the mustard that people leave on the side of their plates!' Colman's is the LARGEST PRODUCER OF MUSTARD IN BRITAIN.

The sixteenth-century immigrant weavers from Holland introduced CANARIES to Norwich. The breeding of them became a local speciality and the Norwich canary soon became distinctive for its colour and song. Norwich Football Club is nicknamed 'The Canaries', and the team strip is yellow.

BORN IN NORWICH

MATTHEW PARKER (1504–75), second Anglican Archbishop of Canterbury and the first to have a wife. He was the ORIGINAL 'NOSEY' PARKER, a nickname given to him by Elizabeth I on account not only of his large nose, but also what she saw as his prying nature.

LUKE HANSARD (1752–1828), recorder of parliamentary debates and proceedings.

MICHAEL BRUNSON, TV newscaster and journalist, in 1940.

RUPERT EVERETT, actor, in 1959.

Edith Cavell

Brave Nurse

In 1865, Edith Cavell was born in an old house on the green at SWARDESTON, just south of Norwich, where her father was the vicar. In 1895, after much travelling, she returned to Swardestone to tend her father through illness and this gave her a desire to become a nurse. She trained at the London Hospital and, in 1907, went to Belgium, where she was put in charge of a training school for nurses just outside Brussels. She was back in Norfolk, weeding her mother's garden, when she heard that Belgium had been invaded by the Germans and insisted on going back, knowing that her school would soon be busy tending to the victims of war.

The school found itself behind enemy lines after the British retreat from Mons in 1914. Although they treated all soldiers, irrespective of nationality, Edith started to help the British soldiers who found their way to the school to escape to neutral Holland. An underground network was set up and, in the year that followed, some 200 allied servicemen were got out of Belgium.

Betrayed by Belgian collaborators, Edith was arrested in August 1915, admitted what she had done, and was sentenced to death by firing squad. The night before her execution, she was visited in her cell by the English chaplain in Brussels, Stirling Gahan. Together they recited the hymn 'Abide with Me' (*see* Brixham, Devon) and Edith uttered the words that appear on her gravestone, 'Standing, as I do, in view of God and Eternity, I realise that patriotism is not enough: I must have no hatred or bitterness towards anyone.'

At dawn, on 12 October 1915, Edith Cavell was taken outside and executed by a firing squad of eight men. Her last words were, 'Please tell my loved ones . . . I am glad to die for my country.' It is said that one of the soldiers in the firing squad, PRIVATE RIMMEL, could not bring himself to fire at Edith and threw down his rifle. He was shot by his commanding officer for refusing to obey orders and hastily buried near Edith's grave.

Nurse Cavell's execution worked as a huge propaganda coup for the Allies and recruitment doubled during the following weeks. Along with the sinking of the *Lusitania*, her execution was instrumental in persuading America to enter the war. After the war, her body was brought back to her native Norfolk and buried in a simple grave by the south door of Norwich Cathedral.

Didlington Hall

Museum of Doom

SIR (HENRY) RIDER HAGGARD (1856–1925), farmer and author of *King Solomon's Mines* and *She*, was born at his family home, WEST BRADENHAM HALL, near SWAFFHAM. In later life, when he returned from his travels, he bought DITCHINGHAM HOUSE, close to the Suffolk border, where he raised his family.

Didlington Hall, a huge red-brick house set in spreading parkland with woods, lakes and follies, near Swaffham, was owned by WILLIAM AMHERST, MP. Built on to the side of the house was a private museum full of Eygyptian antiques and curiosities from around the world, collected together by the Amhersts. As a young man, Rider Haggard was allowed to explore this exotic treasure trove and it inspired much of his writing, especially an Egyptian doll from which he drew the character of 'She Who Must Be Obeyed', the Egyptian Queen, Ayesha, from *She*.

Another young man whose interest in all things Egyptian was sparked by visits to the museum at Didlington was HOWARD CARTER (1874–1939), the man who discovered Tutankhamen's tomb. He was born in nearby

Swaffham and his family were great friends of the Amhersts.

Didlington Hall is no longer there but the park survives.

Holkham

First Bowler

HOLKHAM HALL was completed in 1762 by THOMAS COKE (1697–1776), the first Earl of Leicester, and was inspired by that other Palladian palace, the nearby HOUGHTON HALL of Sir Robert Walpole. In 1777, it became only the second of England's stately homes to open to the public, after Wilton House in Wiltshire.

Coke's nephew and heir, also Thomas Coke (1754–1842), was an innovative landowner and farmer. He pioneered the rotation of crops and the enriching of the soil with manure, and built smart, comfortable houses for his farm workers. He became known as 'COKE OF NORFOLK' and his success at turning the inhospitable sands and saltmarshes of North Norfolk into rich crop-growing fields encouraged farmers throughout Britain to copy his methods.

Thomas's heir, William Coke, was the FIRST MAN IN ENGLAND TO WEAR A BOWLER HAT. In 1849, he placed an order with Lock & Co. of St James's for a hard hat that would protect his head from overhanging branches while he was out shooting on his Norfolk estate. Lock's passed on his requirements to felt hat makers Thomas and William Bowler of Southwark Bridge Road, who devised a new kind of hard hat ready for Coke's approval in December 1849. Coke travelled up to London, walked into the shop, placed the hat on the floor and proceeded to jump up and down on it. He then picked the hat up, dusted it down and inspected it for damage. There was none, so he placed the hat on his head, enquired the price and left. To this day, if you go into Lock's and ask for a 'bowler' they will politely correct you and show you what they prefer to call a 'coke'.

Well, I never knew this ABOUT NORFOLK

The town of WORSTEAD in East Norfolk gives its name to WORSTED, a type of cloth made from wool and produced by Flemish weavers who settled in this part of Norfolk in the 12th century.

MELTON CONSTABLE HALL in North Norfolk became Brandham Hall for the 1971 film of L.P. Hartley's novel *The Go-Between*, starring Julie Christie and Alan Bates. The director Joseph Losey had managed to get the use of the estate for a very reasonable price as the Hall was owned by a local farmer and unoccupied at the time. The building needed redecorating, but exuded just the right aura of gracious decay. The lawns in the garden had been badly neglected though, and had turned brown, so they had to be sprayed with green paint, which caused a certain amount of difficulty for the actresses in their long Edwardian dresses. Melton Constable Hall has now been converted into flats.

The sturdy round tower of the little church, standing above a farmyard at EAST LEXHAM, is over 1,000 years old and is the OLDEST SAXON TOWER IN ENGLAND.

HOUGHTON HALL, a magnificent Palladian palace near King's Lynn, was built by BRITAIN'S FIRST PRIME MINISTER, SIR ROBERT WALPOLE (1676–1745), and was completed in 1735. Walpoles have been Lords of the Manor at Houghton since the 13th century and Sir Robert lies in the family vault at the little flint church in the park. Houghton was both his monument and his retirement home, although he only lived there for three years before he died. He stayed in office for 21 years, so is BRITAIN'S LONGEST-SERVING PRIME MINISTER. Sir Robert Walpole was also the FIRST PRIME MINISTER TO OCCUPY 10 DOWNING STREET. Lying close by is Sir Robert's son, HORACE WALPOLE (1717–97) (*see* Twickenham, Middlesex).

Houghton Hall and the park, with its peacocks and white deer, is open to the public. Displayed in the stable block is a collection of exquisitely painted MODEL SOLDIERS, thought to be the BIGGEST COLLECTION OF ITS KIND IN THE WORLD. It was assembled by the present owner's father, the sixth Marquess of Cholmondeley. In one display cabinet the Battle of Waterloo is recreated in immaculate detail.

DIANA, PRINCESS OF WALES (1961–97) was born at PARK HOUSE on the edge of the royal estate at SANDRINGHAM. The house had been leased by the Queen to Diana's parents, Viscount and Viscountess Althorp. Prince Charles paid a visit to Park House after his marriage to Diana and came across her signature carved into a wooden window frame. He had the whole window moved to Highgrove as a memento for Diana of her childhood home.

VISCOUNT NELSON (1758–1805), ENGLAND'S GREATEST NAVAL HERO and the victor of the Battle of Trafalgar, was born in BURNHAM THORPE. His grandmother was a sister of SIR ROBERT WALPOLE (*see* Houghton Hall).

SIR WILLIAM HOSTE (1780–1828), son of the Rector of Godwick, was born in INGOLDSTHORPE, north of King's Lynn. He was Nelson's protégé and served with Nelson at the Battle of the Nile. After Trafalgar, Hoste became an innovative and daring frigate captain, based in the Mediterranean. He achieved the capture of two fortress cities, Dubrovnik and Kotor, by hauling the guns from his ship up to the top of the surrounding mountains and bombarding them from above. Such dashing exploits inspired C.S. FORESTER to use William Hoste as the model for his nautical hero, HORATIO HORNBLOWER.

ANNA SEWELL (1820–78), author of *Black Beauty*, was born at PRIORY PLAIN in GREAT YARMOUTH.

CAPTAIN CHARLES CUNNINGHAM BOYCOTT was born in BURGH ST PETER in the far south east of Norfolk in 1832. He became a land agent and, in the 1870s, found himself in County Mayo, Ireland, acting as agent for absentee landlord Lord Erne. In 1880, his tenants, spurred on by the Irish Land League under Charles Parnell, demanded a substantial cut in their rents. Boycott refused and Parnell suggested that everyone in the area should suspend all dealings with Boycott. No one would work on his land, household servants downed tools, shops wouldn't serve him and even his mail remained undelivered. It turned out to be a hugely effective tactic and *The Times* in London adopted Boycott's name as a word meaning 'to ostracise or refuse to deal with'. The word has since passed into the English language.

Northamptonshire

County Town: Northampton

County of Spires and Squires
Anon

Peterborough Cathedral

Northampton

Boots, Shoes and Car Chases

Northampton has the biggest outdoor market square in England and is the capital of Britain's shoe-making industry, with Barkers, Church's and Crockett & Jones all having factories in the town.

The first car chase in Britain involving the police occured in Northampton in April 1899. Sergeant McLeod of the Northamptonshire County Police was proceeding on foot along the Weedon Road, in accordance with his duties, when he happened upon a suspicious individual selling forged tickets for the Barnum and Bailey Circus. Upon being challenged, the miscreant scarpered. Being hampered somewhat in terms of agility and speed by his regulation boots (made in Northampton, naturally), Sergeant McLeod flagged down a passing BENZ automobile belonging to a somewhat apprehensive JACK HARRISON, commandeered the vehicle and set off in pursuit.

A hair-raising chase down the Weedon Road ensued, in the course of which speeds of almost 15 mph (24 kph) were reached, and the scoundrel was finally nabbed near FLORE, some 3 miles (5 km) out of town. A beaming Sergeant McLeod was commended by his superiors for his quick thinking and impressive driving skills, and his satisfaction was only slightly tempered when he received a sharp reprimand for exceeding the speed limit of 12 mph (19 kph).

Sulgrave

Stars and Stripes

In 1539, at the Dissolution of the Monasteries, LAURENCE WASHINGTON, a prosperous merchant from the Washington family of Durham, bought the manor of Sulgrave from Henry VIII and built the fine stone house we see there today. His family lived there for the next 70 years.

Above the porch is carved the Washington family coat of arms, three stars above two stripes – the inspiration, it seems, for the American flag. Laurence is buried in the church at Sulgrave, as is his son Robert.

Robert's son, another Laurence, great-great-great-grandfather of George Washington, first President of the United States of America, left Sulgrave and is buried in the church at GREAT BRINGTON, about 12 miles (19 km) to the north. His grandson, John, emigrated to Virginia in 1656 and was George Washington's great-grandfather.

The village of Great Brington stands at the gates to ALTHORP, ancestral home of the Spencers, famous Northamptonshire squires. The first Laurence Washington who bought Sulgrave was a cousin of Lady Spencer of Althorp, and this was the reason he moved to Northamptonshire. DIANA, PRINCESS OF WALES (1961–97), born a Spencer, is buried on an island in the middle of a lake in the grounds of Althorp.

The family of another American hero, BENJAMIN FRANKLIN (1706–90), came from the village of ECTON, just north of Northampton, where they had been since at least 1555. The last Franklin to live in Ecton was Benjamin's uncle, Thomas, who is buried in the graveyard there. Benjamin paid a visit to Ecton to retrace his roots in 1758. The house and smithy owned by his uncle and grandfather are no longer there – in their place is the THREE HORSESHOES INN.

Benjamin Franklin's father, Josiah, emigrated to America in 1683 and settled in Boston. Benjamin, one of 17 children, was one of the five men chosen to draft the American DECLARATION OF INDEPENDENCE in 1776, when he was 70 years old; he also helped to write the AMERICAN CONSTITUTION.

Franklin was primarily a scientist and inventor. He conducted research into electricity, INVENTED THE LIGHTNING ROD, and INTRODUCED THE WORDS BATTERY, CONDUCTOR AND POSITIVE AND NEGATIVE INTO THE ENGLISH LANGUAGE. His other inventions included BI-FOCAL SPECTACLES, the ROCKING CHAIR and the FRANKLIN STOVE. He also discovered the course of the GULF STREAM, and gave these aphorisms to the world:

Early to bed and early to rise makes
a man healthy, wealthy and wise.

Time is Money.

In this world, nothing is certain but
death and taxes.

Easton Neston

A Costly Pile

One of England's finest stately homes, Easton Neston has been in the Fermor Hesketh family, also well-known Northamptonshire squires, since 1535. It stands on the edge of TOWCESTER, the OLDEST

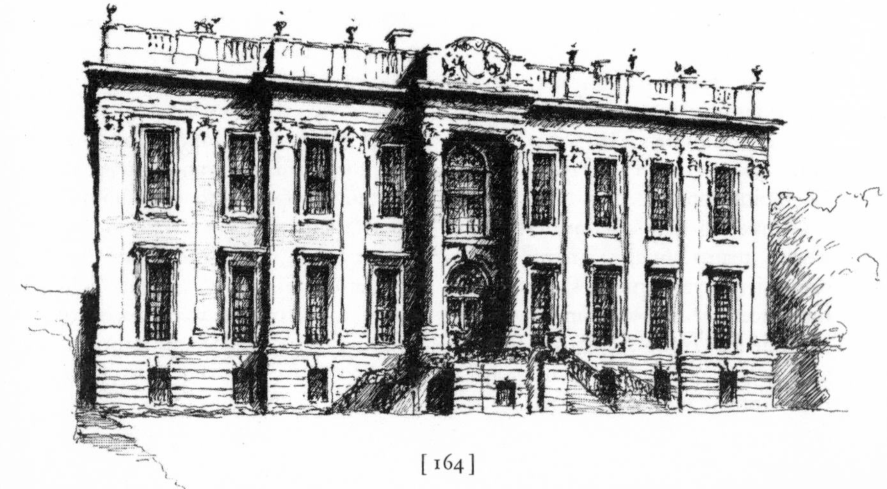

TOWN IN NORTHAMPTONSHIRE, and contains Towcester Racecourse within its grounds. The present house, built by NICOLAS HAWKSMOOR, plus 3,300 acres and the village of Hulcote, was put up for sale for £50 million in 2004 by the present Lord Hesketh.

Lord Hesketh, born in 1950, found fame – but lost a fortune – when, in the 1970s, he set up his own Formula 1 motor-racing team, Hesketh Racing. He hired JAMES HUNT, known as 'Hunt the Shunt', as his driver, and his team raced in the colours of red, white and blue, refusing any sponsorship. They set out to annoy the hidebound racing fraternity by being seen to have fun. Hesketh would send his helicopter for fresh croissants and newspapers and hold wild parties on his yacht.

But behind the amateur bluff, Hesketh Racing meant business. In 1973, Hesketh hired the promising young car designer Harvey Postlethwaite and built his own car, the Hesketh 308, in the stable block at Easton Neston. They developed the car throughout 1974 and, in 1975, came the team's high point when James Hunt won the Dutch Grand Prix at Zandfoort. That year James Hunt came fourth in the World Championship.

Competing with the professional works teams finally proved too expensive, even for Hesketh. The buccaneering, free-wheeling days of rich amateur owners were gone and, at the end of 1975, the team was closed down and the cars were sold. Nevertheless, Hesketh had achieved a great deal. He had injected glamour and fun into the sport, and had given Harvey Postlethwaite, one of Britain's most talented designers, his break. Harvey went on to win two constructors championships with Ferrari. Hesketh also gave James Hunt his chance. Hunt won the World Championship the following year in 1976.

Daventry

First Radar

THE WORLD'S FIRST RADAR STATION was sited at Daventry. In 1935, SIR ROBERT WATSON-WATT (a descendant of JAMES WATT, pioneer of the steam engine), while working at the Radio Research Laboratory at Ditton Park in Slough, was ordered by the chaps at Air Defence to devise a death ray – something that could destroy enemy aircraft with radio waves. Sir Robin replied that he didn't think that that would be possible, but how about using radio waves to detect enemy aircraft?

The defence committee hid its disappointment well and muttered that they supposed that would be better than nothing. So, on 26 February 1935, the Secretary of the Committee, Sir Robin, and his colleague A.F. WILKINS, went down to Daventry and clambered into the back of a Morris van, equipped with a cathode-ray oscilloscope display.

There followed the WORLD'S FIRST PRACTICAL DEMONSTRATION OF RADAR when a Heyford Bomber flying through the shortwave emissions of the BBC Empire station at Daventry at 6,000 ft (1,830 m) was identified from a distance of 8 miles (13 km). The radar technology demonstrated that day went on to become an invaluable weapon during the Battle of Britain in 1940.

Well, I never knew this
ABOUT
NORTHAMPTONSHIRE

ACHURCH, near Oundle, was the birthplace of the illustrator ALFRED LEETE (1882–1933). He worked on *Punch* magazine and designed the First World War recruiting poster 'Your Country Needs You' featuring Lord Kitchener.

THE BELL INN at FINEDON claims to be the OLDEST LICENSED HOUSE IN ENGLAND. There has been an inn on the site since 1042.

RICHARD III was born in FOTHERINGAY CASTLE on 2 October 1452. On 8 February 1587, MARY QUEEN OF SCOTS was beheaded there, in the banqueting hall. She was buried in Peterborough Cathedral, although her son, James I, later removed her body to Westminster Abbey. In 1627, Fotheringay Castle was pulled down and today the scene of such tragedy is tranquil and full of beauty with the River Nene flowing slowly through the meadows round the foot of the castle mound and on past the glorious church.

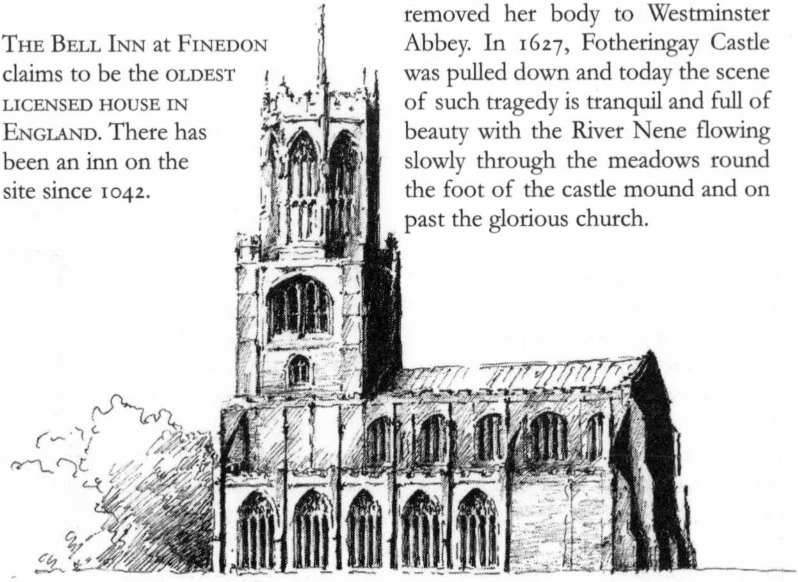

In a remote corner of the grounds of Rushton Hall, near Corby, hidden behind a screen of cedar trees, is the Triangular Lodge, built by Northamptonshire squire Sir Thomas Tresham (1545–1605) and completed in 1597. It is a celebration of the Holy Trinity – Father, Son and Holy Ghost – and the number three. It has three storeys and three sides, each 33 ft long, with three bays, three gables and three triangular windows.

The first tomatoes grown in Britain were cultivated in Britain's first conservatory, built in 1562 at William Cecil's Burghley House.

In 1843, at Lamport Hall, near Kettering, Sir Charles Isham, another of Northamptonshire's squires, introduced the first garden gnomes in England. They were imported from Nuremberg, and Isham used them to hold down the place names at his dinner table. He began to suspect that they were putting his guests off their food and so moved them into the garden. Then he thought they looked a little forlorn, so he imported some Japanese bonsai trees, the first bonsai in England, to create a forest so they could feel at home. The trend-setting garden is still there and can be visited.

Peterborough Cathedral, where Catherine of Aragon is buried, was used as the location for the 1982 TV series of Anthony Trollope's *Barchester Chronicles*, starring Nigel Hawthorne, Alan Rickman and Geraldine McEwan. They originally wanted to film at Salisbury Cathedral, but the magnificent Norman cathedral at Peterborough, tucked away behind unprepossessing shopping precincts and industrial estates, is one of England's hidden gems and, as a result, much quieter and more suitable for filming than Salisbury.

Some 1½ miles (2.5 km) from the village of Naseby, in the heart of England, in the meadows where Shakespeare's River Avon rises, lies a battlefield marked by a stone column. Here, on 14 June 1645, Oliver Cromwell's New Model Army defeated the forces of Charles I, ending the Civil War and altering for ever the balance of power between Monarch and Parliament. The battle turned on two errors by the Royalists. First, Prince Rupert and his cavalry tore through the Puritan ranks with such ease that they grew over-confident and raced off to plunder the enemy baggage waggons. When they returned, the battle was over. Secondly, King Charles, seeing his troops faltering, spurred his horse forward to inspire them on, but was turned back by an anxious attendant. Seeing their king apparently riding away from the fray, his men lost heart and were overwhelmed.

DEENE PARK has been the home of the BRUDENELL family, Northamptonshire squires since 1514. Edmund Brudenell was created EARL OF CARDIGAN by Charles II and his son lived at Deene for over 100 years. The seventh Earl, who was born in Hambleden in Buckinghamshire (*see* Buckinghamshire), rode out from here to lead the CHARGE OF THE LIGHT BRIGADE, which he miraculously survived. He died in 1868 after a fall from his horse, the same one that had carried him safely through the carnage at Balaklava. The horse lived for another four years and its head is now displayed in the White Hall at Deene.

The NENE VALLEY RAILWAY between Peterborough and Wansford was used for the spectacular railway scenes in the 1983 James Bond film *Octopussy*, starring Roger Moore and Maud Adams.

Particularly fine examples of Northamptonshire's famous spires can be found at GLINTON, STANWICK, HIGHAM FERRERS and ST PETER'S, OUNDLE.

Higham Ferrers

NORTHUMBERLAND

COUNTY TOWN: NEWCASTLE-UPON-TYNE

'And the sweet grey-gleaming sky
And the lordly strand of Northumberland'

A.C. SWINBURNE

Tyne Bridge, most famous symbol of Newcastle

Newcastle

Northern Lights

Folk who come from Newcastle are known as GEORDIES because Newcastle was the only town in Northumberland to declare for KING GEORGE I and close its gates against the Jacobite rebels, supporters of James Stuart, the 'Old Pretender'.

ST NICHOLAS'S CATHEDRAL has a rare 15th-century crown spire. In 1644, during the Civil War, SIR JOHN MARLEY, the Mayor of Newcastle, saved the building from being burned down by the Scots, by locking Scottish prisoners inside the tower.

SIR JOSEPH SWAN (*see* Gateshead, Durham), INVENTOR OF THE LIGHT BULB, first demonstrated his bulb at the NEWCASTLE LITERARY AND PHILOSOPHICAL SOCIETY on 3 February 1879, ten months before the American Thomas Edison's first demonstration of his bulb. In 1881, MOSLEY STREET in Newcastle became the FIRST STREET IN THE WORLD TO BE LIT BY ELECTRIC LIGHT. Earlier in the year, Swan had opened the FIRST ELECTRIC LIGHT BULB FACTORY IN THE WORLD at BENWELL in the western suburbs of Newcastle.

Down by the quayside is a street called SANDGATE, once the home of the NEWCASTLE KEEL MEN, skilled boatmen who transferred coal from the quayside to the ships in the middle of the River Tyne. The name came from their flat-bottomed boats, 'keels', a derivation of the word *ceol*, which was an Anglo-Saxon boat. KEEL is the FIRST ENGLISH WORD KNOWN TO HAVE BEEN WRITTEN DOWN.

Newcastle hosted the WORLD'S FIRST DOG SHOW, at the Town Hall, in 1859. There were 60 entries in two classes: pointers and setters. Mr Jobling, judging the pointers, won the setters class with his dog called Dandy, while Mr Brailsford, judging the setters, won the pointers class with his liver and white dog.

Newcastle hosted BRITAIN'S FIRST BEAUTY CONTEST in 1905. The 'Blonde and Brunette Beauty Show', open to all young ladies over the age of 16, was staged at the Olympia Theatre.

Newcastle's BLACK GATE houses the WORLD'S ONLY BAGPIPE MUSEUM.

BORN IN NEWCASTLE

ADMIRAL COLLINGWOOD (1750–1819), who took command at the Battle of Trafalgar after the death of Nelson.

EBENEZER LANDELLS (1808–60), who launched *Punch* magazine.

SIR OVE ARUP (1895–1988), engineer who worked on Coventry Cathedral and Sydney Opera House.

JACK HIGGINS (real name Harry Patterson), author of *The Eagle Has Landed*, in 1929.

ALAN PLATER, playwright, in 1935.

HANK MARVIN (real name Brian Rankin), guitarist with The Shadows, in 1941.

STING (real name Gordon Sumner), singer-songwriter, in 1950.

KEVIN WHATELY, actor famous for his roles in *Auf Wiedersehen Pet* and *Inspector Morse*, in 1951.

JIMMY NAIL, actor, in 1954.

ROWAN ATKINSON, comedian, in 1955.

ALAN SHEARER, England football captain, in 1970.

Bamburgh

Castles and Heroines

Bamburgh has been fortified since at least 547, and it was the FIRST CAPITAL OF NORTHUMBRIA. The oldest part of the present castle is the 12th-century keep, while the rest of the building was restored by Lord Armstrong in the late 19th century.

Bamburgh is the Joyous Guard of Sir Lancelot in *Morte D'Arthur.* Joyous Guard was a formidable castle previously called DOLOROUS GUARD, which Lancelot had captured single-handedly and made his home. He is supposedly buried there.

In 1464, during the Wars of the Roses, HENRY VI held court here after his defeat at the Battle of Hexham.

BAMBURGH CASTLE soon came under seige from Edward IV's artillery, the FIRST CASTLE IN ENGLAND TO COME UNDER CANNON FIRE.

Buried under a fine monument in the churchyard is one of England's nautical heroines, GRACE DARLING (1815–42). Grace's father was the keeper of LONGSTONE LIGHTHOUSE, off the Northumberland coast. At dawn on 7 September 1838, Grace was awoken by a violent storm. Near dawn she spotted a ship, the *Forfarshire*, aground on HARCAR ROCK, about 1 mile (1.5 km) away. Grace and her father rowed out into the pounding waves in the tiny lighthouse coble and managed to pluck five survivors off the wreck and row them back to the lighthouse. They then returned through the storm for the remaining four crew. It was three days before the weather abated and the survivors could be taken to the mainland.

The rescue captured the imagination of the whole country. Grace was pretty and slight and endearingly modest. She became one of the FIRST CELEBRITIES with her picture on the front page of all the newspapers and reporters clamouring for her story. She received hundreds of offers of marriage, and visitors, but continued to live at Longstone lighthouse in order to escape all the attention. In 1842, she died, tragically young, of pneumonia. Grace's early death led to her attaining almost saintly status and she was buried before a huge crowd of mourners, with Queen Victoria personally sending her condolences.

Cragside

House Lights

Commanding a spectacular position in wooded hills above Rothbury is Cragside, a glorious Victorian Gothic pile designed by Norman Shaw, and the FIRST HOUSE IN THE WORLD TO BE LIT BY HYDRO-ELECTRICITY – powered by a lake specially constructed in the garden. Cragside belonged to the engineer SIR WILLIAM ARMSTRONG, who filled the house with his inventions, including a hydraulic service lift and a powered roasting spit. In 1880, he installed Swan light bulbs and Cragside became the FIRST LARGE HOUSE TO BE LIT BY ELECTRIC BULBS (*see* Newcastle, and Gateshead, Durham).

William Armstrong was born in NEWCASTLE in 1810. He was interested in science from an early age and his first enterprise was a hydro-electric generator, inspired by watching a mill wheel at work when he was a young man. He later developed a hydraulic crane that was soon used at docks all over the world. The cranes were built at Armstrong's factory at ELSWICK in Newcastle, immortalised in the Tyneside anthem 'Blaydon Races'.

Concerned at the ineffectiveness of British artillery in the Crimean War, Armstrong moved on to making guns and he designed a BREECH-LOADING RIFLE that was quickly recognised as the BEST GUN IN THE WORLD. He supplied them to both armies in the American Civil War.

In 1894, Armstrong bought and restored BAMBURGH CASTLE. In 1897, his company merged with Joseph Whitworth to form Armstrong Whitworth, which then became Vickers Armstrong (responsible for making the Wellington Bomber). This in turn merged with the Bristol Aircraft Company, which finally became BAC.

Lord Armstrong, who was created a peer in 1887, died at Cragside on 27 December 1900 and was buried in the church at Rothbury on the last day of the century.

Wylam

Cradle of the Railways

The smart Tyneside village of Wylam is the undisputed cradle of the railways, being the birthplace of both GEORGE STEPHENSON and TIMOTHY HACKWORTH.

George Stephenson (1781–1848), known as the 'Father of the Railways',

was born in a small stone cottage beside the River Tyne, now owned by the National Trust. The wooden railway from the Wylam colliery, where his father worked, ran past the front door. After assisting his father at Wylam, George became engineer at Killingworth Colliery, north of Newcastle, where he started to develop his steam locomotives, culminating in the *Rocket*, which achieved a world speed record of 30 mph (48 kph) at the Rainhill trials (*see* Lancashire). The *Rocket* was built at Stephenson's foundry in FORTH STREET, NEWCASTLE, opened in 1823 as the FIRST LOCOMOTIVE FOUNDRY IN THE WORLD. He is buried at Chesterfield in Derbyshire.

TIMOTHY HACKWORTH (1786–1850) worked at the Wylam colliery and helped WILLIAM HEDLEY design his *Puffing Billy*. He was later employed by his former neighbour, George Stephenson, to supervise the locomotive foundry in Newcastle. He came up with the idea of coupling the wheels with rods instead of chains and designed his own locomotive, *Royal George*, using this technique. His *Sans Pareil* competed against Stephenson's *Rocket* at the Rainhill trials, but suffered a cracked cylinder. However, *Sans Pareil* continued in use until 1863, whereas the *Rocket* was taken out of service after two years. Hackworth finally settled in Shildon in Durham and concentrated on building slow but successful, heavy freight locomotives, and is credited as the man who made steam locomotion reliable. He is buried at St John's, Shildon.

Well, I never knew this ABOUT NORTHUMBERLAND

BERWICK-UPON-TWEED has changed hands between the Scots and English 14 times and is the ONLY ENGLISH TOWN NORTH OF THE RIVER TWEED. It is also the ONLY ENGLISH TOWN WHOSE FOOTBALL TEAM PLAYS IN THE SCOTTISH LEAGUE.

KIRKHARLE is the birthplace of LANCELOT 'CAPABILITY' BROWN (1716–83), the landscape gardener. He began his career in the gardens of KIRKHARLE PARK. He is buried at Fenstanton in Huntingdonshire.

ALNWICK CASTLE, home since 1309 to the PERCYS, Dukes of Northumberland, is the SECOND LARGEST INHABITED CASTLE IN ENGLAND – a claim also made by Arundel Castle (*see* Sussex). Windsor Castle is the largest. It has found recent fame as Hogwart's School in the *Harry Potter* films. Other films made at Alnwick include *Robin Hood, Prince of Thieves* with Kevin Costner, and *Elizabeth*, starring Cate Blanchett. The TV comedy series *Blackadder*, starring Rowan Atkinson, also used the castle.

Up river from the three bridges of Berwick at HORNCLIFFE is BRITAIN'S FIRST SUSPENSION ROAD BRIDGE, the UNION CHAIN BRIDGE, built in 1820 by SIR SAMUEL BROWN. He devised a new kind of link for chain cables which allowed for the development of bigger and heavier suspension bridges, a technique adopted by Thomas Telford when constructing his Menai Bridge. Union Bridge has a span of 360 ft (110 m) and links England with Scotland across the River Tweed.

In 1513, James IV of Scotland, three Scottish bishops, 13 earls and most of the Scottish aristocracy were slain at the BATTLE OF FLODDEN, fought near the village of BRANXTON. To this day, it is a bare, windswept, melancholy place. King James set up his headquarters at FORD CASTLE, where he was all too easily distracted by the lady of the house, Lady Heron, who later passed on what she had learned to Henry VIII's English forces, commanded by the Earl of Surrey.

THOMAS BEWICK (1753–1828) is buried in the churchyard at OVINGHAM, on the River Tyne. He was born across the river at CHERRYBURN. One of Britain's finest wood engravers, his work was hugely sought after and he set the standard for book illustration, until the introduction of the photograph. He illustrated *Aesop's Fables* and *The Book of British Birds*, but his masterpiece was *The Chillingham Bull*, carved in 1789. (The herd of white cattle in Chillingham Park is unique and has lived there for at least 700 years.) The BEWICK SWAN was named in his honour.

CHARLES, second EARL GREY (1764–1845), was born in FALLODON. He was Prime Minister from 1830 to 1834 and saw through the Great Reform Act of 1832. There is a monument to him at the top of Newcastle's finest street, Grey Street. He INTRODUCED EARL GREY TEA TO ENGLAND when he was given the recipe by a Chinese mandarin, in return, it is said, for saving the mandarin's life. It is a blend of Indian and Ceylon teas subtly flavoured with bergamot, a kind of orange.

Nottinghamshire

County Town: Nottingham

Robin Hood County

Southwell Cathedral

Nottingham

Bicycles and Boots

Up until the First World War, Nottingham was famed for its Nottingham lace, a by-product of the city's hosiery industry, and it was the LARGEST PRODUCER OF LACE IN THE WORLD. Lace eventually became considered a luxury and the trade declined.

JESSE BOOT was born in Nottingham in 1850. His father owned a herbalist shop, but died when Jesse was young, so Jesse left school at the age of 13 and helped his mother

The recipe for HP Sauce was created in Nottingham by a grocer called F.G. Garton, who began marketing Garton's Sauce in 1903. When he heard that his sauce was being served in the canteen at the Houses of Parliament, he decided to call it HP Sauce. Garton eventually handed over his recipe and the HP brand to Edwin Samson Moore, owner of the Midland Vinegar Company, in return for £150 and the writing off of some unpaid debts. In the 1960s, HP Sauce became known as 'Wilson's gravy', after Prime Minister Harold Wilson, who was rumoured to pour it all over his food. The sauce is now owned by Danone and produced in Aston, Birmingham.

to run the business. He studied pharmacy in his spare time and opened his first chemist's shop in 1877. He was concerned that poorer people could not afford the medicines they needed, since the other chemists in Nottingham all ran a price-fixing cartel. Jesse therefore sold his goods at a much cheaper price, advertising in the local paper and sending a bell ringer round the streets of Nottingham. His became the most popular shop in town and became known as 'THE PEOPLE'S STORE'. Jesse also kept down the price of prescriptions and he soon built up the BIGGEST CHAIN OF CHEMIST SHOPS IN THE WORLD. In 1929, he was created Lord Trent. He died in 1931.

Nottingham is also the home of RALEIGH BICYCLES. At the end of the 19th century, there was a small factory in Raleigh Street, near the town centre, making three bicycles a week. FRANK BOWDEN bought one, rode it for six months in the Pyrenees and liked it so much he bought the company, building it into the BIGGEST BICYCLE MANUFACTURER IN THE WORLD. In the first years of the 20th century, James Samuel Archer invented the Sturmey Archer three-speed gear, which was bought by Raleigh and helped to keep them at the forefront of the industry. In 1960, Raleigh was bought by Tube Investments. With growing competition from the Far East, however, there is uncertainty over the company's future in the 21st century.

Southwell

Apple Leaves

Southwell is perhaps England's least-known cathedral city. This is undeserved, for the cathedral is an exquisite Norman gem, possessed of some of the finest stone carvings in existence, particularly the 'LEAVES OF SOUTHWELL' round the door to the Chapter House.

In a garden at EASTHORPE, on the outskirts of the town, are the descendants of an historic tree. In 1805, the lady of the house transferred some pips from the apple she was eating into a pot. When the seedlings grew up, she took the strongest and planted it in the garden. It sprouted but did not bloom until many years later, by which time the house was owned by a MR BRAMLEY. The tree produced so much fruit that Mr Bramley began to distribute apples around the neighbourhood. They were so good that HENRY MERRYWEATHER, a fruiterer of Southwell, called to see Mr Bramley to ask if he could take some cuttings. Merryweather grew some trees from the cuttings and sent the fruit to the Fruit Committee, who gave it a certificate and the BRAMLEY APPLE was launched. As Henry Merryweather remarked to Mr Bramley, 'Now, Sir, you have the honour of raising, and I have the honour of sending out, the finest apple on earth.'

Newstead

Mad, Bad and Dangerous to Know

On a dark and stormy day, when the wind is howling and the skies are grey, NEWSTEAD ABBEY is the most romantic and ghostly place in Nottinghamshire. It was founded by HENRY II, as a penance for the murder of Thomas à Becket, and being born of such an evil deed seems to have cast an ancient shadow on this beautiful place. In 1540, after the Dissolution of the Monasteries, it was bought by SIR JOHN BYRON, who created a house out of the monastic ruins. The fifth Lord Byron, the poet's great-uncle, retired to Newstead in dissolute disgrace, run out of London after killing William Chaworth of Annesley in a duel at a tavern in Pall Mall. He let the house fall into ruin, wiped out all the deer in the park, neglected the gardens, ill-treated his wife and tenants and finally died alone in the one habitable room left.

The poet, the sixth LORD BYRON (1788–1824), inherited Newstead Abbey when he was ten, but it was in such a state of disrepair that he and his mother had to rent BURGAGE MANOR in SOUTHWELL. Byron moved into Newstead in 1808, after he had taken his degree. The wild, haunting beauty of the place, remote, decayed, full of ghosts,

family history and inevitable doom, added immeasurably to Byron's romantic image and undoubtedly inspired his passionate and rebellious poetry. Byron loved Newstead Abbey and swore never to sell it, but his debts mounted and his hand was forced. He saw it for the last time in 1814, when it was sold to his friend COLONEL THOMAS WILDMAN, who had made a fortune in the West Indies. He began to restore the house and it stayed in private hands until 1931, when it was given to Nottingham Corporation.

Byron is buried in HUCKNALL church, 4 miles (6.5 km) to the south. Next to him lies his daughter, AUGUSTA 'ADA' KING, Countess of Lovelace. She was a talented mathematician who helped CHARLES BABBAGE with his calculating machine, forerunner of the computer. The one-time standard computer language, ADA, was named after her.

Annesley

Hills of Annesley, bleak and barren
Where my thoughtless childhood strayed,
How the northern tempests, warring,
Howl above thy tufted shade.

Now no more, the hours beguiling,
Former favourite haunts I see,
Now no more my Mary smiling
Makes ye seem a heaven to me.

ANNESLEY HALL, where the teen-aged LORD BYRON loved and lost MARY CHAWORTH, his first and saddest passion, stands beside the ruins of a church, across the fields from the poet's home at Newstead Abbey. In the park nearby, is DIADEM HILL, 578 ft (176 m) high, where they would meet and where they finally parted. Byron truly loved Mary, his 'bright morning star of Annesley', who was petite and exquisitely beautiful, but she did not return his feelings and he never recovered from her rejection. 'Had I married Miss Chaworth, perhaps the whole tenor of my life would have been different,' he wrote, and something of the aching sense of loss that runs through his poetry can still be felt here, where his melancholy and self-destruction began.

Lying in the ruined church is WILLIAM CHAWORTH, slain in a duel by Byron's great uncle William, the 'Wicked Lord' from whom Byron inherited his title and the desolate Newstead Abbey.

Mary Chaworth died in 1832, when Annesley Hall was attacked by a mob rioting over the Great Reform Bill.

Gotham

Acting the Goat

Gotham is a simple Nottingham village, and the men of Gotham were simple people with simple ways. We are told in *The Merry Tales of the Mad Men of Gotham*, published in 1540, that they tried to drown eels in the village pond. They built a hedge around a cuckoo's nest so that the cuckoo couldn't fly away. They took their cheeses to the top of the hill and let them roll all the way to Nottingham market on their own. When they got to Nottingham and found the cheeses weren't there, they assumed they must have got lost and gone to York instead, so they all went off to York to look for them. To hide the church bell from invaders, they took it out on the river and sank it, marking the postion with a notch on the side of their boat.

But there may have been method in their madness. In 1200, there were rumours that King John was coming their way for a spot of hunting. If he passed through Gotham, then the village street would become part of the king's highway, and the villagers subject to new taxes. If they all pretended to be mad, however, then the king would stay away, for lunacy was thought to be contagious. It worked. Trouble was, they played the part so convincingly, everyone else thought they were daft as well and the reputation stuck.

In his travels, American writer WASHINGTON IRVING heard this story and he applied the name Gotham to his home city of New York, which he regarded as full of crazy people. Hence the writers of BATMAN adopted the name Gotham City for their version of New York City.

Well, I never knew this ABOUT NOTTINGHAMSHIRE

LITTLE JOHN bell, hanging beneath the dome of the NOTTINGHAM COUNCIL HOUSE, 200 ft (61 m) above the ground, weighs over 16 tons and has the DEEPEST TONE OF ANY BELL IN ENGLAND.

WELLOW, on the edge of SHERWOOD FOREST, has the TALLEST MAYPOLE IN ENGLAND.

LAXTON is the LAST VILLAGE IN ENGLAND TO RETAIN THE STRIP FIELD SYSTEM as used by the Saxons. There are three fields, Mill Field, South Field and West Field, each of 300 acres. One field grows winter grain, one grows spring grain and one is left fallow, and this system is rotated annually. The two cultivated fields are divided into strips and these are allocated, at random, ten strips to each tenant. The idea is to ensure that each tenant gets some poor land as well as some good. The allocation is done annually by an elected jury who makes sure that the land is well tended and rules on any disputes. Rents are paid to the lord of the manor.

The GENETICALLY MODIFIED TOMATO was engineered at NOTTINGHAM UNIVERSITY and was the FIRST GENETICALLY MODIFIED PLANT FOOD APPROVED FOR SALE in both Britain and the United States.

The SCREEN ROOM cinema on Broad Street has only 21 seats and is the SMALLEST PUBLIC CINEMA IN THE WORLD.

NOTTS COUNTY FOOTBALL CLUB, formed in 1862, was a founder member of the Football League and is the OLDEST FOOTBALL CLUB IN ENGLAND.

JOHN BIRD, the television comedian, was born in Nottingham in 1936.

NOTTINGHAM is the home of JOHN PLAYER & SONS cigarettes, now part of Imperial Tobacco. In the 1930s and 40s, their factory in Radford Boulevard was the BIGGEST TOBACCO FACTORY IN THE WORLD.

OXFORDSHIRE

COUNTY TOWN: OXFORD

'Dreaming Spires'

MATTHEW ARNOLD

Radcliffe Camera, the third largest unsupported dome in England

Oxford

Gown . . .

Oxford began at the point on the THAMES where Saxon ox drovers could ford the river, near where FOLLY BRIDGE is today. A small priory grew up nearby and, in 872, KING ALFRED stopped here on his way up river for some refreshment and got into a deep debate with the learned residents that lasted for some days. Oxford's reputation for scholarly pursuits was born. To this day, the River Thames at Oxford is called ISIS, a shortened form of the Latin THAMESIS.

In 1157, King Richard the Lionheart was born where 24 BEAUMONT STREET now stands. His brother, King John, was also born in Oxford, in 1167.

The writer and poet Matthew Arnold spoke of Oxford as the 'city with her dreaming spires'. The view that inspired this description can still be seen from BOARS HILL, about 4 miles (6.5 km) to the south-west of the city.

OSCAR WILDE (1854–1900) was an undergraduate at MAGDALEN COLLEGE, where he gained a first in *literae humaniores*. He was very fond of the May Morning tradition when the choir sing from the top of the beautiful 15th-century MAGDALEN TOWER. In 1505, the FIRST CLOCK TO BE FIXED TO THE OUTSIDE OF A BUILDING IN ENGLAND was unveiled on Magdalen Tower.

SIR JOHN BETJEMAN (1906–84) came up to Magdalen in 1925, bringing with him his teddy bear, Archibald. Archibald was the inspiration for Sebastian's teddy, Aloysius, in *Brideshead Revisited* by Evelyn Waugh (1903–66), who was at Hertford College.

Magdalen College was featured in *Shadowlands* in 1993. The film tells the story of C.S. LEWIS's relationship with his wife, Joy Gresham, who died of cancer in 1960. Lewis (1898–1963) taught at Oxford from 1925 until 1954, and is buried in the churchyard at Headington Quarry, near where he lived at Headington. C.S. Lewis wrote *The Chronicles of Narnia*, a series of books for children about an imaginary land. He was great friends with another writer of fantastic tales, J.R.R. TOLKIEN (1892–1973), author of *The Lord of the Rings*. Tolkien also taught at Oxford and is buried in the Roman Catholic cemetery at WOLVERCOTE, north of Oxford.

Oxford has even dipped its distinctive toe into the world of fashion with OXFORD BROGUES, a hardwearing shoe, and a species of voluminous trouserings, known as OXFORD 'BAGS', which were very popular with students in the 1920s.

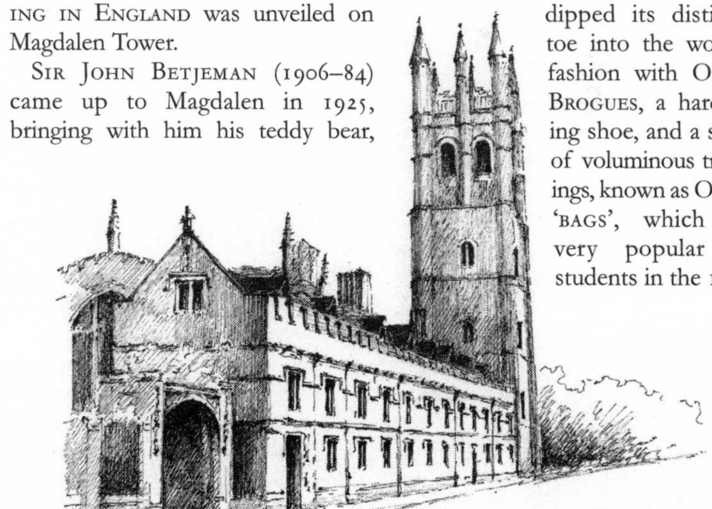

The Other Oxford

... and Town

Oxford is not all about the University. In 1898, the FIRST COMMERCIAL TRAVELLER TO USE A CAR, RALPH FOORT, came from Oxford. And, in 1933, Oxford unwrapped the WORLD'S FIRST LOLLIPOP LADY.

In 1913, WILLIAM MORRIS (1877–1963), a farm labourer's son from Worcester, took over a derelict military college in the little village of COWLEY, to the south of Oxford, and started to make bicycles. At that time, the village wasn't much more than a 12th-century church with a fine view of the dreaming spires, and a creeper-covered 17th-century house. Within 40 years, it had become one of the LARGEST MOTOR CAR PLANTS IN THE WORLD, producing a car every minute.

From bicyles, Morris moved on to making two-seater MORRIS OXFORD cars and, in 1919, he formed MORRIS MOTORS. He introduced the mass production methods of Henry Ford and his four-seater MORRIS COWLEY soon displaced the Ford Model T as Britain's favourite car. The first MORRIS MINOR, designed by SIR ALEC ISSIGONIS (1906–88), rolled off the production line in 1948, and went on to become

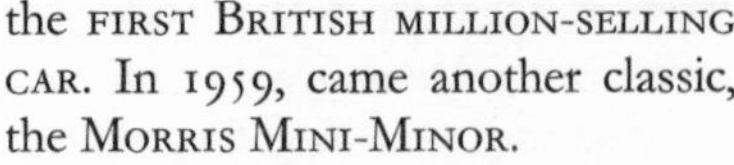

the FIRST BRITISH MILLION-SELLING CAR. In 1959, came another classic, the MORRIS MINI-MINOR.

William Morris was the most successful British car maker of all time and helped change the face of modern transport. Morris merged with Austin in 1952 to become the British Motor Company, the fourth largest car maker in the world at the time. This was then subsumed into British Leyland, which became the Rover Group. Minis, now under the BMW badge, are still made at Cowley today.

Woodstock

A Wonderland Fit for Heroes

Outside the village church at BLADON, near Woodstock, lies SIR WINSTON CHURCHILL (1874–1965), the Prime Minister who led Britain and her Allies to victory in the Second World War.

Winston Churchill was born in BLENHEIM PALACE, the great baroque pile just across the park, built for the Duke of Marlborough in honour of his victory at Blenheim in 1704. JOHN CHURCHILL from Axminster, Devon, the first Duke of Marlborough (1650–1722), is the ONLY BRITON EVER TO HAVE RISEN FROM A COMMONER TO A DUKE IN ONE GENERATION.

At the gates of Blenheim, lies the town of Woodstock, where HENRY II built a bower for his mistress the 'FAIR ROSAMUND' and surrounded her with a maze. When Henry was away, his wife

In 1874, queues began to form outside the Oxford shop of Frank Cooper, demanding marmalade. Cooper's wife, Sarah Jane, was selling the surplus of her own robustly flavoured, premium marmalade, made from a recipe handed down to her by her mother. It became hugely popular, particularly with the dons, and to satisfy demand Frank Cooper had to open a factory next to the railway station. The recipe remains unchanged to this day, although the marmalade which, strictly speaking, should be called Sarah Jane Cooper's Mother's Oxford Marmalade, is no longer made at the original factory. Frank Cooper's company was eventually bought by Heinz, and is now part of the RHM group. Robert Scott took a jar of Frank Cooper's Oxford Marmalade to Antarctica, where it was found, years later, buried in the snow.

Queen Eleanor, found her way through the maze by following a strand of Rosamund's silken dress that had unravelled behind her. The Queen gave the mistress a choice, either to drink from a poisoned draught or to retire to a nunnery. Whichever the Fair Rosamund chose, she was eventually buried beneath the chapel of the nunnery at GODSTOW in 1177 and never saw Henry again.

THE TROUT INN at GODSTOW was a favourite haunt of *Inspector Morse*, as well as many Oxford undergraduates, and the picturesque waterside pub has featured in many episodes of the TV series starring John Thaw.

GODSTOW is also where Charles Dodgson (LEWIS CARROLL) brought ALICE LIDDELL and her sisters for a picnic, entertaining them with *Alice's Adventures in Wonderland* while they rowed up the river from Folly Bridge. Alice Liddell was the daughter of the Dean of CHRIST CHURCH, where Dodgson was a lecturer in mathematics. It is possible to glimpse, through a gateway, the garden at Christ Church where Alice played, and to see the very tree branch on which the Cheshire Cat appeared before vanishing, leaving just a grin left behind.

Well, I never knew this ABOUT OXFORDSHIRE

NORTH STOKE, by the River Thames, is the last resting place of DAME CLARA BUTT (1872–1936), who had 'THE MOST GLORIOUS VOICE EVER HEARD'. With her powerful and distinctive contralto, she was renowned for her range and 'cavernous' lower register. Her recording of 'Land of Hope and

Glory' was the best-selling record of its day and Sir Thomas Beecham declared that 'on a clear day you could have heard her across the English Channel'. She was buried to the strains of her own rendition of 'Abide with Me' (*see* Brixham, Devon).

In the little Norman church with the Saxon tower at CAVERSFIELD, just north of Bicester, is the OLDEST INSCRIBED BELL IN ENGLAND, marked with the words 'In honour of God and St Laurence, Hugh Gargatt and Sibilla his wife had these bells erected'. It has hung there since the 12th century, and has rung out the news of Crécy and Agincourt, Bosworth Field, Trafalgar and the Charge of the Light Brigade.

The 16th-century KELMSCOTT MANOR was the Oxfordshire home of WILLIAM MORRIS (1834–96), poet, Pre-Raphaelite painter, craftsman and social reformer. He moved there in 1871, and is buried beneath a stone slab in the churchyard. The house is open to the public in the summer.

RADCOT BRIDGE, dating from *c.*1150, is the OLDEST BRIDGE OVER THE RIVER THAMES. In 1387, HENRY BOLINGBROKE smashed down the central arch to thwart the Earl of Oxford's men, who had been sent to hunt him down by his cousin, Richard II. The pursuers, taken by surprise, were all either captured or drowned. Twelve years later, Henry had Richard II murdered in Pontefract Castle and was crowned Henry IV.

In a small, oak-panelled study at the top of the massive, square kitchen tower of the manor house at STANTON HARCOURT, the poet ALEXANDER POPE spent two summers translating Homer's *Iliad.* In the church lies ROBERT HARCOURT, Standard Bearer to Henry VII at the Battle of Bosworth Field in 1485. Hanging above his tomb is the very flag he carried into battle and waved in triumph over the corpse of the vanquished King Richard, ushering in the age of the Tudors.

Kelmscott Manor

Headington Hill Hall

One well-known resident of the town HEADINGTON was the tycoon ROBERT MAXWELL (1923–91), who rented HEADINGTON HILL HALL from Oxford City Council and lived there for 32 years until his mysterious death in 1991. He called the 51-room house, built in 1824 for the Morrell brewing family, 'the best council house in the country'. Others called it Maxwell House. Maxwell ran his Pergamon Press from the stables. The main road from London into Oxford passes under an ornate iron footbridge built in 1877 to link two sections of the estate. The house is now part of Oxford Brookes University and can be visited by appointment.

EDWARD THE CONFESSOR (1005–66) was born in ISLIP, on the edge of Otmoor, to the north east of Oxford.

Behind the Magdalen College deer park, in the churchyard of ST CROSS, lies the author of *The Wind in the Willows*, KENNETH GRAHAME (1859–1932). He is buried in the same grave as his son, Alastair. The tales of river-bank folk that became *The Wind in the Willows* were made up as bedtime stories for Alastair and were published in 1908. While an undergraduate at Oxford, Alastair committed suicide by lying down on a railway track, a tragedy from which Grahame never recovered. Alastair was thought to have possessed many of the excessive characteristics found in Toad. MAPLEDURHAM HOUSE, a beautiful red-brick, Elizabethan house on the River Thames near Reading, was the original for TOAD HALL.

Buried nearby in the same churchyard is the writer and theatre critic KENNETH TYNAN (1927–80). In 1965, he was the FIRST PERSON EVER TO MOUTH AN OBSCENITY ON TELEVISION. He also devised the nude musical *Oh Calcutta!* for the West End.

Rutland

County Town: Oakham

Multum in Parvo

Much in a small place

Oakham

Horseshoes and Pie

The Great Hall is all that is left of OAKHAM CASTLE, built in the 12th century. It is ENGLAND'S OLDEST AND BEST-PRESERVED MEDIEVAL CASTLE HALL and is unusual in that it was built separately from the rest of the castle. Inside is a remarkable array of over 200 horseshoes, hanging from the walls. William the Conqueror's farrier lived at Oakham and, since that time, there has been a custom that every peer of the realm, on a first visit to Oakham, should hand over a horseshoe to the Lord of the Manor. The oldest in this unique collection is that left by Edward IV in 1470. The newest was presented by Prince Charles in 2003.

In 1619, JEFFREY HUDSON, a soldier and courtier who grew to a height of only 3 ft 6 in (107 cm), was born in a small thatched cottage, still standing in Melton Road. Until the age of 30, Jeffrey remained 18 in (46 cm) tall. At the age of nine, he was taken under the wing of the Duke of Buckingham, who lived at Burley-on-the-Hill. During a visit by Charles I and his wife, Henrietta

Maria, Jeffrey sprang out of a pie that was served up to the royal guests. Was not that a dainty dish to set before a king? Much more imaginative than four and twenty blackbirds. The Queen took an instant liking to him and his 'sprightly ways' and Jeffrey Hudson went off to London and soon became a favourite at court.

Titus Oates

Spin

Titus Oates was born in OAKHAM in 1649, son of a Baptist minister. It soon became apparent that his grasp of the Baptist faith was shaky. First he became an Anglican minister, then a curate, then a Navy chaplain, each time being dismissed for drunkenness and sodomy. He then experimented with becoming a Catholic and a Jesuit, later claiming that this was a ruse to learn their secrets.

In 1678, Titus Oates took his vivid imagination to Charles II's London, and found the capital awash with stories of plots, from Protestants striving to keep the Catholic James from the succession, to Catholics scheming to kill Charles so that James could claim the throne and properly restore the Catholic faith. In London, Oates got together with a number of prominent anti-Catholics, and told Charles II of a 'Popish Plot' to assassinate him, which he had overheard while masquerading as a Jesuit. Although the king did not believe him, leading Whigs, such as the Earl of Shaftesbury, used Oates's story as an excuse to round up Catholics and introduce an Act excluding Catholics from Parliament.

Titus Oates's Popish plot took on a life of its own; Catholics were persecuted and run out of town, with many being sent to the scaffold. Finally, in 1681, Charles II lost patience with Oates. Not a shred of evidence had been unearthed to substantiate the plot and Oates had begun to denounce all who opposed him, including the Duke of York and the king himself. Oates was thrown into prison and, in 1683, Charles turned the tables by using the rumours of the Rye House Plot – a Protestant plan to ambush and assassinate Charles II and his brother James on their way back to London from the races at Newmarket – to rid himself of his Protestant opponents, such as the Earl of Shaftesbury, who fled into exile. Titus Oates remained in prison until William of Orange came to the throne in 1688, at which point he was pardoned and given a small pension on which to retire. He died in 1705.

Barleythorpe

The Yellow Earl

BARLEYTHORPE HALL, just outside OAKHAM, was the home of Hugh Cecil Lowther, the fifth EARL OF LONSDALE (1857–1944), known variously as 'The Yellow Earl', 'England's greatest sporting gentleman' and 'Lordy'. He was given the nickname The Yellow Earl because of his love for the colour yellow. His bedroom, his cars, his servants' uniforms were all varying hues of yellow. In the 1930s, he was president of Arsenal Football Club and, to this day, the Arsenal away strip is yellow in his honour.

England's greatest sporting gentleman was the first President of the National Sporting Club. A keen boxing fan, he organised the FIRST EVER BOXING MATCH WITH GLOVES. He also introduced BOXING'S OLDEST CHAMPIONSHIP BELT, the valuable LONSDALE BELT, made from gold and porcelain and presented to the champion of each British weight division. The first belt was won by lightweight boxer FREDDIE WELSH in 1909. The first British heavyweight to win the Lonsdale Belt, in 1911, was 'BOMBARDIER' BILLY WELLS, known to millions as the man who bangs the gong at the beginning of

Rank films. The only man ever to win three Lonsdale belts is HENRY COOPER.

'Lordy' was a *bon vivant* who loved cigars, on which he spent £3,000 a year. He is one of only two men – the other being Winston Churchill – to have a Cuban cigar size named after him. The LONSDALE CIGAR SIZE is 6 in (15 cm) long and has a 42 ring gauge.

In the early 20th century, Lord Lonsdale was twice Master of Rutland's COTTESMORE HUNT. The Cottesmore was founded in 1695 by Thomas Noel, who purchased a pack of hounds brought down from Lowther Castle in Westmorland by the Earl's ancestor Henry, Viscount Lowther (*see* Westmorland).

Barleythorpe Hall is now a residential care home run by Rutland County Council.

Tolethorpe Hall

He Gave his Name

The 14th-century Tolethorpe Hall, 2 miles (3 km) north of Stamford, has been the home of the STAMFORD SHAKESPEARE COMPANY since 1977. They put on an annual season of plays in June, July and

August, in the Rutland Open Air Theatre, situated in the grounds. The auditorium is protected by a permanent high-tensile canopy, which is the ONLY THEATRE STRUCTURE OF ITS TYPE IN EUROPE.

In 1550, ROBERT BROWNE was born in Tolethorpe Hall. He grew up to lead the first group of religious separatists after the Reformation and his followers became known as BROWNISTS. He questioned the authority of the established Church of England and, in 1581, had to flee to Holland where, in 1582, he wrote and published the first exposition of Congregational principles. His ideas were adopted by several separatist groups, such as the Quakers (*see* Leicestershire), Baptists and the Pilgrim Fathers. Indeed, many of Browne's treatises were eventually incorporated into the AMERICAN CONSTITUTION.

Well, I never knew this
ABOUT
RUTLAND

WHITWELL, a tiny village just to the north of Rutland Water, is twinned with PARIS. A few years ago, the Chairman of Whitwell parish council, keen to boost the profile of the village, wrote to the Mayor of Paris, Jacques Chirac, to investigate the possibility of twinning the two communities. Conscious of the Mayor's busy workload, the Chairman generously suggested that he would only expect an answer if it was in the negative and that, if he had not received a reply within 15 days, he would take that as Chirac's assent to the scheme. The Chairman did not receive a reply from Chirac and, hence, Whitwell is now twinned with Paris. It says so on the village signs.

The church in the tiny village of TICKENCOTE, just off the A1 near Stamford, has the FINEST AND MOST ELABORATE NORMAN CHANCEL ARCH OF ANY CHURCH IN THE COUNTRY. The Norman vaulting of the roof is glorious and the only other example of its kind in England is above the choir of Canterbury Cathedral.

Since 1858, Rutland has been associated with RUDDLES BEER, real ale brewed at LANGHAM, just north of Oakham. In 1997, Morland's, who had taken over Ruddles, closed the Langham brewery, which has now been demolished. Greene King, present owners of Ruddles, have since revived Ruddles Beer, but it is now brewed in Bury St Edmunds, Suffolk.

In 1619, at NORTH LUFFENHAM, south of Rutland Water, VINCENT WING was born, one of the FIRST ASTROLOGERS and forerunner of such sages as Patric Walker, Russell Grant and Jonathan Cainer. In those days, astrology and astronomy were closely linked and Wing was foremost a mathematician, whose predictions were based on mathematical study of the heavens. His forecasts were published in a hefty volume called *A Dreadful Prognostication*, which terrified 17th-century England, while his astronomical almanac was standard reading for scholars and forecasters alike. All were written from his study in Rutland.

UPPINGHAM SCHOOL has the LARGEST PLAYING FIELDS OF ANY SCHOOL IN ENGLAND.

RUTLAND WATER covers the LARGEST SURFACE AREA OF ANY ARTIFICIAL LAKE IN EUROPE and in England is second in surface area only to the natural Lake Windermere.

In the room with the imposing oriel window over the north porch of STOKE DRY church, the GUNPOWDER PLOT was much discussed. Next to the church once stood the house where SIR EVERARD DIGBY was born in 1578. Brought up a Protestant, he was converted to Catholicism by a Jesuit priest and, with all the zeal of a convert, he organised and financed the plan devised by Robert Catesby to blow up Parliament and King James. The plot was foiled and he went to the scaffold, along with the other surviving plotters, in 1606.

Shropshire

County Town: Shrewsbury

'The country that lies between the dimpled lands of England and the giant purple steeps of Wales.'

Mary Webb

Ironbridge, Coalbrookdale

Shrewsbury

Birthplace of the Skyscraper

Shrewsbury, set in a loop of the River Severn, is the county town of Shropshire. The early spelling was 'Shroesbury' or 'Shrowesbury', which seems to point us towards how the name should be pronounced.

The street plan of Shrewsbury has not changed since the days of medieval sleuth, Brother Cadfael of Shrewsbury Abbey, portrayed on television by Sir Derek Jacobi. Cadfael was the creation of Edith Pargeter (1913–95), who wrote under the name Ellis Peters and was born on the edge of Shrewsbury at Horsehay.

Outside the Shire Hall is the tallest Doric column in the world, 133 ft (40.5 m) high, crowned with a statue of Lord Hill (1772–1842), who fought under Wellington at the Battle of Waterloo.

Shrewsbury is the BIRTHPLACE OF THE SKYSCRAPER. In a rather dingy outskirt, down by the canal, stands the DITHERINGTON FLAX MILL, FIRST STRUCTURE IN THE WORLD TO BE BUILT AROUND AN IRON FRAME. CHARLES BAGE, who built Ditherington Flax Mill in 1796, was able to take advantage of being close to the new ironworks at nearby Coalbrookdale. Flax dust being highly flammable, Bage was looking to create a fireproof environment for his mill, and he achieved this by replacing wooden beams with an iron frame. As an added advantage, the frame design created much more space, doing away with the need for structural pillars. This iron frame technique, invented in Shrewsbury, was used nearly a century later when they were rebuilding Chicago, and is still the preferred method of constructing skyscrapers all over the world.

CHARLES DARWIN (1809–82), originator of the Theory of Evolution, was born in Shrewsbury, and went to Shrewsbury School.

SANDY LYLE, golfer, winner of the US Masters in 1988, was born in Shrewsbury in 1958.

Coalbrookdale

Founding Fathers of the Industrial Revolution

The modern world began in 1709, at Coalbrookdale, a deep, dark Shropshire valley on the River Severn, full of iron ore and coal. In that year, an ironmaster named ABRAHAM DARBY discovered a way of producing cast iron using coal instead of charcoal. It took an awful lot of trees to provide the charcoal to make a ton of iron and English woodlands were diminishing fast. Suddenly, at a stroke, high grade iron could be produced in unlimited quantities. Machines and structures of incredible strength could be made. Like a secret recipe, Darby passed on his knowledge only to his son, Abraham Darby II, who improved and perfected his father's methods. Then, in 1779, the grandson, Abraham Darby III, built the most visible and enduring symbol of the age, the IRONBRIDGE, THE FIRST METAL BRIDGE IN THE WORLD. It has a span of 100 ft (30.5 m) and is still in use by pedestrians, having closed to traffic in 1931.

All along Coalbrookdale are the birthscars of the Industrial Revolution: the furnace site where Abraham Darby I developed his coke smelting process, the coal mines, rusting pieces of iron. At BLISTS HILL is the HAY INCLINED PLANE, where boats were lifted on iron rails from the River Severn to the Shropshire Canal, 200 ft (61 m) above at the top of the hill.

Down river at BROSELEY, in 1787, ironmaster JOHN Wilkinson (*see* Westmorland) built the WORLD'S FIRST IRON BOAT. Everywhere there are bridges made from iron, gates and fences, clock towers and railings.

For somewhere that had such a profound effect on the world, it is strangely quiet and peaceful now, as if resting from its labours.

Ludlow

Of Princes and Poets

In the Middle Ages, LUDLOW CASTLE was the central stronghold of the Welsh Marches, commanding the whole border region and much of Wales. The term 'March' comes from the Anglo-Saxon '*mearc*', meaning boundary. The castle was the home of three tragic princes. The PRINCES IN THE TOWER, Edward and his brother Richard, Duke of York, lived most of their short lives there, until the death of their father, Edward IV, in 1483. From here, the new king, Edward V, set out to be crowned in London, but he and his brother were waylaid at Stony Stratford by their uncle Richard's men and taken to the Tower of London, never to be seen again.

Henry VII's eldest son, PRINCE ARTHUR, also lived here with his young wife, CATHERINE OF ARAGON. She had a walk made for her round the castle, still called QUEEN'S WALK,

The year 1634 saw the first performance of John Milton's masque, Comus, *at Ludlow Castle, in honour of the Earl of Bridgwater becoming Lord President of the Council of the Marches. The parts were played by the earl's children and the story is set in an enchanted forest. A young girl, parted from her brothers, is waylaid by Comus, a pagan god of Milton's invention. The brothers rescue their sister with the help of Sabrina, goddess of the River Severn, who is summoned by the song 'Sabrina fair, listen where thou art sitting, under the glassy, cool, translucent wave'. Summer performances of Shakespeare are now held every year in the ruins of the castle's Great Hall where* Comus *was performed, with the tiny, round Norman chapel of Mary Magdalen as a backdrop.*

and here they would stroll together and plan their lives on the English throne. After only a few months of happy marriage Arthur died, aged just 16, and Catherine's fate as tragic consort to Henry VIII was sealed. Prince Arthur lies in a glorious chantry tomb at Worcester Cathedral, but his heart was sealed in a silver casket and is buried beneath the chancel of Ludlow's church.

Buried in Ludlow's church is the poet A.E HOUSMAN (1859–1936), author of *A Shropshire Lad.* Although forever associated with Shropshire, Housman was born in Worcestershire and had never even been to Shropshire when he began his great work. However, he did have a view of the Clee Hills in Shropshire from his home at Perry Hall, and these 'blue remembered hills' became his inspiration.

Matthew Webb

First Cross Channel Swimmer

Matthew Webb (1848–83), the FIRST MAN TO SWIM THE ENGLISH CHANNEL, was born in DAWLEY, just north of Ironbridge. On 24 August 1875, he dived into the water off the Admiralty Pier at Dover and re-emerged at Calais after 21 hours and 45 minutes. As he waded ashore, the passengers of a passing mailship, *The Maid of Kent*, sang 'Rule Britannia'. On his return to Dawley, Webb was treated to a town procession for which, it was noted, even the local prize pig stood up with its front trotters on the wall of its sty to applaud the returning hero.

In 1883, Captain Matthew Webb lost his life attempting to swim through the whirlpools at the foot of the Niagara Falls. His head was dashed upon a rock and his body recovered downstream four days later.

Thomas Parr

Oldest Man

At GREAT WOLLASTON, just off the road from Shrewsbury to Wales, stands a small thatched cottage, birthplace and home of the OLDEST ENGLISHMAN WHO EVER LIVED.

Thomas Parr was born in 1483. He lived to see ten monarchs on the throne, from the Plantagenet Edward IV, through all the Tudors to the Stuart Charles I. He joined the army at 17, returning when he was 35 to run the family farm. He married for the first time when he was 80, had an affair and an illegitimate child when he was 100 and married again at 122.

When he was 152, the Earl of Arundel took him up to London to meet Charles I, who asked the secret of his long life. 'Moral temperance and a vegetarian diet,' he replied. Unfortunately, the foul stench of London polluted his lungs, which had thrived on fresh Shropshire air, and he died in November 1635. He is buried in Westminster Abbey.

Well, I never knew this
ABOUT
SHROPSHIRE

In the gardens of LINLEY HALL, MORE, close to the border with Wales, are the descendants of the FIRST LARCH TREES PLANTED IN ENGLAND. In the 18th century, Robert More of Linley Hall, a keen botanist and a friend of Sweden's CARL LINNAEUS, went on a trip to the Tyrol with the Duke of Atholl and they both returned with several young larches. There was a race to see who could plant their trees first and Robert More won by a day.

At BRIDGNORTH, is a leaning tower that has a slant three times that of Pisa. The Leaning Tower of Pisa is 5 degrees out of true, the Leaning Tower of Bridgnorth, 17 degrees. It is all that is left of the 12th-century castle keep and owes its tilt to Oliver Cromwell's forces, who tried to blow it up during the Civil War.

BRIDGNORTH has the ONLY INLAND CLIFF RAILWAY IN ENGLAND. With a vertical rise of 111 ft (34 m), it links the Low Town with the High Town.

At ACTON BURNELL, are the ruins of the OLDEST FORTIFIED MANOR HOUSE IN ENGLAND, built in 1284 by Edward I's chancellor, ROBERT BURNELL. Next to it, in the grounds, are two stone gables, all that remain of a tithe barn known as the 'PARLIAMENT BARN'. Here, in 1283, Edward I called the FIRST ENGLISH PARLIAMENT TO WHICH THE COMMONS WERE DIRECTLY SUMMONED.

In the village church at ACTON BURNELL, there are monuments to members of the LEE family, who owned the village in the 16th and 17th centuries. They are ancestors of RICHARD HENRY LEE, whose signature is on the AMERICAN DECLARATION OF INDEPENDENCE, and GENERAL ROBERT E. LEE, who commanded the Confederate Forces in the American Civil War.

The ancient timbered town of SHIFNAL is supposed to be the model for MARKET BLANDINGS in the novels of P.G. WODEHOUSE. The nearby estate of Weston Park in Staffordshire, the country seat of the Earls of

Bradford, is said to have inspired the idea of Blandings when Wodehouse was living at STABLEFORD, a few miles away. The gardens, terraces and lake are much as described in the books, although the castle itself is thought to be Sudeley Castle in Gloucestershire and Lord Emsworth has an uncanny similarity to the eighth Duke of Devonshire at Chatsworth, who was known to be fond of his prize pig.

Alas, poor Yorick! I knew him, Horatio,
A fellow of infinite jest, of most excellent fancy.

The people of CONDOVER knew him too, for Shakespeare's Yorick is RICHARD TARLTON, born here in the middle years of the 16th century. He was content just to look after his father's pigs, but his earthy wit soon attracted the attention of the Earl of Leicester, who took Richard to London, where Elizabeth I was so taken with him that she made him COURT JESTER. His face was disfigured in a bear-baiting accident, but he used this to his advantage, making such terrible faces that the Queen was known to weep with laughter.

In the church at CONDOVER is the FIRST SCULPTURE FASHIONED BY G.F WATTS (1817–1904), the Victorian artist (*see* Compton, Surrey), a monument to THOMAS CHOLMONDELEY.

Alone in open fields in the grounds of BOSCOBEL HOUSE, near SHIFNAL, stands the ROYAL OAK, where CHARLES II hid from the Roundheads after the Battle of Worcester. It has been badly plundered by souvenir seekers over the years and is now rather forlorn.

OSWESTRY FOOTBALL CLUB are the ONLY ENGLISH TEAM TO PLAY IN THE WELSH FOOTBALL LEAGUE.

WILFRED OWEN (1893–1918), the First World War poet, was born in OSWESTRY.

Somerset

County Town: Taunton

'Sweet Somerset, I will never leave thee.'

Anon

Bath Abbey

Bath

Spa

Bath has given us BATH STONE, BATH CHAIRS, BATH BUNS, BATH OLIVERS – and SHORTHAND.

Bath stone, a golden limestone, originally came from a number of quarries on COMBE DOWN, south of Bath, owned by RALPH ALLEN (1694–1764), known as 'The Man of Bath'. He made his fortune by developing postal routes, based in Bath, that formed the foundations of today's postal system. It was thanks to Ralph Allen that Bath is the postmark on the WORLD'S FIRST STAMPED ENVELOPE, bearing a Penny Black, addressed to a house in Peckham and sent on 2 May 1840.

Bath chairs are a kind of wheelchair, usually hooded, devised in Bath in the 18th century, for use by invalids. Bath buns are a kind of rich, sweet bun, much enjoyed by visitors coming to Bath to take the waters.

Bath Olivers are a kind of plain, dry biscuit eaten after drinking the waters, to take away the bitter taste. The recipe was invented by DR WILLIAM OLIVER in the mid-18th century. Just before he died, he passed on the secret to ATKINS, his coachman, who opened a shop in Green Street and made a fortune.

The WORLD'S FIRST PHONOGRAPHIC SHORTHAND SYSTEM (a method of rapid handwriting based on sound) was devised by ISAAC PITMAN in 1837, and was first taught at the Mechanics Institute, 3 Bath Street, in 1839.

Kelston

The first W.C.

The WORLD'S FIRST WATER CLOSET was designed in 1589 by SIR JOHN HARINGTON (1561–1612), godson to Queen Elizabeth I, and installed in his house at Kelston, near Bath. It was similar in nearly all respects to the modern flush lavatory, with a reservoir of water standing in the bowl to prevent odours from the pipe and a cistern for holding the water that flushed the contents away and cleansed the bowl.

Harington wrote a book about his invention called *The Metamorphosis of Ajax*, a pun on the word 'jakes', a slang word for lavatory, in which he expressed the hope that his 'privie in perfection' would be widely adopted by the better sort. It could be locked to prevent unauthorised use and needed to be emptied twice a day, although 'once was enough provided it was used by no more than twenty people'.

The book, which is full of smutty innuendoes and puns, proved decidedly popular and caused something of a scandal, resulting in Harington being banned from Court. Queen

Elizabeth was, however, something of an obsessive when it came to matters of hygiene and had even been known to 'take a bath once a month, whether she need it or no'. Discreetly, she asked Sir John to install one of his 'Johns' in her palace at Richmond and, to avoid embarrassment, they agreed to refer to the device as her 'throne'. This, and the original at Kelston, were the only water closets built by Harington. It was not until 1778, nearly 200 years later, that water closets were produced in any quantity, by London cabinet maker Joseph Bramah.

East Coker

Evolutionary Tales

T.S. ELIOT (1888–1965), the American-born poet, is buried in ST MICHAEL'S church at East Coker. Eliot, born in St Louis, Missouri, came to study at Oxford for a year in 1911 and decided to stay in England, becoming naturalised in 1927. He was able to trace his roots to East Coker, where his family had lived for many years until leather-maker Andrew Eliot sailed to New England in the mid-17th century. Andrew settled in Salem and was on the jury for the infamous witch trials. Now there is a permanent Eliot presence in the village underneath a memorial tablet that says 'Remember T.S.Eliot, Poet'.

Also lying in the church is WILLIAM DAMPIER (1652–1715), who circumnavigated the globe three times and was the FIRST ENGLISHMAN TO SET FOOT ON AUSTRALIA. In January 1688, Dampier was aboard the English pirate ship *Cygnet* when it beached on the coast of north-west Australia, somewhere near King Sound. While the ship was being repaired, he took copious notes of the local fauna. He had an interest in natural history and would often crew for pirate ships or cargo vessels as a way of getting to distant places where he could study new species. His observations influenced Charles Darwin's theory of evolution, explained in *The Origin of Species*, and Dampier's travels also provided inspiration for Jonathan Swift's *Gulliver's Travels*.

Athelney

Oops!

Rising out of the marshes at Athelney is a little hill with a round church on top called the BURROW MUMP. It was near here, in 878, that KING ALFRED sought refuge from the Norsemen in a swineherd's hut. His forces were scattered, he was weary from constant battle, he had the weight of a kingdom on his shoulders. For the swineherd's wife, however, there were more important matters . . .

Ca'sn thee mind the ke-aks, man,
An' doossen zee 'em burn?
I'm boun thee's eat 'em vast enough
Az zoon as tiz the turn.

Alfred's mind wandered, the cakes were burnt and he was roundly scolded for his carelessness, a good lesson in priorities. The experience revitalised him. He regrouped and defeated the Danes at EDINGTON, forcing their leader, Guthrum, to come to his palace at WEDMORE and negotiate a withdrawal from Wessex to a line north and east of Watling Street – the Danelaw.

Quantocks

Xanadu

CLEVEDON, which has ONE OF BRITAIN'S EARLIEST AND MOST BEAUTIFUL PIERS, built in 1896, is where SAMUEL TAYLOR COLERIDGE and his wife Sara spent their honeymoon. On New Year's Eve, 1796, Coleridge and his young wife settled into a small cottage belonging to their friend, Tom Poole, at NETHER STOWEY in the Quantock Hills. In the following July, WILLIAM WORDSWORTH and his sister DOROTHY took a lease on ALFOXDEN, a large country house, now the ALFOXTON hotel, at nearby HOLFORD. During their walks together across the hills, the two poets came up with the idea of writing a collection of poems under the title *The Lyrical Ballads*.

The time they spent together tramping the Quantock Hills turned out to be just a beginning for Wordsworth, but for Coleridge they were his golden years of poetry. On a walk to WATCHET, he began his masterpiece 'The Rime of the Ancient Mariner'. And it was while staying at a farmhouse in WITHYCOMBE, above Porlock, that Coleridge fell asleep and had the dream that inspired his unfinished fantasy, 'Kubla Khan', which begins: 'In Xanadu did Kubla Khan, a stately pleasure dome decree.' A stranger from Porlock called while he was writing and when the visitor had left Coleridge realised that the dream had gone too.

Cheddar

Cheesy

CHEDDAR CHEESE was discovered over 800 years ago, when a milkmaid accidentally left a pail of milk inside a cave at CHEDDAR GORGE, after a secret tryst. When she went back to get the milk, it had turned into a delicious, crumbly new substance, thanks to the unique conditions in the cave. The constant temperature of 7°C was found to be ideal for the cheese to mature in and Cheddar cheese was born. Henry II declared it to be the best cheese in Britain.

Cheddar cheese-making skills were exported to the New World and it is now made in Canada, the USA, Australia and New Zealand, as well as Ireland. The caves of the Cheddar Gorge are no longer used for storage, as the cheese attracted vermin, but the conditions are replicated at local farms.

Cheddar Gorge is the BIGGEST GORGE IN BRITAIN and is 500 ft (152 m) deep at its deepest point.

Well, I never knew this ABOUT SOMERSET

The MANOR HOUSE at CRICKET ST THOMAS was used as the setting for the TV series *To the Manor Born*, starring Penelope Keith. It is now an hotel.

At BURRINGTON COMBE, a deep gorge in the Mendip Hills, we can find the ROCK OF AGES. In about 1775, AUGUSTUS TOPLADY, the curate of Blagdon, was passing through the gorge when a violent storm blew up and he was forced to take shelter in a cleft of rock. While he was there, with the thunder rolling and the wind howling, he passed the time by composing a hymn:

Rock of Ages, cleft for me,
Let me hide myself in thee.

ST CULBONE'S church, hidden away in a secluded dell by the sea, not far from Porlock, is the SMALLEST CHURCH IN ENGLAND, measuring just 35 ft (10.5 m) by 12 ft (3.7 m).

The church at OARE was the setting for many of the scenes from *Lorna Doone* by Richard Blackmore (1825–1900). His grandfather was the vicar here and Blackmore's visits as a boy had a powerful effect. Lorna Doone is married in this church and Carver Doone fires the shot that spills Lorna's blood on the altar steps.

TARR STEPS, across the RIVER BARLE at WINSFORD on Exmoor, is thought to date from about 1000 BC, which would make it the OLDEST BRIDGE IN ENGLAND.

The SWEET TRACK, on the Somerset Levels, near WESTHAY, west of Glastonbury, dates from 4000 BC and is the OLDEST KNOWN ROADWAY IN THE WORLD. Named after RAY SWEET, who discovered it in 1970, the track extended across the reedy swamps for just over 1 mile (1.5 km), from a ridge at Shapwick to the little island of Westhay. It consists of a walkway made from oak planks, supported by crossed poles of alder and hazel, driven into the ground at an angle and pegged at the sides. Most of the original track is now protected and preserved where it was found.

KEINTON MANDEVILLE, near Somerton, is the birthplace of John Henry Brodribb – better known as SIR HENRY IRVING (1838–1905), considered the greatest actor of his time and the FIRST ACTOR TO BE KNIGHTED. His celebrated partnership with the actress Dame Ellen Terry lasted for 27 years. The small grey stone house where he was born has been renamed Irving House. He is buried in Westminster Abbey.

WELLOW, near Bath, is the birthplace of JOHN BULL (1562–1628), organist at the Chapel Royal and the man who wrote the music for the NATIONAL ANTHEM. In 1613, several of his keyboard compositions appeared in *Parthenia*, the FIRST BOOK OF VIRGINAL MUSIC TO BE PUBLISHED IN ENGLAND, the virginal being an early keyboard instrument.

Buried inside a unique little island church in the middle of the lake at

ORCHARDLEIGH PARK, is the patriot and Poet Laureate SIR HENRY NEWBOLT (1862–1938), best known for his *Sea Songs*, which include Drake's Drum: 'Drake he was a Devon man an' he ruled the Devon seas.' He was also responsible for the following lines, familiar to every public schoolboy:

There's a breathless hush in the close
tonight,
Ten to make and the match to win . . .
Play up! play up! and play the game!

EVELYN WAUGH (1903–66), author of *Brideshead Revisited*, is buried in the churchyard of St Peter and Paul in COMBE FLOREY, where he lived.

Staffordshire

County Town: Stafford

'the fields and moors of Staffordshire . . .
warmly surveyed by the sun . . .
spread out undulating'

Arnold Bennett

Lichfield Cathedral

Lichfield

Ladies and Gentlemen

LICHFIELD CATHEDRAL is the ONLY CATHEDRAL IN ENGLAND TO HAVE THREE SPIRES. They are known as the LADIES OF THE VALE.

On the corner of BREADMARKET STREET, facing the Market Square, stands the house where SAMUEL JOHNSON (1709–84) was born, above his father's bookshop. It is now a museum to his memory. Always known as Dr Johnson, he started a school at EDIAL HALL, just outside the town, but only three pupils turned up, one of them being DAVID GARRICK, who became a great friend. Garrick was born in Hereford, but spent his first 20 years living in Lichfield before accompanying Dr Johnson to London, where he was to find fame as an actor. Dr Johnson is considered to be the FOUNDER OF THE MODERN ENGLISH BIOGRAPHY, but he is best remembered for compiling the FIRST COMPREHENSIVE DICTIONARY OF ENGLISH, forerunner of all modern English dictionaries. He is also renowned for pithy aphorisms, including:

'When two Englishmen meet their first talk is of the weather.'

'Depend upon it, Sir, when a man knows he is to be hanged in a fortnight, it concentrates his mind wonderfully.'

'The triumph of hope over experience.'
(on second marriages)

In the marketplace at UTTOXETER, there is a statue of an aged Dr Johnson standing with his head bowed in sorrow and remorse. On a foul wet day in 1780, when he was 70 years old, Dr Johnson came here and stood all morning, bare-headed in the rain, as a penance for his disobedience when, as a young man, he had once refused to accompany his father to Uttoxeter market.

Close to Dr Johnson's birthplace, is the house where ELIAS ASHMOLE (1617–92) was born. His collection of rarities, which were bequeathed to him by botanist John Tradescant, formed the basis of BRITAIN'S FIRST PUBLIC MUSEUM, the ASHMOLEAN MUSEUM in Oxford, opened in 1683.

EDWARD WIGHTMAN, the LAST PERSON TO BE BURNED FOR HERESY IN ENGLAND, was put to death in the Market Square, Lichfield in 1612.

Stoke-on-Trent

The Potteries

Stoke-on-Trent is comprised of Arnold Bennett's five towns, STOKE, BURSLEM, LONGTON, HANLEY and TUNSTALL, plus a sixth, FENTON. It is the centre of the English pottery industry, and hence is known as the Potteries. Standing on rich clay soil, pottery has been made here since the Middle Ages, but the Potteries' rise to world renown began with JOSIAH WEDGWOOD (1730–95), born in BURSLEM, who opened his first factory near Hanley in 1769. He built a village for his workers and called it ETRURIA, in honour of a classical vase he had admired and mistakenly thought was Etruscan. For himself, he built the still-standing ETRURIA HALL, where his son, Thomas, was born in 1771.

During the 18th and 19th centuries, a number of household names established themselves in the Stoke area, including DAVENPORT, MINTON, COPELAND and DOULTON. JOSIAH SPODE became celebrated for his fine china, which incorporated crushed animal bone. All these pottery works can be visited.

Thomas Wedgwood, son of Josiah, was one of the FIRST PIONEERS OF PHOTOGRAPHY. He knew that silver nitrate was blackened by exposure to sunlight and tried to think of a way to turn this to a practical application. By moistening a sheet of white paper with a solution of silver, placing a fern leaf on it and exposing the whole lot to the sun, he obtained what could be regarded as the FIRST EVER PHOTOGRAPH. By constructing a crude camera and letting in sunlight through a shutter, he improved on his technique, but couldn't find a way to make the picture permanent. He died in 1805, at the age of 34, before he could perfect his ideas, but not before he had invented the principle of photography, based on using the action of light to make pictures. He is buried at Tarrant Gunville in Dorset.

Wolverhampton

A Rare Signature

It was in Wolverhampton that they found the 'MOST VALUABLE SIGNATURE IN THE WORLD', that of BUTTON GWINNETT. Gwinnett was born in Gloucestershire, in 1732, and came to live for several years as a rather unsuccessful trader in Wolverhampton. In 1765, he emigrated to America and settled in Savannah, Georgia. He was one of the three men from Georgia who signed the DECLARATION OF INDEPENDENCE in 1776. In 1777, he was killed in a duel and largely forgotten.

After a while, the signatures of all those who had signed the Declaration became collectors' items, particularly as a complete set, fetching extraordinary prices. It turned out that Button Gwinnett's signature was by far the most rare, by virtue of his being pretty much of a nobody. Only 36 examples of his signature were found, which meant that only 36 collectors could own a complete set.

The search became frantic, the rewards offered enormous, and news of it eventually filtered through to a Wolverhampton historian. The name Button Gwinnett rang a bell and some gentle research unearthed the fact that Gwinnett had been a subscriber to the town's Bluecoat School. In 1761, he had attended three meetings at the school, and on each occasion he had signed the minutes! There were three signatures and each of them was sold for a fortune. Even to this day, the signature of Button Gwinnett, an Immortal Nobody, is amongst the most sought-after in the world.

The Compleat Angler

Gone Fishing

IZAAK WALTON, author of *The Compleat Angler*, was born in STAFFORD in 1593. *The Compleat Angler* is a gentle story of three men on a fishing trip in Hertfordshire, and it paints a wistful picture of an idyllic rural life now lost. As Charles Lamb said to Samuel Coleridge, 'it breathes the very spirit of innocence, purity and simplicity of heart . . . it should sweeten a man's temper at any time to read it, it would Christianise every angry, discordant passion . . . pray make yourself aquainted with it'.

Izaak Walton spent as much time as he could fishing on the River Dove in BERESFORD DALE, where, in 1674, his friend, Charles Cotton, had built a stylish little FISHING TEMPLE, now a place of pilgrimage for all anglers. The tranquil life of a fisherman left Walton completely unprepared for the perilous escapade into which he was plunged at the age of 58. He was an ardent Royalist and, after the Battle of Worcester in 1651, while staying at

Stafford, he received an urgent summons from his friend GEORGE BARLOW, who lived in an isolated farmhouse at BLORE, near Market Drayton. When he arrived at BLORE PIPE HOUSE, Walton was hurried inside by his host, who pressed a small package into his hand. 'Guard this with your life, Izaak,' he hissed. 'It belongs to the King.'

Walton opened up the package and found himself gazing upon a jewel of such lustre and magnificence that he could only gasp. 'What is this?' he cried. 'It is the lesser George,' his friend replied, 'one of the Crown Jewels of our noble sovereign King Charles. His aide, Colonel Blagg, came hot from the battlefield and left it here in my safe keeping. But I fear he has been taken and it will not be long before I am searched. The Roundheads are coming and they must not discover it here. Pray find a way to return it to the King. Now fly! If you are caught it will be the Tower for you!'

Izaak Walton loved the thought of adventures and so, instead of berating his friend for landing him in such a predicament, he slipped out of the farmhouse and melted into the Staffordshire mist. He returned home by devious ways and then went on to London, passing unsuspected through the Roundhead patrols, the dangerous gem secreted about his person. Once in London, Walton was able to get a message through to Colonel Blagg in the Tower of London. Emboldened by the knowledge that his charge was safe, Blagg managed to effect his escape from the Tower, collect the jewel from Walton and carry it to France where he rejoined Charles II in exile.

Colonel Blagg was loosely connected to the Smith family who, 150 years later, were to found W.H. Smith, the newsagent. Their first newsagents shop was opened in 1792, in Little Grosvenor Street, London, by Henry Walton Smith, father of William Henry (*see* Hambleden, Buckinghamshire). The Walton part of his name is said to come from Izaak Walton, in honour of the great service he did their ancestor Colonel Blagg.

Calwich Abbey

'Man is born free, and everywhere he is in chains'

Calwich Abbey, overlooking the River Dove near ELLASTONE,

was built on the site of an old monastery by BERNARD GRANVILLE in the early 18th century. It was a beautiful spot and attracted many famous visitors, including HANDEL and ANNA SEWELL, author of *Black Beauty*.

In 1766, the French author and political philosopher JEAN-JACQUES ROUSSEAU (1712–78) came to live at nearby WOOTTON HALL, now demolished. He had been run out of France for publishing *Le contrat social*, which, with its slogan of Liberté, Equalité, Fraternité, was to become the bible of the French Revolution. Rousseau would often visit Calwich Abbey, since Bernard Granville was the only person in the district to speak French. He caused great alarm to Granville's sister, Mrs Delany, by avidly courting her niece, Mary Dewes, who was flattered by the attentions of such a celebrated man.

In the winter, the Granvilles closed up Calwich Abbey and moved down to London, leaving the unbalanced Rousseau prey to his paranoid fears of imaginary persecution and danger. The peace of deepest Staffordshire began to get to him and he would alarm the simple villagers of Wootton by wandering the lanes in a sweeping black cape and black cap, muttering to himself in French and rolling his eyes with suspicion if anyone approached. He finally cracked and fled back to France.

Well, I never knew this ABOUT STAFFORDSHIRE

One summer's day, during the reign of Queen Victoria, a young couple came to walk beside the beautiful LAKE RUDYARD, a few miles north of Stoke-on-Trent. The young man got down on his knees at the water's edge and asked the young lady to marry him. Joyously she said yes, and when their son was born a while later in India, LOCKWOOD and ALICE KIPLING named him RUDYARD, in memory of that wondrous day.

WILLENHALL has taken advantage of the coal and iron and steel works in the area to become the CAPITAL OF ENGLAND'S LOCKMAKING INDUSTRY. The town produces 90 per cent of the country's locks and keys and is home to UNION LOCKS and YALE, as well as the National Lock Museum.

WALSALL is home to BRITAIN'S FIRST STATUE TO A WOMAN other than royalty. It was erected in 1886, in memory of SISTER DORA PATTISON, a much-loved local nurse.

BURTON-ON-TRENT is the BREWING CAPITAL OF BRITAIN and the home of

MARMITE. A 13th-century abbot began brewing here, but Burton was originally a prosperous textile town. This industry declined and then, in 1777, WILLIAM BASS, attracted by the clear waters of the River Trent, set up a brewery and over the following years many household brewing names followed. Drawn to Burton-on-Trent by the abundance of brewer's yeast, The Marmite Food Company was established in a disused malt house and produced the world's first jar of Marmite in 1902. A *marmite* is a French cooking pot, like the one pictured on the label, and is used for making a famous French soup, *petite marmite*.

Across the River Trent at GREAT HEYWOOD is ESSEX BRIDGE, which, at over 100 yd (90 m), is the LONGEST PACK HORSE BRIDGE IN ENGLAND. It was built in Elizabethan times by the EARL OF ESSEX, as a short cut to Cannock Chase. It leads to the grounds of Shugborough Park, home of the society photographer Patrick Lichfield.

FLASH, in the far north of Staffordshire, is the HIGHEST VILLAGE IN ENGLAND, with an elevation of 1,518 ft (463 m) above sea level. Flash stands near the border of three counties – Staffordshire, Cheshire and Derbyshire – and was once the haunt of fraudsters, forgers and thieves, who could evade county sheriffs by nipping across the county borders. This gave rise to the expression a bit 'flash', meaning sham or not genuine.

ALTON TOWERS began its life as a major tourist attraction in the 1890s, when the 20th Earl of Shrewsbury, CHARLES HENRY TALBOT, whose family had owned the estate since the 15th century, began to organise fêtes, firework displays and balloon festivals in the grounds. In 1901, he developed the TALBOT MOTOR CAR and one of his Talbots became the FIRST MOTOR CAR TO EXCEED 100 MPH (161 kph). He sold Alton Towers in 1924, and it passed through many hands until, in 1980, 500 acres were turned into an amusement park. BRITAIN'S FIRST DOUBLE CORKSCREW ROLLER COASTER attracted huge crowds and, today, Alton Towers is the BIGGEST THEME PARK IN BRITAIN. It also boasts the LARGEST FAST FOOD RESTAURANT IN BRITAIN, the TALBOT.

Suffolk

County Town: Ipswich

'A most beautiful prospect which ministereth unto the inhabitants a full choice of beautiful and pleasant situations.'

Robert Reyce, from *Suffolk in the 17th Century*

Framlingham Castle

Bury St Edmunds

Patron Saint of England?

Bury St Edmunds, once county town of Suffolk, grew up around the shrine of King Edmund the Martyr, who was butchered by Danish invaders in 869. A huge cathedral was built on the site of the original abbey in 1095, and here, at the high altar, the barons of King John, led by Stephen Langton, swore to call the king to account, a meeting that led to the signing of *Magna Carta* in 1215.

Places that played a part in the story of King Edmund can be found all over Suffolk. Just outside Bures, near Sudbury, the simple, thatched St Stephen's Barn stands on the site of the tiny church in which 15-year-old Edmund was crowned King of East Anglia on Christmas Day 855. At Hoxne, near the Norfolk border, Edmund met his death at the hands of the Danes in 870. Fleeing back to Framlingham after his defeat at the BATTLE OF THETFORD, he ran into a search party at Hoxne and hid beneath the wooden bridge across the river, on the edge of the village green. A bridal party, crossing the bridge, saw Edmund's gold spurs reflected in the water and pointed him out to the enemy. He was dragged out, tied to an oak tree, whipped and shot at with arrows, all in an effort to make him renounce the Christian faith. When he refused, he was beheaded and his body flung into the bushes.

Housed in the Queen Anne manor house at 8 Angel Hill is the Gershom Parkington Collection. The finest collection of time-keeping instruments in the world, it was bequeathed in 1953 by Frederic Gershom Parkington, in memory of his son John, who was killed in the Second World War. Here, amongst the clocks, watches and sundials, we learn that grandfather clocks take their name from a song written in 1876 by the American Henry Clay Work, which begins, 'My grandfather's clock was too big for the shelf'.

The oak tree lived until 1848 and, when it was cut down, an old arrow head was found buried deep in the trunk. A stone cross stands in its place and a screen was made from the timber and placed in the church at Hoxne. Edmund's body was re-united with the head and buried in the chapel at a nearby monastery, where an old farmhouse called the Abbey now stands. His body was removed to St Edmundsbury Abbey in the 10th century. The stream became known as the GOLDBROOK and, to this day, it is thought to be very unlucky for a bride to cross the bridge on her wedding day.

In ST MARY's church in Bury St Edmunds, on the corner of the Abbey gardens, is the tomb of MARY TUDOR, sister of Henry VIII and Queen of France. In 1514, as a young girl of 18, she married King Louis XII of France, who was 52 and had just lost his wife. He died on New Year's Day, 1515, and Mary returned to marry her first love, the DUKE OF SUFFOLK. Their granddaughter was LADY JANE GREY, whose reign as Queen of England lasted just nine days – an even shorter span than her grandmother Mary Tudor's two months as Queen of France.

River Orwell

Animal Farm, Follies and Old Sea Dogs

ERIC BLAIR (*see* Sutton Courtenay, Berkshire), author of *1984* and *Animal Farm*, took his pen name, GEORGE ORWELL, from the River Orwell. He often stayed in Suffolk with his parents, who lived at SOUTHWOLD.

At ORWELL PARK, now a preparatory school, on the north bank, lived ADMIRAL EDWARD VERNON (1684–1757). He became a national hero during the War of Jenkins's Ear, for capturing Portobello in Central America from the Spanish in 1739. He was given the nickname 'OLD GROG', for his habit of wearing a coat made from grogram, a strong, coarse mix of silk and mohair. It was on his suggestion that the seaman's daily ration of rum was diluted with water, a recipe that became known as GROG.

Vernon commanded a combined English and American attack on Cartagena in 1741. One of the officers under his command was Lawrence Washington, half-brother of George Washington, first President of the United States of America. Lawrence named his house in Virginia MOUNT VERNON, in honour of his commanding officer. George Washington inherited the house in 1761 and lived there for 45 years.

GRIMSTON HALL, on the north bank, near TRIMLEY ST MARY, was the home of THOMAS CAVENDISH (1555–92), known as 'The Navigator', and the SECOND ENGLISHMAN TO CIRCUMNAVIGATE THE WORLD. He was the first Englishman to see the island of St Helena, where Napoleon was later exiled. He died at sea.

Situated on the south bank of the River Orwell is FRESTON'S TOWER, ENGLAND'S OLDEST FOLLY. It was built in the days of Henry VIII by Lord de Freston, as a place to study for his daughter Ellen. Each floor was set aside for a different subject.

The Lower Room to charity from 7 to 8 o'clock
The Second to working tapestry from 9 to 10
The Third to music from 10 to noon
The Fourth to painting from 12 to 1
The Fifth to literature from 1 to 2
The Sixth to astronomy at even

Edward FitzGerald

Old Fitz

Edward FitzGerald (1809–83), translator of the *Rubaiyat of Omar Khayyam*, was born in BREDFIELD HOUSE, just outside WOODBRIDGE. His family then moved to BOULGE HOUSE, 1 mile (1.5 km) down the road, where he lived until the age of 28, when he set himself up in a cottage at the entrance to the driveway. He later moved to a farmhouse at MELTON and then, in 1860, after a brief and unsuccessful marriage at the age of 47, went to live above a shop at No. 10 on the north side of MARKET HILL in WOODBRIDGE. He spent his declining years at LITTLE GRANGE in NEW STREET.

Both FitzGerald and his domineering mother were children of first cousins. Blessed with a private income, he was able to give full rein to his eccentricity, and would often wander around the quays of Woodbridge dressed like a tramp, smoking a pipe, with a bottle of porter in his hand. Something of a hermit, he was nonetheless a brilliant scholar. When a friend of his, EDWARD COWELL, sent him a copy of the *Rubaiyat* – a meditation on life that celebrates the pleasures and complexities of living – that he had found at the Bodleian Library in Oxford, FitzGerald became captivated and set about translating it into English:

A Book of Verses underneath the Bough
A Jug of Wine, a Loaf of Bread – and Thou

The Moving Finger writes, and, having writ
Moves on . . .

Known to all as 'Old Fitz', Edward FitzGerald is buried beneath the tower of the isolated church in the grounds of his old home Boulge House. The roses that bloom on his grave come from cuttings off the bush that grows on the grave of Omar Khayyam in Naishapur.

Well, I never knew this
ABOUT
SUFFOLK

The WORLD'S FIRST COMMERCIAL MOTORISED LAWN MOWER was built by RANSOME'S of IPSWICH in 1902. ROBERT RANSOME perfected a new kind of plough share in 1803 and this led to him becoming a pioneering manufacturer of agricultural tools. He began making lawn mowers in 1832, building a licensed version of the world's first lawn mower invented by Edwin Budding of Stroud (*see* Gloucestershire). Ransome's is now the WORLD'S LARGEST MANUFACTURER OF LAWN CARE EQUIPMENT.

The castle at ORFORD was the FIRST CASTLE IN BRITAIN TO BE BUILT IN THE SHAPE OF A POLYGON. This did away with the need for a fourth tower and made it more difficult to undermine the fortifications. BENJAMIN BRITTEN opened two of his operas, *Noye's Fludde* and *Curlew River*, here. SIR ROBIN WATSON-WATT (a descendant of James Watt, inventor of the steam engine) did his experiments with radar here, which led, in 1937, to the establishment of the WORLD'S FIRST RADAR STATION down the coast at BAWDSEY MANOR.

The church of ST MARY THE VIRGIN at DENNINGTON, 3 miles (5 km) north of Framlingham, possesses the ONLY SCIAPOD IN BRITAIN. A sciapod is a mythical desert creature from North Africa that hops around on one huge foot, which it raises into the air to act as a sunshade, while sleeping. This sciapod is carved on to a bench end in the central aisle.

LOWESTOFT NESS is BRITAIN'S EASTERNMOST POINT. The composer Benjamin Britten was born in LOWESTOFT in 1913.

The white weatherboarded mill at WOODBRIDGE, built in 1792, is the ONLY REMAINING WORKING TIDE MILL IN BRITAIN.

Henry VIII's daughter MARY sheltered in FRAMLINGHAM CASTLE during the attempt, in 1553, to put Lady Jane Grey on the throne. Later, as Queen Mary, she visited Framlingham with her husband, King Philip of Spain.

While living at the OLD GRANGE in SHILLING STREET, LAVENHAM, in the early 18th century, JANE TAYLOR sat at a tiny top-floor window and watched the stars glittering in the sky. She was moved to write a poem which began, 'Twinkle Twinkle, Little Star'.

The revolutionary FRAMLINGHAM CASTLE was built at the end of the 12th century by ROGER BIGOD, second Earl of Norfolk. It was the FIRST CASTLE IN ENGLAND TO BE BUILT WITHOUT A KEEP. Instead, the curtain walls acted as defence for a much larger area within. The Bigods, described by the Suffolk writer Julian Tennyson as 'about the toughest brood ever hatched in England', came across with William the Conqueror, saw themselves as kings of East Anglia and were in constant conflict with the monarch of the day. Their name passed into the language as 'BIGOT', meaning 'a prejudiced person intolerant of any opinions other than his own'.

NEWMARKET is the headquarters of English horseracing, breeding and training and of the Jockey Club. Begun under James I in 1605, racing really became established under Charles II. In 1683, the town was razed to the ground by fire and the only building left from then is believed to have belonged to Nell Gwyn. One of Newmarket's racecourses, the ROWLEY MILE, is 2½ miles (4 km) long and 176 ft (53 m) wide, the LONGEST AND WIDEST HORSERACING STRAIGHT IN THE WORLD.

SUTTON, a little village on the River Debden, was the birthplace of MARY SEWELL (1797–1884). The mother of Anna Sewell, Mary was an author in her own right. She was a Quaker and much concerned about the plight of orphans. Her work, *Mother's Last Word*, about two orphan boys, was the FIRST EVER WORK IN ENGLISH TO SELL OVER ONE MILLION COPIES.

Willy Lott's Cottage

JOHN CONSTABLE (1776–1837), English landscape painter, was born in EAST BERGHOLT. Nearby, on the River Stour, which forms the border with Essex, are FLATFORD MILL and WILLY LOTT'S COTTAGE, immortalised in his paintings such as *Flatford Mill* and *The Hay Wain*. The scenery is almost unchanged since Constable's day.

Surrey

County Town: Guildford

'among English counties there are few that can compete in charm or delight with Surrey'

George Williamson

Leith Hill

High Point

Leith Hill, at 965 ft (294 m), is the HIGHEST POINT IN SOUTH EAST ENGLAND. The top of LEITH HILL TOWER is 1,029 ft (314 m) above sea level and, looking eastward, there is nothing higher between here and the Ural mountains in Russia. The tower was built in 1766 by RICHARD HULL of LEITH HILL PLACE, who is buried underneath – head down so that he will be the right way up to meet his Maker when the world is turned upside down on Judgement Day.

Leith Hill Place, which stands on the slopes of Leith Hill, is 17th century and belonged in the 19th century to JOSIAH WEDGWOOD II. Local legend has it that the house fell into disuse and when it was opened up again by Josiah's daughter every room was found to be piled high with priceless pieces of Wedgwood. Josiah Wedgwood's daughter was the mother of the composer RALPH VAUGHAN WILLIAMS (1872–1958), who grew up here from the age of three. In 1905, he founded the Leith Hill Music Festival, for which he was principal conductor for 50 years.

Dorking

A Pilgrim Father

At Dorking is the ONLY SURVIVING HOUSE IN ENGLAND THAT BELONGED TO ONE OF THE MAYFLOWER PILGRIM FATHERS. WILLIAM MULLINS was born in Dorking, in 1572, and became a prosperous shoemaker. In 1612, he bought a large house in WEST STREET, now numbers 58 to 61. It is uncertain why he decided to sell up and emigrate to the New World but, in 1620, he and his wife Alice and his two younger children, Priscilla and Joseph, joined the *Mayflower* at Rotherhithe and sailed to America.

William, Alice and Joseph all died at New Plymouth in the winter of 1621. Priscilla married the *Mayflower's* cooper, John Alden, and together they founded the neighbouring town of Duxbury. They went on to have 11 children and their descendants include the poet Henry Longfellow, Presidents John Adams and John Quincy Adams and Vice-President Dan Quayle. Priscilla was immortalised in Longfellow's poem 'The Courtship of Miles Standish'.

LAURENCE OLIVIER (1907–89), the actor and director, was born in Dorking.

Just outside Dorking is DENBIES, the LARGEST VINEYARD IN BRITAIN.

Compton

Unique Double Sanctuary

The CHURCH OF ST NICHOLAS at Compton is one of England's hidden treasures. Set back above the pretty main street under two enormous cedar trees, it has an unassuming exterior, but inside there is startlingly beautiful Norman work with a remarkable DOUBLE SANCTUARY, UNIQUE IN BRITAIN, and two noble chancel arches, the smaller built in 1080. The upper sanctuary is protected by a fragile 12th-century wooden screen carved out of a single plank of oak, from a tree that was growing when Alfred was king. It is the OLDEST SCREEN IN ENGLAND.

Behind the altar is a tiny window of rare Norman stained glass showing the Madonna holding her Child, which dates from 1175, ONE OF ONLY TWO SUCH NORMAN WINDOWS IN ENGLAND.

Two minutes' walk away, down a leafy lane, is the WATTS GALLERY, completed in 1904 and dedicated to the work of G.F. WATTS (1817–1904), who was known as the Victorian Michelangelo.

Nearby is the unusual terracotta WATTS CHAPEL, designed by his second wife Mary Watts and built by the villagers. G.F. Watts' first wife was the actress Dame Ellen Terry (*see page 104*). It stands at the heart of a new cemetery that the Wattses laid out on the hillside because the St Nicholas churchyard was full. The Wattses are buried at the top of the slope.

Abinger

'Left to itself, there is not a safer place in England than Abinger.'
E.M. Forster

In 1924, the author of *A Passage to India*, E.M. FORSTER (1879–1970), inherited a house at WEST HACKHURST, near Abinger, where he lived for the next 20 years.

ABINGER COMMON, high up in the Surrey hills, has a claim to being the OLDEST VILLAGE IN ENGLAND. Dug into the Greensand fields, behind Abinger Manor, is a MESOLITHIC PIT DWELLING, excavated by Dr Leakey in 1950, and estimated to be some 7,000 years old.

In the garden of the 17th-century ABINGER MANOR house is a NORMAN CASTLE MOTTE, now grassed over and planted with trees and flowers. The house was built by the diarist JOHN EVELYN, as a place for him to stay when visiting his elder brother, who lived at the family's main residence, WOTTON HOUSE, a short walk away. John Evelyn was born at Wotton House in 1620, and came quickly into the family fortune, which was based on the manufacture of gunpowder. Well travelled and knowledgeable, he became a great favourite at the court of Charles II and his diaries which, like Pepys's, were not meant for publication, give a wonderful insight into English life from before the Commonwealth until the days of Queen Anne. Evelyn loved trees and gardening and designed the exquisite gardens at nearby ALBURY PARK, as well as those at Wotton. He died in 1706 and is buried at Wotton church. The Evelyn family are still Lords of the Manor.

The Incomparable SIR MAX BEERBOHM (1872–1956), caricaturist and author, lived at Abinger Manor Cottage during the Second World War.

The actress PRUNELLA SCALES, Sybil in *Fawlty Towers*, was born in Abinger in 1932.

Albury

The Silent Pool

ALBURY PARK is a Tudor house remodelled by PUGIN, who also designed the village of Albury. The gardens were laid out by JOHN EVELYN, for his friend and neighbour HENRY HOWARD, the sixth Duke of Norfolk, and include terraces, a 200-ft (61-m) tunnel burrowed into the hillside and the LONGEST YEW HEDGE IN ENGLAND. Later, the house came into the hands of the Duke of Northumberland, and the Dowager Duchess of Northumberland lived here until her death in 1965. It was used as the location for the Scottish wedding in the film *Four Weddings and a Funeral*.

Buried somewhere under the ruined chancel of the redundant Saxon church next door is WILLIAM OUGHTRED (1575–1660), who, as well as being parson here for 50 years, was one of the leading mathematicians of his day. He invented the SLIDE RULE and the MULTIPLICATION SIGN (x). He expired from joy when he heard of the Restoration of Charles II to the throne.

At ABINGER HAMMER, just down the road, stands KING JOHN'S HOUSE, an impressive, red-brick Jacobean building that stands on the site of a royal hunting lodge. While riding through the forest one day, King John surprised a nymph bathing in a deep limpid pool, so startling her that she retreated into the water until she

was out of her depth and drowned. The waters of the pool have remained as still and clear as crystal ever since, earning it the name the SILENT POOL. Although just a short walk away from the busy A25, there is an air of tranquillity and peace here that is tremendously soothing. Tendrils of river weed reach for the surface like tresses of hair and sometimes, if you strain to hear, a young girl's voice can be heard softly singing.

Brooklands

Ghosts, Glory and Glamour

Passengers gazing idly out of the train window as they trundle out of WEYBRIDGE Station, heading for the south coast, little realise that the dull, commonplace industrial landscape they see before them hides a thrilling story of glory, ghosts and glamour. Here, beneath the pre-fabs and the factories, lies the legend that is Brooklands, the FIRST MOTOR RACING CIRCUIT IN THE WORLD.

Brooklands was built on his own land by motor racing enthusiast HUGH LOCKE KING. The circuit was 3¼ miles (6 km) in length, 100 ft (31 m) wide, and included two long straights, one of over ½ mile (800 m). The most celebrated features were the two sections of banking, 30 ft (9 m) high, that were designed to help cars achieve the maximum possible speeds.

Brooklands opened in June 1907 and, for the next three decades, it was at the very centre of British motor sport, hosting scores of races, festivals and record attempts and welcoming all the pioneers and heroes of the day. On 15 February 1913, PERCY LAMBERT became the FIRST PERSON TO COVER 100 MILES (161 KM) IN AN HOUR, travelling 103 miles 1,470 yards in 60 minutes. In October that year, he returned and attempted to break his own record. He had averaged 110 mph (177 kph) for 120 laps when a rear tyre burst and his car careered off the track and disintegrated, killing him instantly. He is buried at Brompton Cemetery in London.

The FIRST BRITISH GRAND PRIX was held at Brooklands on 7 August 1926, during which the fastest lap was set at 85.99 mph by SIR HENRY SEGRAVE in a Talbot. Segrave went on to become the only British racing driver to win a Grand Prix in a British car for 32 years. He died in 1930 attempting the world water speed record on Lake Windermere.

There were many land speed records set at Brooklands, the last in 1922 when Kenelm Lee Guinness set an official world land speed record of 133.75 mph in a Sunbeam. The car was later purchased by Sir Malcolm Campbell (1885–1949) and developed into the first of his famous record-breaking Blue Bird cars, three of which were built at Brooklands by Thomson & Taylor.

One of the most glamorous racers of the 1920s was COUNT LOUIS ZBOROWSKI, who won many times at Brooklands in his monster, aeroengined, self-built racing cars, each called CHITTY CHITTY BANG BANG after the noise made by their crude exhaust pipes. Chitty I was eventually retired after it shed a tyre and left the banking at high speed, demolishing a timing box and giving the timing official inside a nasty fright. After Count Zborowski's death at Monza in 1924, Chitty I was bought by the Conan Doyle brothers, sons of the creator of Sherlock Holmes, and used for speed trials in the 1930s. She was subsequently abandoned to rot at Brooklands. It was this car that inspired Ian Fleming's children's story *Chitty Chitty Bang Bang.*

Brooklands was also at the forefront of British aviation. On 8 June 1908, ALLIOTT VERDON ROE (*see* Lancashire), became the FIRST ENGLISHMAN TO ACHIEVE POWERED FLIGHT when he flew 75 ft (23 m) across the track in his own hand-built aeroplane. Unfortunately, this was not recorded officially and the prize of the first official flight by an Englishman went to John Brabazon in 1909 (*see* Isle of Sheppey, Kent).

In 1939, at the outbreak of the Second World War, Brooklands was closed as a motor racing circuit and taken over by the government for the production of miltary aircraft, including the Hurricane fighter plane and the Wellington bomber. Over the years, as it became derelict and overgrown, eerie footsteps could be heard in the quiet hours of the morning, along with revving engines and squealing tyres, and sometimes a ghostly man in white overalls and a helmet was seen walking across the car park towards the banking, before disappearing. Could it have been Percy Lambert, haunting the scene of his finest triumphs and ultimate fate? Today, however, much of the site has been restored and you can visit the Brooklands Museum.

Woking

The War of the Worlds

THE SHAH JEHAN MOSQUE in Woking was opened in 1889 and is the OLDEST MOSQUE IN BRITAIN. It was built to serve students from the nearby Oriental Institute, which is no longer there but is commemorated in the name Oriental Road.

H.G. WELLS (1866–1946) lived at Woking at the end of the 19th century and during this time he wrote *The War of the Worlds*, published in 1898. The book opens on Woking's HORSELL COMMON, where the Martians land. When a radio adaptation of *The War of the Worlds* read by Orson Welles, and set in New Jersey, was broadcast in America, there was mass panic!

H.G. Wells had a ten-year affair, and a son, Anthony, with the Irish-born novelist DAME REBECCA WEST (1892–1983), who is buried in plot 81 at BROOKWOOD CEMETERY on the outskirts of Woking, the BIGGEST CEMETERY IN BRITAIN. DODI FAYED (1955–97), son of Harrods owner, Mohamed Fayed, is also buried here. He died in the car crash that took the life of Princess Diana in 1997.

Surrey Iron Railway

The World's First Public Railway

Dotted about Surrey are a number of hidden glimpses of one of the WORLD'S EARLIEST RAILWAYS. On display in the memorial gardens off Quality Street at MERSTHAM, near Redhill, are four plate rails from the CROYDON MERSTHAM AND GODSTONE RAILWAY, which was part of the Surrey Iron Railway, the WORLD'S FIRST PUBLIC RAILWAY, opened in 1803. It was constructed by the canal builder, WILLIAM JESSOP, to carry stone from the local quarries at Merstham, through Croydon to Jessop's wharf on the River Thames at Wandsworth. Trains of up to 15 wagons were drawn by 'a miserable team of lame mules' until steam began to take over and the line was abandoned in 1846. The track bed was incorporated into the main London to Brighton line, although a short stretch can still be seen running alongside the A23 at HARPS OAK, north of Merstham.

A little further north along the A23, beside the Little Chef at HOOLEY, is a small brick bridge that carried DEAN LANE over the old railway. At MITCHAM, there is a building called STATION COURT, which used to be MITCHAM STATION on the Surrey Iron Railway and has some claim to being the OLDEST RAILWAY STATION IN THE WORLD. The wall of the RAM BREWERY in York Road, WANDSWORTH, is aligned along the route of the old railway and there is a plaque set in the wall that commemorates this.

Well, I never knew this ABOUT SURREY

The 18th-century SHALFORD WATER MILL, near GUILDFORD, timber-framed and hung with tiles, was rescued, restored and given to the National Trust in 1932 by the elusive and mysterious 'FERGUSON'S GANG'. In the 1930s, using Shalford Mill as their headquarters, this group went about England rescuing derelict buildings and preserving what they

saw as the country's valuable heritage from developers. Another of their gifts to the National Trust was the Town Hall at Newport on the Isle of Wight. Nobody knows to this day who Ferguson was or who were the members of his gang. They would turn up at the National Trust offices in London, wearing cloaks and masks and calling themselves names like Bill Stickers, Sister Agatha, Erb or Old Biddy. Then they would hand over bundles of notes to the Secretary, as an endowment fund for a particular project, and disappear back into the busy streets, never tarrying for more than 30 seconds.

On OUTWOOD COMMON stands the OLDEST WORKING POST MILL IN ENGLAND. Built in 1665, it used to be one of a pair, the CAT AND THE KITTEN, but the Kitten, a smock mill, collapsed in 1960. In 1666, the villagers of OUTWOOD watched the flames of the Great Fire of London from the top floor of the mill.

P.G. WODEHOUSE (1881–1975), comic author and creator of Jeeves, was born in GUILDFORD.

WOKING is home to the MCLAREN FORMULA ONE MOTOR RACING TEAM.

Nestling beside a red-brick manor house (now a school), on the banks of the River Mole at STOKE D'ABERNON, is a 10th-century grey flint church containing one of England's treasures. On the floor of the chancel is the brass of SIR JOHN D'ABERNON, who died in 1277. It is the OLDEST BRASS IN ENGLAND and the ONLY ONE TO SHOW A KNIGHT WITH A LANCE.

SUSSEX

COUNTY TOWN: LEWES

'Yea, Sussex by the sea.'

RUDYARD KIPLING

Brighton

London by the Sea

Brighton became one of Britain's first seaside resorts towards the end of the 18th century, when DR RICHARD RUSSELL wrote about the health benefits of bathing in the sea at the tiny fishing village of BRIGHTHELMSTONE. One of the first people to register at 'Dr Brighton', as it became known, was the PRINCE REGENT, who rented a small farmhouse there in 1783. He enjoyed it so much that he bought the farmhouse and commissioned Henry Holland, and then John Nash, to convert it into the flamboyant BRIGHTON PAVILION. Here he could escape the confines of the Court in London and indulge in more raffish pursuits. Hence Brighton's reputation as the home of the 'dirty weekend'. Appropriately, Brighton was also the FIRST SEASIDE RESORT TO OFFICIALLY SANCTION A NUDIST BEACH.

The oldest hotel in Brighton is the OLD SHIP, which once belonged to NICHOLAS TETTERSELL, owner of the coal brig on which the future Charles II escaped to France after his defeat at the Battle of Worcester in 1651. To commemorate the event, the Old Ship organises an annual Royal Escape yacht race from Brighton to Fecamp on the Normandy coast.

The METROPOLE HOTEL was the finishing post for the EMANCIPATION RUN in 1896. This was the first LONDON TO BRIGHTON CAR RUN, held to celebrate the abolition of the rule that required every mechanised road vehicle to be preceded by a man holding a red flag. The event still takes place every year on the first Sunday in November.

BRITAIN'S FIRST LICENSED CASINO, the METROPOLE CASINO, opened in the Clarence Room of the Metropole Hotel in 1962. It has now moved to Preston Street, where it still proudly sports the original Metropole logo.

Brighton's magnificent GRAND HOTEL was the site of the worst political assassination attempt since the Gunpowder Plot of 1605. On the morning of 12 October 1984, an IRA bomb ripped apart four floors of the hotel where the Prime Minister, Margaret Thatcher, and members of the Conservative Party were staying during their party conference. Five people were killed and over 30 injured.

On the sea wall below Marine Parade, to the east of the Palace Pier, is a plaque marking the site of the CHAIN PIER, the WORLD'S FIRST SEASIDE PLEASURE PIER. Opened in 1823, it was constructed like a suspension bridge by SIR SAMUEL BROWN, who had built the world's first suspension road bridge across the River Tweed in 1820 (*see* Northumberland). The pier acted as the terminus for the cross-channel service to Dieppe. It was destroyed by a storm in 1896, although the two entrance kiosks on the shore were saved and now flank the entrance to the Palace Pier.

BRIGHTON MARINA is the LARGEST MARINA IN EUROPE.

Hastings

Dawn of the Norman Age and the Television Age

On the clifftop at Hastings are the scant remains of the FIRST CASTLE BUILT IN ENGLAND BY WILLIAM THE CONQUEROR. Down by the pier, is the CONQUEROR'S STONE, on the spot where William is supposed to have eaten his first breakfast in England.

Upstairs Downstairs, *Coronation Street*, *Fawlty Towers*, *Life on Earth*, Al-Jazeera and *Big Brother* – all owe their existence to 21 LINTON CRESCENT, Hastings, for it was here that the 'TELEVISION AGE' was born. It was in this building, in 1923, that television pioneer JOHN LOGIE BAIRD (1888–1946) succeeded in transmitting shadowy images of a man's hand, and thus ensured that life would never be the same again. Logie Baird's equipment consisted of a cardboard disc cut out of a hat box, a tin plate, a bicyle lamp lens, sealing wax and some darning needles.

In 1924, as his experiments became more sophisticated, Baird had to move to the upper floor of 8 QUEENS AVENUE, but was soon asked to leave after an unfortunate accident involving 12,000 volts that flung him, stunned, across the room and fused the whole building. After a scuffle on the pavement outside with his irate landlord, Mr Tree, John Logie Baird gathered up his stuff and returned to London. In 1941, he retired to a house by the railway station at Bexhill-on-Sea, where he died in 1946.

Comedian JO BRAND was born in Hastings in 1957, as was 'Baby' Spice Girl, EMMA BUNTON, in 1979.

Arundel

Gormenghast

ARUNDEL CASTLE claims to be the SECOND LARGEST CASTLE IN ENGLAND – along with Alnwick (*see* Northumberland) – and is the home of the Dukes of Norfolk. The extraordinary Gothic skyline of towers and battlements, perched above the marshes, was the inspiration for the fantastical castle in Mervyn Peake's *Gormenghast*, and the scene was

painted by J.M.W. TURNER from the Black Rabbit pub down by the river.

The present castle, grouped around the old Norman keep, was restored in the days of Henry, the 15th Duke, who inherited it in 1860, at the age of 13. Vastly rich, he became eccentric and would shuffle around town dressed in shabby clothes with a long, unkempt beard. Once, while he was waiting on the platform at Arundel Station for a friend to arrive, an imperious lady summoned him to carry her case, thinking he might be grateful for a little honest work.

'Here, my man, is a penny for you,' she said, pressing the coin into his hand. 'No doubt it's the first honest penny you've ever earned.' He murmured in reply, 'Indeed it is.'

This Duke was also responsible for Arundel's Roman Catholic CATHEDRAL OF OUR LADY, built in 1868 and designed by JOSEPH HANSOM, inventor of the Hansom cab.

Hartfield

Home of Winnie-the-Pooh

IN 1925, A.A. MILNE bought COTCHFORD FARM, just south of Hartfield, not far from East Grinstead, and found in ASHDOWN FOREST the perfect setting for his tales about the adventures of a 'bear with very little brain'. A little further up the road is the five hundred acre wood, which inspired the HUNDRED ACRE WOOD, and dotted around the area are many of the scenes that appear in the books.

Poohsticks Bridge

It is still possible to recognise a number of these places, as E.H. SHEPARD drew his memorable illustrations in Ashdown Forest. Any walk through the trees becomes a wonderful guessing game as to which beech tree might be Piglet's home or which was the oak tree where Pooh floated up into a bee's nest on the end of a balloon, or which sad and boggy patch was Eeyore's gloomy place.

POOHSTICKS BRIDGE, a little wooden bridge that crosses the Posingford Stream deep in POSINGFORD WOOD, can be reached, after a stiff muddy walk, from a small car park just off the B2026 as it climbs the hill towards UCKFIELD.

Further up the B2026, towards the top of Ashdown Forest, is an old quarry that is ROO'S SANDY PIT, and right at the summit is GALLEON'S LEAP (GILS LAP), the enchanted place where they 'could see the whole world spread out'. Across the road is a pond by the site of where Pooh discovered the North Pole.

Uppark

How the Other Half Live

Beautiful 17th-century Uppark stands high on the South Downs above HARTING. It was devastated by fire in 1989, but sympathetically restored by the National Trust. In 1774, the house was inherited by SIR HARRY FETHERSTONHAUGH, something of a rake, who brought down from London a beautiful young 'escort' from Cheshire named EMMA HART and installed her in a cottage on the estate. She would often dance naked on the dining table for the delectation of Sir Harry's guests – good preparation, perhaps, for becoming the most famous mistress in Europe, Nelson's EMMA HAMILTON.

In 1880, 14-year-old H.G. WELLS came to stay for Christmas, 'downstairs' at Uppark, where his mother was housekeeper. Snowed in for two weeks, he spent the time writing and was intrigued by the contrasts between upstairs and downstairs. He later said that this time at Uppark had opened his eyes to the world and changed his life.

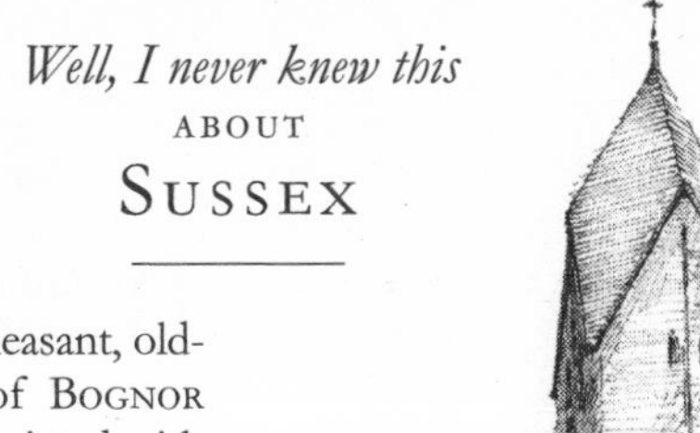

Well, I never knew this ABOUT SUSSEX

'BUGGER BOGNOR.' The pleasant, old-fashioned, sandy resort of BOGNOR REGIS will forever be associated with this expression, supposedly the last words of GEORGE V when, just before he died, he was assured by his doctor that he would soon be well enough to holiday at his favourite seaside town ('Regis' was added in his honour). *The Times* reported that his last words were a concerned, 'How is the Empire?', while the official line is that he said, 'Gentleman, I am sorry for keeping you waiting like this. I am unable to concentrate.' His doctor, meanwhile, asserted that the king's last words, on being given a massive shot of morphine, were 'God damn you!' King George V died on 20 January 1936.

At WORTHING, a plaque on the Esplanade marks the site of the house where OSCAR WILDE wrote *The Importance of Being Earnest.* He was staying here in the summer of 1894 to escape his creditors in London, and was inspired to write the play by an article in the *Worthing Gazette* about a baby in a hamper that had been found at King's Cross Station. It took him just 21 days to write the play, which he described as 'the best I have ever written'. He named his hero Jack Worthing in honour of the town.

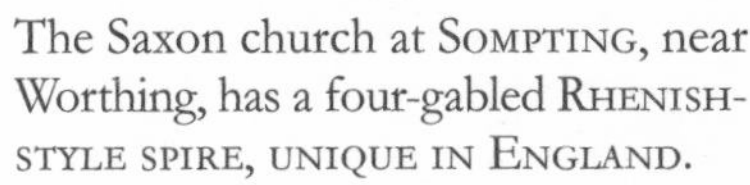

The Saxon church at SOMPTING, near Worthing, has a four-gabled RHENISH-STYLE SPIRE, UNIQUE IN ENGLAND.

'Away to sweet Felpham, for heaven is there,' wrote WILLIAM BLAKE (1757–1827). You can still see Blake's Cottage, in Blake's Lane, FELPHAM, where he lived from 1800 to 1803 and where he wrote 'Jerusalem'. SIR HUBERT PARRY (1848–1918), who later set 'Jerusalem' to music, lived along the coast at RUSTINGTON.

In 1906, the writer HILAIRE BELLOC (1870–1953) bought the white smock windmill near his home at SHIPLEY, south of Horsham. He would doff his cap to his 'beautiful Mrs Shipley' whenever he passed by and there is now a plaque to his memory above the windmill door.

The church at STEYNING possesses what is often described as the most magnificent Norman arch in England, dating from around 1100, and a superb display of rich Norman carving. A notable student at the Grammar School was JOHN PELL (1611–85), who became a mathematician and gave his name to PELL'S EQUATION (the indeterminate quadratic equation y2 = nx2 + 1), which, apparently, was first studied 1,000 years previously by Brahmagupta. Of wider interest, perhaps, is the fact that he invented the DIVISION SIGN (÷). John Pell was born in SOUTHWICK, near Brighton, which was also the birthplace of the singer DAME CLARA BUTT (1873–1936).

In Saxon times, the lovely church at WORTH stood alone as a welcome refuge deep in the dark impenetrable forest of Anderida. It lies in the middle of a wide clearing at the gates to the Bishop of Horsham's home, with just a couple of old timbered houses in sight. The Victorians added a short spire and the 20th century surrounded it with a new town, CRAWLEY, and the M23, but some-

how the church retains an air of seclusion, the roar of traffic deadened by the trees. None of this can prepare you for the breathtaking interior, three supreme Saxon arches built over 1,000 years ago when Sussex was remote and savage. The chancel arch is the LARGEST SAXON ARCH SURVIVING IN BRITAIN, possibly the world, and an incomparably beautiful masterpiece.

The playwright SIR DAVID HARE was born in BEXHILL-ON-SEA in 1947.

WARWICKSHIRE

COUNTY TOWN: WARWICK

Shakespeare's County

Handsworth

Founding Fathers of the Industrial Revolution

ST MARY'S church at Handsworth, north-west of the city centre, is, perhaps, the most important shrine in Britain to the Industrial Revolution. Here, lying beside each other, are three of the Founding Fathers: MATTHEW BOULTON, JAMES WATT and WILLIAM MURDOCK.

In 1765, Matthew Boulton opened the BIGGEST FACTORY IN THE WORLD, the SOHO MANUFACTORY, on HANDSWORTH HEATH outside Birmingham. He also put up accommodation for the factory workers, turning the tiny village of Handsworth into an industrial town. The factory made metalware products such as coins, tokens, ormolu and silver plate.

James Watt arrived in Birmingham in 1774 to oversee the use and production of his steam engines by Boulton. They went into partnership as BOULTON & WATT and, in 1796, opened the Soho Foundry by the canal for the production of steam engines.

Boulton & Watt opened offices in Cornwall, where demand for their steam engines from the tin and copper mines was growing. To oversee their operations there, they sent William Murdock, already a pioneer in steam engines. While in Cornwall, Murdock invented a gas lighting system (*see* Redruth, Cornwall), which was put to use in the Soho Manufactory, making it the FIRST FACTORY IN THE WORLD TO BE LIT BY GAS.

In its heyday, Boulton & Watt was the BIGGEST AND BEST-KNOWN INDUSTRIAL CONCERN IN THE WORLD. As Matthew Boulton said, 'We are providing what all the world desires to have – power!'

Soho Manufactory

Later in his life, Matthew Boulton INVENTED MODERN COINAGE, making coins of consistent weight and design. In 1797, his Soho Mint was commissioned to make coins for George III. As part of the process, Matthew Boulton developed a system whereby a strip of metal went into the works one end and coins emerged from the other; in other words, he had invented the PRODUCTION LINE.

Matthew Boulton lived at SOHO HOUSE in Handsworth from 1766 until his death in 1809. It was the FIRST CENTRALLY HEATED HOUSE IN ENGLAND since Roman times and became a meeting place for some of the greatest engineers, scientists and thinkers of the age, including members of the Lunar Society.

Soho House

The Lunar Society

Lunatics All

The Lunar Society was a group of brilliant engineers, scientists, inventors and thinkers who met in and around Birmingham between 1765 and 1813. Their preferred venue was Soho House in Handsworth, the home of Matthew Boulton, and they would schedule their meetings each month for the Monday nearest the full moon, so that there was plenty of light for the journey home along the dangerous, unlit roads. Hence the name Lunar Circle, or Lunar Society or, as they sometimes called themselves, the 'Lunatics'.

The members of the Lunar Society were hugely powerful and influential, leaders and designers of the revolution that was sweeping the world, the Industrial Revolution. At meetings they would discuss not only the new inventions and the science behind them, but how that science and invention could be applied to the real world of industry, medicine, transport, education, politics and social issues. They knew that they were changing the world and they had the confidence to believe that they were changing it for the good of mankind.

Their outlook was 'liberal'. They abhorred slavery and tyranny, whether of church or state, and sympathised with the ideals behind both the French and American revolutions, yet at the same time they believed in capitalist self-help and the need for success to be rewarded. Leading members of the Lunar Society included :

MATTHEW BOULTON (1728–1809) of Boulton & Watt, who, as the leading industrialist of the day, developed modern-day industrial practice with the first workers' insurance schemes and sick pay.

JAMES WATT (1736–1819), of Boulton & Watt, who was the inventor of the world's first practical steam engines, which provided power for the new factories springing up across the country. The unit of power, the 'WATT' is named after him.

WILLIAM MURDOCK (1754–1839), who worked for Boulton & Watt and was the inventor of the gas light.

ERASMUS DARWIN (1731–1802), who was a poet, inventor, botanist and father of 14 children. He published a theory of evolution 60 years before his grandson, Charles, and developed a steering system that was adopted by Henry Ford, and a mechnical copying machine. He also foresaw the use of steam-powered propulsion:

Soon shall thy arm, Unconquered
Steam! afar
Drag the slow barge, or drive the rapid
car
Or on wide waving wings expanded bear
the flying chariot through the fields of
air.

JOSIAH WEDGWOOD (1730–95), the Father of English pottery, who was also a grandfather of Charles Darwin (*see* Stoke-on-Trent, Staffordshire).

JOSEPH PRIESTLEY (1733–1804), discoverer of carbon dioxide, carbonated (fizzy) drinks, nitrous oxide and oxygen.

JAMES KEIR (1735–1820), a chemist who discovered a way of making affordable soap.

RICHARD LOVELL EDGEWORTH (1744–1817), an inventor who published books on educational theory. He was the father of the novelist MARIA EDGEWORTH.

WILLIAM SMALL (1734–75), a mathematician and philosopher, who was also a mentor of Thomas Jefferson, third President of the United States of America. The Lunar Society was deeply upset when Small died tragically young at the age of 40. He was replaced by . . .

WILLIAM WITHERING (1741–99), a doctor and botanist. He discovered the benefits of digitalis, which is extracted from the foxglove plant, in the treatment of heart disease.

Historic Coventry

Bareback Rides

Coventry was established in 1043 when EARL LEOFRIC OF MERCIA founded an abbey here. His wife, LADY GODIVA, was the FIRST WOMAN TO BE MENTIONED IN THE DOMESDAY BOOK. She is also renowned for pleading with her husband to reduce his taxes on the people of Coventry, which she felt were unfair and holding back the development of the town. Leofric agreed to lower them only if she rode through the town naked. To his amazement and horror, she did, and the townsfolk showed their gratitude by staying indoors and not looking. The mischievous 'PEEPING TOM', who did take a peek and was struck blind, was a 17th-century Puritan addition to the story.

The phrase 'TO SEND TO COVENTRY', meaning to ignore or ostracise, originated during the English Civil War, when Royalist captives were sent to the town, which was a Parliamentary stronghold, and the townsfolk were discouraged from having anything to do with them.

Coventry was the ONLY ENGLISH CITY TO LOSE A CATHEDRAL TO BOMBING during the Second World War. On 14 November 1940, ST MICHAEL'S CATHEDRAL was almost totally destoyed during a devastating air raid. The spire was saved and, at 295 ft (90 m) it is the THIRD TALLEST SPIRE IN ENGLAND.

Coventry's new cathedral, built at right angles to the old and facing north–south, was opened in 1962. The tapestry behind the altar took GRAHAM SUTHERLAND seven years to complete and, when it was finished, was the BIGGEST TAPESTRY IN THE WORLD.

In the 1969 film *The Italian Job*, the scenes where the Mini-Coopers are driven at speed through the catacombs of Rome were, in fact, filmed in the huge sewer pipes beneath the streets of Coventry.

Industrial Coventry

Home of British Bicycles

In 1870, JAMES STARLEY and WILLIAM HILLMAN of the COVENTRY MACHINISTS COMPANY produced the FIRST ENGLISH-MADE BICYCLE called the ARIEL. It was of a 'penny farthing' design, hugely unstable and difficult to ride. In order to demonstrate this new marvel, Starley and Hillman rode the 96 miles (154 km) from London to Coventry in one day, arriving at Starley's house in Coventry just as the Cathedral clock struck midnight. They both had to be helped down from their machines and were seen walking with an extra wide gait for some days afterwards.

In 1874, Starley and Hillman brought out a ladies' version of the Ariel specially adapted to be ridden side-saddle. The awkward sitting position and complicated pedal and crank mechanism, allied to the billowy dresses of the day, made controlling one of these contraptions a challenge beyond all but the most daring. Several courageous young women had to be sent home with serious bruises and contusions sustained after plummeting to earth from the high saddle. Starley and Hillman were surprised and disappointed at the paucity of demand for their invention. The ladies' Ariel was quietly dropped after Hillman narrowly avoided a major catastrophe, getting into a serious and irretrievable wobble while attempting to ride home on one. He decided to make cars instead.

In 1877, James Starley invented the DIFFERENTIAL as a means of enabling him to keep up with his son when they went out riding together on one of his tandems. His basic design is used in motor cars to this day.

The FIRST SAFETY BICYCLE was developed by Starley's nephew, John Kemp Starley, who introduced the ROVER SAFETY in 1885. This was the forerunner of the modern bicycle, with wheels of equal size, a diamond frame and geared chain drive. His design has changed very little to this day.

Rugby

Home of Rugby Football

Although it is an important railway junction and industrial centre, the town of Rugby is celebrated across the world as the home of the great game of RUGBY FOOTBALL. The school where it all began dominates the town and, on the DOCTOR'S WALL overlooking the school close, there is a granite plaque that commemorates the occasion, in 1823, when WILLIAM WEBB ELLIS, 'with a fine disregard for the rules of football . . . first took the ball in his arms and ran with it'. Today, countries as diverse as Argentina, France, Japan, Western Samoa and South Africa all compete every four years for the William Webb Ellis Trophy at the Rugby World Cup, first won in 1987 by New Zealand.

Little knowing that he had carved his name in history, William Webb Ellis went on to enter the Church and became Rector of St Clement Danes in the Strand in London. In 1855, a picture of him appeared in the *Illustrated London Post* after he had given a rousing sermon about the Crimean War. He died in the South of France in 1872 and is buried at Menton, near Nice, on the French Riviera.

The most celebrated Headmaster of Rugby School was DR THOMAS ARNOLD, who reigned there from 1828 until 1842. He is buried in the school chapel. Nearby there is a statue of one of his pupils, THOMAS HUGHES (1822–96), who wrote *Tom Brown's Schooldays*, which was based on his own time at Rugby. Another well-known old boy is the poet RUPERT BROOKE (1887–1915), who was born in Rugby, at 5 Hillmorton Road, and whose father was a house-master at the school.

Tolkien's Middle England

Middle Earth

Professor J.R.R. Tolkien (1892–1973), author of *The Lord of the Rings*, voted Britain's best-loved book, grew up in Birmingham and drew many of his influences from the area. Born in South Africa, he came to live in the tiny village of SAREHOLE, between Birmingham and Solihull, when he was three. He and his brother spent many happy hours exploring the nearby SAREHOLE MILL (once owned by Matthew Boulton), and this was to become the SHIRE MILL from *The Hobbit*. They were frequently being chased off by the mill owner's son, whom they nicknamed the 'White Ogre', as he was always covered in flour.

Near to the mill was the mysterious MOSELEY BOG, a pond once used for supplying the mill with water and now hidden away in a patch of neglected woodland where nothing ever seemed to have happened, and which became Tom Bombadil's OLD FOREST.

Sarehole was Tolkien's Shire. The village was quiet and rural when Tolkien first moved there, but the creeping spread of industrial Birmingham soon began to encroach and this development is reflected in *The Lord of the Rings* when the pastoral beauty of the Shire is menaced by the grime and ugliness of a harsh, industrial evil.

In 1904, Tolkien's mother died, and he and his brother went to live with their aunt near EDGBASTON, close to the city centre. Here he discovered the Two TOWERS: MINAS TIRITH and MINAS MORGUL. One was PERROT'S FOLLY, nearly 100 ft (30.5 m) high and built in 1758 by John Perrot. The other was a Victorian tower belonging to the Edgbaston waterworks.

Sarehole Mill has been restored (largely thanks to a donation from Tolkien) and is now a museum. Moseley Bog still exists, as do the two towers, and they can all be visited.

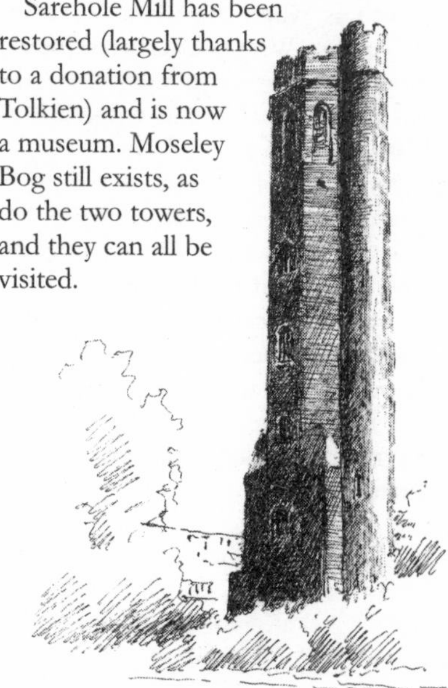

Perrot's Folly

Well, I never knew this ABOUT WARWICKSHIRE

SIR THOMAS MALORY, author of the definitive book on the legend of King Arthur, *Le Morte D'Arthur*, was born in 1420 at NEWBOLD REVEL, near Rugby, where his father was Lord of the Manor. He inherited large estates in 1433 and became MP for Warwickshire, but got caught up in the Wars of the Roses while serving under the Earl of Warwick and spent much of his time in and out of prison. He was finally sent to Newgate Prison in London in 1468, which is where he wrote *Le Morte D'Arthur*. WILLIAM CAXTON, who printed the book in 1486, wrote in the preface that 'it was reduced into English (from a French story) by Syr Thomas Malory, Knight, in the ninth year of the reign of Edward IV' (1470). In the story, Malory paints a vivid picture of the horrors of prison life that was clearly drawn from his own experiences. He was never to know of the acclaim his work won for him, as he died in Newgate in 1471 and is buried in the nearby Grey Friars.

In 1895, in BIRMINGHAM, FREDERICK LANCHESTER built the FIRST PETROL-DRIVEN FOUR-WHEEL CAR EVER MADE IN BRITAIN.

In 1930, OSCAR DEUTSCH opened the WORLD'S FIRST ODEON CINEMA in BIRMINGHAM. ODEON stands for 'Oscar Deutsch Entertains Our Nation'.

BIRMINGHAM was comprehensively bombed during the Second World War and much of the city centre is modern. One noble building that survives from the city's Victorian grandeur is the TOWN HALL, opened in 1834 and designed by JOSEPH HANSOM (1803-82), inventor of the Hansom cab (*see* Leicestershire).

WESTMORLAND

COUNTY TOWN: APPLEBY

'I do not know in all my country . . . a place more naturally divine'

JOHN RUSKIN

Kirkby Lonsdale

Ruskin's View

Kirkby Lonsdale, with its charming narrow streets and grey stone houses perched above the River Lune (from which it derives its name), was the favourite town of the Victorian author and critic JOHN RUSKIN (1819–1900). The view across the Lune valley from the churchyard is known as RUSKIN'S VIEW, which he described as 'one of the loveliest in England and therefore in the world'.

Just outside the town, spanning the River Lune with three grand arches, is one of England's finest ancient bridges, the DEVIL'S BRIDGE, built in the 12th century. The story goes that it was put there by the Devil at the request of an old woman who could not get across the fast-flowing river to retrieve her cow. All he asked for in return was the soul of the first living thing to cross the bridge. The old woman agreed but, instead of going over herself, as the Devil had anticipated, she went to fetch her dog and threw a bun on to the bridge so that the dog ran after it, straight into the arms of the Devil. According to folklore, a dog has no soul, so poor old Beelzebub was thwarted and slunk away in a sulk.

The girl's school at CASTERTON, 1 mile (1.5 km) up the road, was attended by the BRONTË SISTERS and was the model for LOWOOD, the school in *Jane Eyre*.

Grasmere

'The Loveliest Spot That Man Hath Ever Found.'
William Wordsworth

Grasmere is WILLIAM WORDSWORTH's village. Here he lived, here he spent his happiest days and wrote his greatest poetry, and here he rests, beneath a simple gravestone in a corner of the churchyard by the river.

Wordsworth came to Grasmere in 1799, when he was 29. With his sister, DOROTHY, he moved into DOVE COTTAGE, a tiny 17th-century former inn, set into the hillside at Town End, 2 minutes' walk from the centre of the village. From the moment they arrived, Dove Cottage became a social hub, with an assortment of poets and artists always visiting and often staying, even though there was hardly room for a couple. SAMUEL COLERIDGE moved into Greta Hall, in Keswick, in 1800, and would regularly walk over to Dove Cottage and stay, as would ROBERT SOUTHEY and THOMAS DE QUINCEY.

In 1802, Wordsworth married and brought his bride, MARY, to Dove Cottage, which almost proved too much for Dorothy, who locked herself in her room and sobbed. When SIR WALTER SCOTT came to stay, he found the cottage so lacking in certain comforts that he would sneak off to the Swan Inn up the road for a fortifier, under the guise of going for a bracing walk. Scott's subterfuge was revealed when he and his host went up to the Swan to hire a pony and the landlord tried to hustle them into Scott's regular seat by the window, expressing surprise that he was in so much earlier than his usual time.

Dove Cottage

Wordsworth himself usually wrote outside in the garden when the house was full, and would shout to himself above the hubbub. All this activity obviously worked for Wordsworth, for he wrote some of his best work at Dove Cottage, including 'I Wandered Lonely as a Cloud' (*see* Cockermouth, Cumberland) and 'My Heart Leaps up when I Behold, a Rainbow in the Sky'.

By 1807, with a growing family, Dove Cottage had become too small, even for the Wordsworths, and they moved to ALLEN BANK, a larger house nearby, then to the OLD VICARAGE and, finally, in 1813, to

RYDAL MOUNT, near Ambleside, where they lived until William died in 1850. He is buried in the churchyard of ST OSWALD'S at Grasmere, along with his wife Mary, sister Dorothy, daughter Dora and her husband, and Samuel Coleridge's son Hartley, who had rather attached himself to the Wordsworths after being abandoned by his father at Greta Hall.

Lowther

Lowther! in thy majestic pile are seen
Cathedral pomp and grace in apt accord
With the baronial castle's sterner mien

Thus did Wordsworth describe LOWTHER CASTLE, standing in 3,000 acres of fine parkland, once the grandest house in Westmorland, now its most spectacular ruin. There have been many houses on this site, which has been the seat of the Lowther family, now EARLS OF LONSDALE, since the days of Edward I. Many of them lie in the family mausoleum in St Michael's church at the Castle gates. The present Castle, a fine example of Gothic revival architecture, was completed in 1814, and was the first work of ROBERT SMIRKE, who went on to design the British Museum.

At the end of the 19th century, Lowther Castle was inherited by Hugh Lowther, fifth Earl of Lonsdale, known as the 'Yellow Earl' (*see* Barleythorpe, Rutland). Whenever he was in residence the Castle would resound with the chatter of royalty, politicians, sportsmen and artists, and the narrow lanes around Askham would be full of the Earl's fleet of yellow motor cars. The Yellow Earl was passionate about cars and was thrilled when the Kaiser arrived for a visit in a brand new Benz, complete with new-fangled chauffeur.

After the death of the fifth Earl in 1944, the Castle was abandoned and the contents removed, while the roof was stripped in 1957. Today, all that is

left is a shell, although attempts are being made to raise funds for the Castle's restoration.

Helvellyn

Man's Best Friend

Helvellyn is BRITAIN'S THIRD HIGHEST MOUNTAIN and Westmorland's highest point at 3,118 ft (950 m). It is one of only four peaks in England over 3,000 ft (914 m). Above RED TARN is a track along the top of a high ridge of rock, which in places is only 3 ft (90 cm) wide, and with an awesome drop on either side, called STRIDING EDGE. In clement weather it is relatively safe, and the views are breathtaking, but when the wind blows and the cloud comes down Striding Edge becomes truly perilous.

In 1805, a young artist named CHARLES GOUGH fell to his death from the narrow path and lay undiscovered for three months. When his body was finally located, the searchers were led to the spot by the sound of pitiful whimpering and there they found Charles Gough's faithful terrier, lying with his head on his master's cold face, weak with hunger and sorrow, too feeble even to growl or wag his tail. He wouldn't be parted from his master as they carried the young artist down the mountain, as if hoping still to hear his whistle and walk with him once more across the open windswept hills. Later that year, WILLIAM WORDSWORTH, HUMPHRY DAVY and SIR WALTER SCOTT tackled Striding Edge together and were greatly moved by the story. As Scott wrote:

How long didst thou think that his
silence was slumber?
When the wind waved his garment,
how oft didst thou start?

Well, I never knew this
ABOUT
WESTMORLAND

On the water meadows below BROUGHAM HALL, in sight of Penrith across the River Eamont, the LAST BATTLE ON ENGLISH SOIL was fought on 18 December 1745, the final scuffle of the '45 Rebellion. A detachment of Highlanders managed to hold up the pursuing Duke of Cumberland here while their main body escaped north across the Scottish border. There were few casualties. Brougham Hall, half-castle, half-country house, has been the seat of the Brougham family on and off since 1400. Edward VII and George V both visited it in the early 20th century, earning it the title the Windsor of the North. It is currently being restored.

The curious little BRIDGE HOUSE at AMBLESIDE was built in the 18th century as an apple store for Ambleside Hall. It was constructed over Stock Beck in order to avoid land taxes.

JOHN WILKINSON (1728–1808), the FIRST IRONMASTER, was born in CLIFTON in Westmorland. He invented a cylinder boring machine that improved James Watt's steam engines so that they could be used as a practical power source and became the sole manufacturer of Boulton & Watt engines for 25 years (*see* Handsworth, Warwickshire). He set up a practical coke smelting ironworks in COALBROOKDALE, where he constructed the WORLD'S FIRST IRON BOAT, to transport his iron goods along the River Severn. He was also one of the principal sponsors of the first iron bridge. His sister married Joseph Priestley, a member of the Lunar Society (*see* Warwickshire). He is buried in Ulverston. His name is remembered in the WILKINSON'S SWORD brand.

AMBLESIDE stands at the head of LAKE WINDERMERE, which is the LARGEST LAKE IN ENGLAND; 10½ miles (17 km) long, but less than 1 mile (1.6 km) wide.

In June 1930, the famous racing driver SIR HENRY SEGRAVE died on LAKE WINDERMERE when his boat hit a submerged log and disintegrated while he was attempting to set a new world water speed record (*see* Brooklands, Surrey).

On BELLE ISLAND, in the middle of LAKE WINDERMERE, opposite Bowness, is the FIRST ROUND HOUSE BUILT IN ENGLAND, completed in 1774.

Wiltshire

County Town: Trowbridge

'At peace in my tall windowed Wiltshire room'

Siegfried Sassoon

Wilton House, the first stately home in England to be opened to the public

Salisbury

Barchester Towers

The ancient, unchanging city of Salisbury slumbers at the meeting place of five rivers, exuding history and utter Englishness. It is the model for Anthony Trollope's 'Barchester'.

The view of Salisbury Cathedral across the water meadows of the River Avon has been voted the loveliest view in England and was painted by Constable from the gardens of the Bishop's Palace.

The foundation stone of the Cathedral was laid in 1220, and the building was finished just 38 years later, with the result that Salisbury is one of the few English cathedrals to have been completed in a single architectural style, Early English. The spire, added in 1334, is 404 ft (123 m) high, the highest spire in England. It stands on marshy ground, with foundations just 6 ft (1.8 m) deep, and leans 2½ ft (75 cm) out of true. Inside the Cathedral is the oldest working clock in Europe, dating from 1386.

The Cathedral Close is the largest in Britain and is flanked with beautiful houses, one of them occupied by the former Prime Minister, Edward Heath.

The actor Michael Crawford was born in Salisbury in 1942.

Fonthill Abbey

He Flew Too High

Drive west from Wilton, take a B road to Fonthill Bishop, turn left through a handsome stone gatehouse and you will find yourself in another world. There are terraces, lakes, noble trees and an air of anticipation, for this is obviously the parkland of some grand estate. But where is the great house? Go on past the crossroads at the Beckford Arms and there, on the right, is a small, forlorn, ruined tower, set amongst the trees, dreaming of lost wonders. This is all that remains of one of the most astonishing and gloriously preposterous private palaces ever built, WILLIAM BECKFORD'S FONTHILL ABBEY.

William Beckford, born in 1760, was the richest man in England. When he was five, he received piano lessons from nine-year-old Mozart; at the age of ten, he inherited a fortune, derived from Jamaican sugar plantations. He toured Europe, met Voltaire and began to build up a vast art collection. In 1784, he became an MP and, in 1786, wrote a Gothic novel called *Vathek*, about a man who builds a high tower so that he can see all the world. Rather like Horace Walpole before him, (*see* Twickenham, Middlesex), the story came to Beckford in a dream.

He had to leave Parliament after a messy homosexual affair, and went into exile on the Continent, during which time his wife died, giving birth to their second daughter. He returned to England in 1796, and engaged the architect JAMES WYATT to help him build the most wondrous Gothic house in England.

Fonthill Abbey was a mix of cathedral and Dracula's Castle, with vast entrance doors 40 ft (12 m) high, cloisters, turrets and spires, and miles of long corridors, all filled with priceless paintings and sumptuous furniture. The most spectacular feature was the central tower, Beckford's Folly, which soared above the surrounding hills,

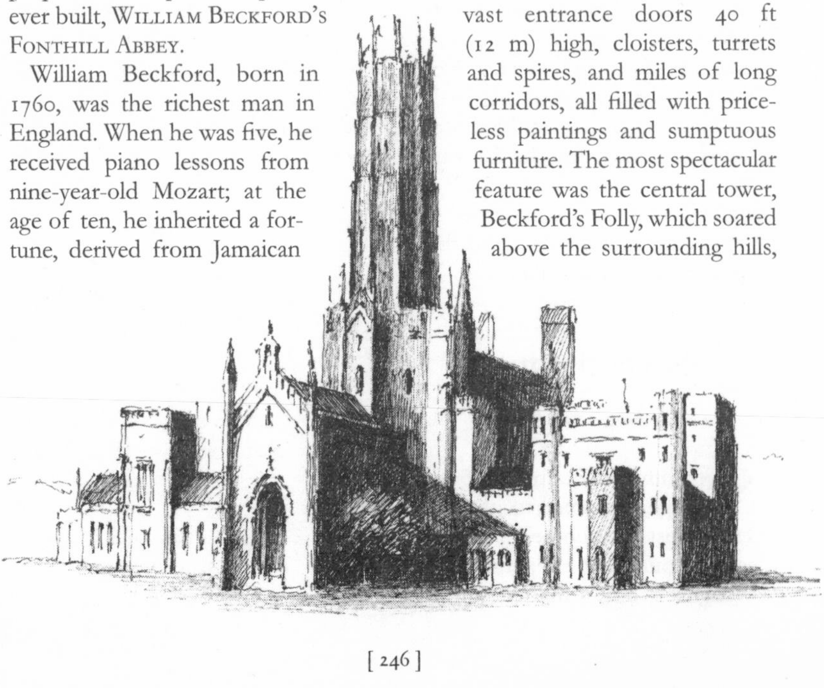

300 ft (91 m) into the sky, setting in stone Beckford's vision from *Vathek*. The lower section of this fantastic creation was made from stone too thin to bear the weight and the tower twice fell to the ground. Each time it was rebuilt, on the third occasion, in 1800, just in time to welcome Lord Nelson and Emma Hamilton, who were entertained with candle-light masques, concerts by the finest musicians in Europe and rich banquets.

They were almost the last people to visit Fonthill Abbey, for William Beckford, shunned and derided for his homosexuality, sent his two daughters to live with relations, built an 8-mile (13-km) wall around the park and shut himself away, living alone in his monstrous citadel, becoming more and more reclusive and eccentric. Finally, the expense of Fonthill broke even Beckford, and, in 1822, he sold the Abbey and went to live in Bath. Shorn of its creator and purpose, the tower fell down for the last time in 1825, and the rest of the building was almost completely demolished soon afterwards. William Beckford died in 1844 and is buried at Bath.

Sevenhampton

Fleming, Ian Fleming

Sevenhampton is a picture-postcard village, too small to notice, that seems lost in slumber. Nothing, it seems, could ever happen here, even though it is only 5 miles (8 km) from the beating heart of Swindon, Wiltshire's largest town. The church lies in a field on the edge of the village, in the company of a few trees. Walk in through the gate and turn left down a barely visible path and you will see a gaunt obelisk standing amongst the gravestones. On it is an oval plaque that reads: 'In memoriam Ian Fleming B. 28 May 1908 D. 12 Aug 1964.' Here, in this modest grave, lies the greatest spymaster of them all, creator of the ultimate secret agent, James Bond, 007.

IAN FLEMING came from a banking family and was educated at Eton. During the Second World War, he worked for the Intelligence Service, reaching the rank of Commander, the same rank as Bond. After the War, he built himself a house on the island of Jamaica called Goldeneye. In 1952, he married Ann, former wife of Lord Rothermere, who was expecting his child, born later that year. He also wrote his first Bond story, *Casino Royale*. He was to write 12 Bond novels in all. The name James Bond came from a real ornithologist whose book, *Birds of the West Indies*, Fleming had seen at the island's airport shop. He also wrote the children's story, *Chitty Chitty Bang Bang* (*see* Brooklands, Surrey).

In 1960, suffering failing health, due to a bad heart, he returned to England and bought the demolished Warneford Place in Sevenhampton, which he rebuilt as SEVENHAMPTON PLACE in 1963. Ian Fleming died in 1964. Buried with him are his wife, Ann, and only son, Caspar.

Two of the Bond films include scenes shot in Swindon. In 1984, for *A View to a Kill*, the inside of the Renault building was used for scenes featuring Roger Moore as James Bond and Patrick McNee as Sir Godfrey Tibbett. Then, in March 2000, Swindon's futuristic Motorola factory at Groundwell doubled as an oil pumping station in *The World Is Not Enough*, starring Pierce Brosnan as Bond.

Box

A Mystery

Driving through the village of Box, on the A4, it is possible to catch a glimpse of the western entrance to a Victorian engineering wonder, Box TUNNEL. When it was built, in 1837, by Isambard Kingdom Brunel, it was thought, at 1¾ miles (2.8 km) in length, to be the longest tunnel in the world. In fact, the Sapperton tunnel, on the Thames and Severn Canal in Gloucestershire, completed in 1789, is over 1,000 yd (914 m) longer. It was, however, the LONGEST RAILWAY TUNNEL IN THE WORLD.

Box Tunnel is on the London to Bristol railway line and is completely straight, descending a 1 in 100 gradient from the east. Brunel designed it so that the sun would shine all the way through the tunnel on one day each year, his birthday, 15 April.

When digging out the tunnel, the engineers came across large quantities of Bath stone, good for building, and a number of stone mines were excavated at the same time. Access to these mines was through a separate, smaller tunnel entrance, built alongside the eastern portal of the main tunnel.

After the stone had been removed, great empty caverns were left and these were utilised by the government during the Second World War, for storing ammunition and other sensitive material, as well as for secret experiments and weapons projects. An underground communications centre was created and connected by a series of shafts to the RAF centre at RUDLOE MANOR, situated directly above the tunnel. The caverns were linked together by tunnels, while railway stations and platforms, along with accommodation facilites, were constructed, until, eventually, a whole subterranean city had been established under Box Hill.

Box Hill was within easy reach of London by fast train and, during the Cold War, the site was converted into a bomb-proof nuclear bunker known as BURLINGTON, where the government and the Royal Family could retire to in the event of a nuclear strike.

Virtually from its inception, Box Hill has excited speculation and conspiracy theories. The small side tunnel at the eastern end looks almost too convincingly disused, boarded up and hidden behind undergrowth. There are some who suspect that Rudloe Manor is used for monitoring UFOs. Others are convinced that Box Hill is a vast secret laboratory or computer nerve centre . . .

Well, I never knew this ABOUT WILTSHIRE

The architect SIR CHRISTOPHER WREN (1632–1723) was born in EAST KNOYLE, a little village near the border with Dorset and Somerset, where his father was the rector. Christopher was born in lodgings above HASLAM'S SHOP, where KNOYLE HOUSE now stands. The Wren family had been forced to move there temporarily, after a fire at the Rectory.

Below WIN GREEN, high up on the Wiltshire downs, where Cranborne Chase swoops down to the Nadder valley, sits ASHCOMBE HOUSE, home of pop singer MADONNA and her husband, Guy Ritchie. The house used to be the home of photographer SIR CECIL BEATON (1904–80), who is buried not far away in All Saints churchyard at Broad Chalke.

In the churchyard at ALVEDISTON, is the grave of SIR ANTHONY EDEN, first Earl of Avon (1897–1977), the Prime Minister brought down by the Suez crisis.

Housed in the CROFTON PUMPING STATION, near GREAT BEDWYN, is the OLDEST WORKING STEAM-DRIVEN BEAM ENGINE IN THE WORLD, made by Boulton & Watt (*see* Handsworth, Warwickshire) in 1812. It is still used for its original purpose of pumping water up to the summit level of the Kennet and Avon Canal.

MARLBOROUGH vies with Stockton-on-Tees and Appleby, in Westmorland, for the WIDEST HIGH STREET IN ENGLAND. The famous college stands on the site of an old castle and it is said that Merlin the Wizard is buried in the school grounds under Maerl's Barrow.

South of Marlborough is MARTINSELL HILL, favourite viewpoint of the Old Marlburian art historian and Stalinist spy ANTHONY BLUNT (1907–83). His ashes were scattered on the hillside here.

Lying next to the A4, between Devizes and Marlborough, is the

LARGEST MAN-MADE MOUND IN EUROPE, SILBURY HILL. It covers an area of 5½ acres, is 130 ft (40 m) high and was constructed approximately 4,000 years ago. Nobody knows why, and countless excavations have failed to discover skeletal remains or any other clues. It is assumed that Silbury has some connection to the nearby AVEBURY STONE CIRCLE.

BOWOOD HOUSE, near CALNE, is the seat of the MARQUESS OF LANSDOWNE and boasts the LARGEST AREA OF MOWN LAWN IN ENGLAND. It was at Bowood, while tutoring the first Marquess's sons, that JOSEPH PRIESTLEY (1733–1804) discovered oxygen. His laboratory inside the house is preserved as it was then.

The ORIEL WINDOW at LACOCK ABBEY is the subject of the WORLD'S OLDEST PHOTOGRAPH, taken by WILLIAM FOX TALBOT in 1835. Fox Talbot's work laid the foundations of modern photography, although he

could never have foreseen that the cloisters of his old home would one day serve as the classrooms of HOGWART'S in the *Harry Potter* films. Lacock Abbey, and the unspoiled old-world village of Lacock, are owned by the National Trust and are much in demand as film locations.

Worcestershire

County Town: Worcester

'Who travels Worcester county
Takes any road that comes
When April tosses bounty
To the cherries and the plums'

John Drinkwater, poet, dramatist, critic and actor

Worcester

Royal Sauce

WORCESTER CATHEDRAL, where King John and Henry VII's eldest son, Prince Arthur, are buried, forms a glorious backdrop to Worcestershire Cricket Ground across the River Severn, a setting often voted the MOST PERFECT IN ENGLISH CRICKET.

Perhaps the best-known product to come from Worcester is LEA & PERRINS WORCESTERSHIRE SAUCE, made from a recipe brought back from India in 1835 by a former GOVERNOR OF BENGAL, the third LORD SANDYS. He gave two Worcester chemists, John Lea and William Perrins, the recipe to a spicy concoction he had grown rather partial to during the time of the Raj, and asked them to brew him up a large batch. This they did, but the results were hugely disappointing: the mixture was nothing like the original and 'tasted filthy'. Lea and Perrins stashed the unwanted brew in the cellar and forgot about it.

Some months later, when they came to clear out the cellar, they decided to give the mixture a tentative sip before they threw it out and, to their joy and astonishment, it had matured into the spicy condiment known and loved across the world today. They purchased the recipe from Lord Sandys and never looked back.

The sauce is made today by the French-owned company Danone, at a heavily-guarded factory in the Midland Road, right next to Worcester Shrub Lane Railway Station. The gates are barred and the public kept well away for fear of industrial espionage. Even in these days of compulsory labelling, the recipe remains top secret.

BERROW'S WORCESTER JOURNAL, established in 1690, is ENGLAND'S OLDEST NEWSPAPER.

Earl Baldwin of Bewdley

Worcestershire's Prime Minister

STANLEY BALDWIN was born in LOWER PARK HOUSE in the handsome riverside town of BEWDLEY in 1867. His father, Alfred, owned an ironworks at WILDEN, near Kidderminster, and here Stanley Baldwin learned about the business world, working for the family firm. The church at Wilden, built by his father, has a remarkable display of windows by EDWARD BURNE-JONES, who was Alfred Baldwin's brother-in-law. Alfred is buried in the churchyard.

In 1908, Stanley took over from his father as Conservative MP for Bewdley. He was Prime Minister three times, from 1923 to 1924, again from 1924 to 1929, during which term he faced the General Strike, and, finally, from 1935 to 1937, when he had to deal with the Abdication crisis. During his last period in office, he infuriated Winston Churchill by refusing to re-arm in the face of the growing military might of Germany.

Baldwin's grandparents, the Rev. James Macdonald, a Methodist minister, and his wife, Hannah, are buried just outside Bewdley in the churchyard at Ribbesford. One of their daughters married the painter EDWARD POYNTER, another SIR EDWARD BURNE-JONES, a third became the mother of RUDYARD KIPLING and a fourth the mother of STANLEY BALDWIN.

For many years, Baldwin lived south of Bewdley at ASTLEY HALL, a fine 19th-century house with exceptional views, now a residential home. He died in 1947, and is buried in Worcester Cathedral.

Malvern

Spring Water and Sports Cars

THE MALVERN HILLS are the OLDEST HILLS IN ENGLAND, rising to 1,395 ft (425 m) at the summit of the highest hill, the WORCESTERSHIRE BEACON. The whole of Middle England is visible from these ancient, rounded heights, as are the three cathedrals that host the Three Choirs Festival: Worcester, Hereford and Gloucester.

The poet WILLIAM LANGLAND (1332–1400) was inspired to write *Piers Plowman* on the slopes of the Malvern Hills (*see* Ledbury, *pages 104–5*):

Meatless and moneyless, on Malvern hills,
I mused upon this dream and went upon my way

Pure spring water filtering down from the hills turned Malvern into a spa town during Victorian times, although its healing powers were first mentioned as far back as 1622, in Bannister's *Breviary of the Eyes.* The water was first bottled and sent out across England in the days of James I, and its popularity was assured after Malvern spring water was presented to Queen Victoria at the Great Exhibition of 1851.

In 1842, Doctors WILSON and GULLY set up a hydrotherapy cure in the centre of Great Malvern, which involved drinking lots of water, hikes on the hills, rub-downs by matron and plenty of cold showers in the form of water jets from above and below.

The Queen takes Malvern Water with her wherever she travels and over one million bottles are sold throughout the world every year. It is bottled by Schweppes, who are now part of Coca Cola, at COLWALL, on the western side of the hills, although anyone can fill up for free from one of the 70 wells in the area.

Buried in the churchyard of ST JAMES'S, at West Malvern, is the writer's friend, PETER MARK ROGET (1779–1869), whose *Thesaurus of English Words and Phrases* was first published in 1852. He was also Secretary of the Royal Society for 22 years and a co-founder of London University.

In 1910, a garage owner, H.F.S. MORGAN, from Malvern Link, unveiled his single-seater three-wheeler at the Olympia Motor Show and found himself inundated with orders. He had originally made the car just for his own amusement, with a little help from *Rocket* builder George Stephenson's grandson, STEPHENSON PEACH, who was the engineering master at Malvern College.

H.F.S. Morgan went into production with a two-seater version of his car in 1911, attracting the attention of the Managing Director of Harrods, who displayed a Morgan in the store window – the only car ever to be so privileged.

Morgan approached a number of the big motor car manufacturers to see if they would be interested in producing his car, but they all turned him down. This determined him to remain independent and make his cars individually by hand, a tradition maintained to this day. Morgan's grandson, Peter Morgan, ran the company until his death in 2003. Morgans are still hand made at the factory in PICKERSLEIGH ROAD, Malvern Link, their home since 1918.

Harvington Hall

Priest Holes

HARVINGTON HALL, situated between KIDDERMINSTER and BROMSGROVE, is a wonderfully romantic gabled house from Tudor times, reached by two fine bridges across a moat, redolent of mystery and adventure. It possesses the finest collection of priest holes of any house in the country, all the work of that master builder of hiding places, NICHOLAS OWEN.

In the 17th century, such was the persecution of Catholics that priests and Jesuits were under constant threat of imprisonment and execution. They needed somewhere to hide from the soldiers intent on hunting them down and many of the big houses of that time contained secret rooms and passageways where those at risk could conceal themselves while the house was being searched.

Nicholas Owen was born the son of a carpenter and was himself a skilled builder and joiner. He worked as a servant for the English Jesuit martyr, EDMUND CAMPION, and was deeply affected by his arrest and capture at Lyford (*see* Berkshire). He went on to become assistant to the Jesuit superior in England, FATHER HENRY GARNETT, and travelled the country with him, designing and building priest holes wherever he went.

Priest holes had to be constructed with several uses in mind. They had to be reasonably comfortable and have somewhere to store food, because searches could last for days or even weeks if the hunter decided to move in with the suspect family. There needed to be ventilation, but no chinks where candlelight might be seen, and the entrance had to be imaginatively disguised. They had to

be constructed in secrecy too, in case any of the household staff were informers, and for that reason Owen usually worked alone and at night.

The priest holes at Harvington are particularly ingenious. Four of them are grouped around the main staircase, linked by secret passageways with trapdoors and moving panels. One is reached by removing a false set of stairs and has an opening by which food can be passed through from the Banqueting Hall. Another has an escape route whereby the priest could let himself down to the moat using a windlass.

In 1606, Owen was finally captured, along with Father Garnett and two others, at HINDLIP HOUSE, just north of Worcester, as a result of the anti-Catholic hysteria following the Gunpowder Plot. They were forced to emerge from their hiding places after three days without food or water and Owen died a few weeks later under torture.

Hindlip House is gone, but Harvington Hall is now an hotel and Owen's priest holes can be examined. Who knows how many more there are waiting to be discovered all over England?

Well, I never knew this ABOUT WORCESTERSHIRE

SIMON DE MONTFORT (1208–65), the 'Father' of the 'Mother of Parliaments', is buried beneath the high altar of the ruined abbey at EVESHAM, the spot marked by a rough-hewn granite cross. Up on GREEN HILL, at the top of the town, is an obelisk that marks the spot where he fell during the Battle of Evesham in 1265, defeated by Prince Edward, the future Edward I.

In 1582, WILLIAM SHAKESPEARE stayed in the black-and-white timbered OLD BULL INN at INKBERROW, west of Alcester, on his way to

Worcester to collect his marriage certificate. The inn is the model for the AMBRIDGE village pub in *The Archers*, BBC Radio 4's soap opera.

MADRESFIELD COURT, 3 miles (5 km) south of Malvern, has never been bought or sold since records began. It has been the home of the LYGON family since the 13th century. The house stands in the middle of a large moat and the original 12th-century Great Hall still lies at the core of the house, which was extended as a Tudor manor and then restored in Victorian Gothic style in 1865. The CHAPEL, decorated in 1902 as a wedding present for the seventh Earl from his wife, is considered the MOST BEAUTIFUL EXPRESSION OF THE ARTS AND CRAFTS STYLE IN BRITAIN. EVELYN WAUGH is said to have modelled the FLYTE family and their great house on the Lygons of Madresfield in his novel *Brideshead Revisited.*

The FIRST POINT-TO-POINT was held at MADRESFIELD in 1836.

In the churchyard of ST JOHN THE BAPTIST, at BROMSGROVE, are the graves of two railwaymen, THOMAS SCAIFE and JOSEPH RUTHERFORD, who were killed when their steam locomotive blew up while climbing the nearby LICKEY INCLINE, the STEEPEST GRADIENT ON THE BRITISH MAIN LINE NETWORK. Scaife was killed instantly on 10 November 1840. Rutherford died the next day.

Near TARDEBRIGGE, to the east of Bromsgrove, is the LONGEST FLIGHT OF LOCKS IN BRITAIN: 58 locks over a distance of 16 miles (26 km) on the Worcester and Birmingham Canal.

YORKSHIRE

COUNTY TOWN: YORK

County of the White Rose

York Minster, largest medieval Gothic cathedral in Northern Europe

Leeds

St Michael and the Frenchman

Leeds was the star of the very FIRST MOVING PICTURES ever seen. French photographer LOUIS ALME AUGUSTIN LE PRINCE (1842–90) was a designer at WHITLEY PARTNERS in Leeds, the family engineering firm of his wife, Elizabeth. In early October 1888, using a single-lens camera he had designed at his workshop in Woodhouse Lane, he filmed members of the Whitley family in the garden of his father-in-law Joseph's house in OAKWOOD GRANGE ROAD, ROUNDHAY, a suburb of Leeds. The film can be dated prior to 24 October, because Le Prince's mother-in-law, Sarah, who appears in the film, died on that date. Also featured are Joseph Whitley, a Miss Harriet Hartley and Le Prince's eldest son. Later that same month, from a second floor window of HICKS BROS., the iron-mongers, Le Prince filmed the moving traffic on LEEDS BRIDGE.

The films were such a success that Le Prince was now ready to demonstrate his breakthrough to the world. On 16 September 1890, after a quick visit to see his brother in France, Le Prince boarded a train at Dijon bound for Paris, with all his equipment and film, but was never seen again. No trace of him was ever found, despite intensive investigations, and his disappearance remains an unsolved mystery to this day. He gave Leeds immortality and vanished.

Londesborough

A Supreme Act of Faith

Londesborough shelters behind a group of trees in a hollow on the bare windswept Wolds, high above the silver Humber. It is a tiny place that occupies a great place in English history for here, in the Saxon palace where Londesborough Park now stands, the GREAT COUNCIL of 627 met.

The matter before KING EDWIN OF NORTHUMBRIA and the Council was whether to adopt Christianity or to continue with the old pagan beliefs. On the Christian wing was Paulinus, emissary of the Pope, and Edwin's wife, Ethelberta, daughter of the Christian Queen Bertha of Kent. On the pagan side were the king's hardened warriors and the Chief Priest, Coifi. Edwin was resistant to change, and the debate was deadlocked when an old man rose from the back of the hall and said, 'The life of man is like a sparrow that flies out of the night into a brightly lit hall, tarries for a moment and then flies out of the other door back into the dark. What is before us and what lies after we do not know. If this new doctrine will tell us anything of these mysteries, let us follow it.'

Such was the power of his words that Edwin was decided and so was his Chief Priest. 'I have worshipped the pagan gods all my life and they have not made me rich,' he declared. With the blessing of King Edwin, Coifi leapt on his horse and rode like the wind to GOODMANHAM, where the pagan shrine stood. Calling on all who could hear to follow him, he thrust his spear through the door, destroyed all the pagan idols within and burned everything to the ground. It was a supreme act of faith by one who had lived his whole life in fear and service of these pagan images, and it sent a powerful message throughout the northern kingdom that the Christian God now reigned. A small church now stands on the site of the former shrine. King Edwin was baptised in York, where York Minster now stands.

Bradford

Brontës and the Railway Children

The 1970 film of *The Railway Children*, which made a star out of Jenny Agutter, was filmed on the KEIGHLEY AND WORTH VALLEY RAILWAY, west of Bradford. OAKWORTH STATION, in the middle of the 5-mile (8-km) long branch line, was the children's local station, base of the porter Perks (Bernard Cribbins), and where their father (Iain Cuthbertson) appears out of the steam at the tearful conclusion of the film. The setting for the paper chase and the landslide was the MYTHOLMES TUNNEL, just outside Oakworth Station. The children's home, THREE CHIMNEYS, is BENTS FARM, a private house near Oxenhope, which can be seen from the public footpath through 'Top Field'.

Next stop on the line is HAWORTH, grey, cobbled and steep, where the Brontë family came to live at the Parsonage in 1820, and where the sisters were inspired by the bleak moors to write their remarkable works. All are buried in the family vault beneath the church, except for Anne, who is buried at Scarborough. Charlotte, Emily, Anne and their brother, Branwell, were all born in the little dining room at 74 Market Street in THORNTON, a village 5 miles (8 km) to the south east, near Bradford, where their father was the curate. The house can be visited by appointment.

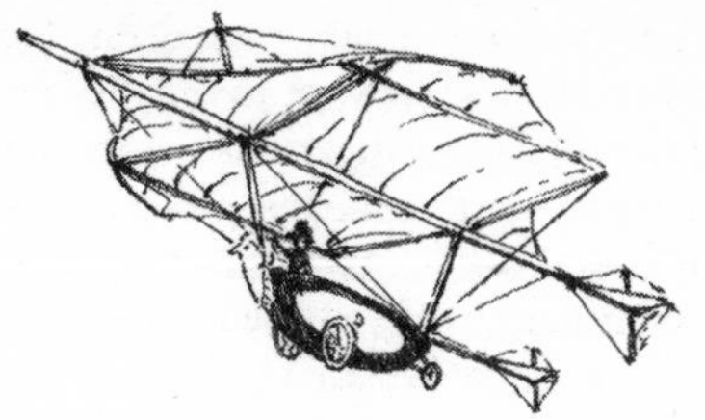

Brompton

The Flying Coachman

THE FIRST TRUE AEROPLANE FLIGHT in history took place in 1853 at BROMPTON HALL, the ancestral home of SIR GEORGE CAYLEY (1771–1857), a few miles west of Scarborough. Sir George had been mulling over the theory of flight since he was a boy and his observations of gliding seagulls had led him to believe that the idea of flapping wings was not going to

Haworth Parsonage

work. Instead, a suitably curved flat wing and the forward motion of the plane would create the necessary lift.

Sir George disappeared into his laboratory, tidied away the seat belts and caterpillar tracks he had already invented, but couldn't find a use for, and set about constructing himself a glider based on scientific principles. After a few false starts, he emerged, blinking into the light, towing behind him a monoplane, equipped with kite-shaped cloth wings of about 500 sq ft (46 sq m), an adjustable tail plane and fin, a boat-shaped cockpit to carry the pilot and a flimsy tricycle undercarriage. He wheeled the ensemble to the edge of a small valley in the grounds and sat back to ponder his next problem. Who was going to fly the thing?

Naturally he, Sir George, could not. That would be self-indulgent. He was an important man of advanced years, an MP no less. Besides, his wife, who disapproved of his experiments, would not have allowed it, and although Sir George was brave, he was not rash. No, he decided it would be prudent to swallow his disappointment and give some other fellow a stab. But who?

At that moment, Sir George's coachman, JOHN APPLEBY, sauntered past, eyeing the machine with considerable scepticism. He had seen many such contraptions before. 'Ah John,' said Sir George, 'just the chap.' By now, the entire household of Brompton had gathered to watch the fun and, before he knew what was happening, the unfortunate coachman found himself manoeuvred into the tiny cockpit and perched on the edge of the abyss. Willing farm hands pulled him into position and the hapless coachman hurtled off down the slope. The ground fell away and then up he soared, into the Yorkshire sky, like a bird.

He opened an eye and, for a moment, there was a sensation of utter peace, floating in the breeze like an autumn leaf. Then, with dreadful suddenness, the other side of the valley loomed up and, in the words of Sir George's ten-year-old granddaughter, he 'came down with a smash'.

John Appleby had joined the gods, the FIRST MAN EVER TO FLY IN AN AEROPLANE. The intrepid coachman extricated himself from the wreckage, brushed down his uniform, rose to his full height and fixed his excited employer with a watery eye. 'Sir George, I wish to give notice. I was hired to drive, not to fly!' With that he turned on his heels and limped away into history.

Sir George Cayley was too old to build on his triumph that day, but that flight in a Yorkshire garden led directly to the Wright brothers success at Kitty Hawke 50 years later. His legacy was a true understanding of the nature of flight. As he wrote in his notebook, 'When I am gone you may find the seeds of thought in these scrawls.'

Cundall

A Thankful Village

A few miles to the east of Ripon, the River Swale winds its way south through England's biggest vale, the Vale of York. Sitting quietly beside the river is the tiny village of CUNDALL. There is a church, restored in 1854, with a beautifully carved cross, probably Saxon, standing in the tree-lined churchyard. Away across the fields is the old Hall, now a farmhouse. There is a smattering of houses at the crossroads. On the surface a pleasant, but unremarkable Yorkshire village. But Cundall is blessed like few other villages, for it is one of England's most rare – a THANKFUL VILLAGE.

The term Thankful Village was first used by ARTHUR MEE in the 1930s and refers to those villages whose men and women all came home safely from the First World War. They were distinctive in having no war memorials, although some had monuments, usually in the church, in gratitude for their good fortune.

Among the thousands of villages in England, Arthur Mee reckoned there were, at most, 31 Thankful Villages, although he could only positively identify 24. These are listed below:

Bedfordshire
STANBRIDGE, near Leighton Buzzard

Derbyshire
BRADBOURNE, north of Ashbourne

Gloucestershire
COLN ROGERS, deep in the Cotswolds
LITTLE SODBURY, where William Tyndale began to translate the Bible into English (*see* page 91)
UPPER SLAUGHTER, near Stow-on-the-Wold

Leicestershire
WILLESLEY, near Ashby-de-la-Zouche

Norfolk
OVINGTON, south east of Swaffham

Nottinghamshire
MAPLEBECK, north of Southwell
WIGSLEY, north of Newark
WYSALL, south of Nottingham

Rutland
TEIGH, north of Oakham

Somerset
AISHOLT, north of Taunton
CHELWOOD, west of Bath
RODNEY STOKE, near Cheddar
STANTON PRIOR, near Bath
STOCKLINCH, near Ilminster
TELLISFORD, south of Bath
WOOLLEY, north of Bath

Suffolk
ST MICHAEL, in the Waveney valley

Wiltshire
LITTLETON DREW, near Chippenham

Yorkshire
CATWICK, north of Beverley
CAYTON, near Scarborough
CUNDALL, see above
NORTON-LE-CLAY, near Ripon

Well, I never knew this
ABOUT
YORKSHIRE

The towering walls of RICHMOND CASTLE, built in 1080 and perched high above the River Swale at the head of Swaledale, are the OLDEST ORIGINAL CASTLE WALLS IN BRITAIN that are still standing.

The 'TOFFEE TOWN' of HALIFAX was the home of the 'Toffee King', JOHN MACKINTOSH. In 1890, he opened a confectionery shop in KINGS CROSS LANE, with his new bride, VIOLET. They wanted to have a speciality product to make a name for the shop and decided to try combining soft American caramel with brittle English butterscotch to produce a high-quality toffee. It became so popular that Mackintosh's Toffee outsold everything else in the shop and, in 1899, they had to move to a factory in Queens Road. This was burnt down in 1909 and they moved again to ALBION MILLS, near the railway station, now their permanent home.

In 1936, Mackintosh's introduced a chocolate and toffee assortment which took its name from a sentimental play by James Barrie, author of *Peter Pan*, called *Quality Street.* The product image was based on the main characters of the play, a soldier and his young lady. Quality Street is still made in Halifax, although Mackintosh's is now part of Nestlé.

KIRKLEES, just north of Huddersfield, is traditionally the burial place of ROBIN HOOD. Feeling poorly, he came here to KIRKLEES PRIORY to be tended by his cousin, the Prioress, little knowing that she was in league with his enemy, Sir Roger of Doncaster. In the guise of healing him, the Prioress bled Robin to death. His Merry Men arrived to late to save him and he was helped too a window, where he shot an arrow into the air from his trusty bow asking that he should be buried where it landed. A stone tablet marks the spot in a wooded glade above the River Calder. The gatehouse of the Priory is still there, although the Priory itself has been replaced by the Jacobean Kirklees Hall.

HOLMFIRTH is the home of *Last of the Summer Wine*, the LONGEST RUNNING TELEVISION SITUATION COMEDY IN THE WORLD, which was first aired in 1973. Many of the locations used in the show are instantly recognisable, such as Nora Batty's house near Upper Bridge and Sid's café across from the church.

HOLMFIRTH has a fine pedigree in film-making, with many slapstick silent pictures being made in the town by BAMFORTH AND CO., founded in 1870 by James Bamforth of Station Road. As well as being pioneers of silent movies, the company found lasting fame with their saucy postcards, usually featuring buxom ladies and their weedy husbands.

RIPON is BRITAIN'S OLDEST CITY. It was granted a charter by ALFRED THE GREAT in 886.

High up on ARKENGARTHDALE MOOR, situated on a minor road from Brough to Richmond, is BRITAIN'S HIGHEST PUBLIC HOUSE, the TAN HILL INN, which stands 1,723 ft (525 m) above sea level.

The gorgeous GEORGIAN THEATRE ROYAL in RICHMOND was founded in 1788 and is the OLDEST THEATRE IN BRITAIN STILL IN ITS ORIGINAL PREMISES.

PONTEFRACT is known as the 'LIQUORICE TOWN'. Liquorice comes from the Middle East and was introduced to Pontefract by the Crusaders. It was grown by monks for medicinal purposes and although they tried to grow it in many other towns it only flourished in Pontefract, possibly because of the rich clay soil. Liquorice comes from the long roots of the liquorice bush and is one of the sweetest substances known. Liquorice is still produced in Pontefract, in particular the Pontefract cake, which is a disc of liquorice shaped like a coin.

PONTEFRACT is also known for having the LARGEST CIRCULAR FLAT RACECOURSE IN EUROPE.

Gazetteer

Interesting locations and places open to the public

Map references are taken from the Ordnance Survey 'Landranger' series.
NT = National Trust (*www.nationaltrust.org.uk*)

Bedfordshire

Cockayne Hatley
Map 153, ref TL *256 496*
Twinwood – Glenn Miller Museum
Tel 01234 350413
www.twinwoodevents.com
John Bunyan – Slough of Despond, Stevington
Map 153, ref SP *991 537*

Berkshire

Bear Wood House
Map 175, ref SU *777 691*
Sounding Arch
Map 175, ref SU *902 810*
Jethro Tull – Basildon
Map 175, ref SU *612 793*
Prosperous Farm
Map 174, ref SU *329 651*
Oakley Court
Tel 01227 785 467
www.moathousehotels.co.uk
Lyford Grange
Map 174, ref SU *396 946*

Buckinghamshire

Stoke Poges Church
Map 175, ref SU *975 827*
Pinewood Studios
Tel 01753 651700
www.pinewoodshepperton.com
Newport Pagnell – Tickford Bridge
Map 152, ref SP *877 438*

Cambridgeshire

Foul Anchor
Map 131, ref TF *466 177*
Sawston Hall
Map 154, ref TL *488 491*
Parson Drove
Map 143, ref TF *390 090*
Wimpole Hall NT

Cheshire

Northwich – Winsford Salt Mine
Map 118, ref SJ *657 680*
Anderton Boat Lift
Map 118, ref SJ *648 753*
Tel 01606 786777
www.andertonboatlift.co.uk
Lyme Park NT

Cornwall

Bude Castle – Stratton Museum, Bude, EX23 8LG
Tel: 01288 353576

St Just
Map 204, ref SW *848 357*
St Piran's Observatory
Map 200, ref SW *768 564*
Morwenstow – Parson Hawker's Hut
Map 190, ref SS *199 153*

Cumberland

Sellafield Visitor Centre
Tel 01946 727027
www.sellafield.com
Scale Force Waterfall NT
Map 89, ref NY *151 173*
Cockermouth NT

Derbyshire

Melbourne Hall
Tel 01332 862502
www.melbournehall.com
Chatsworth
Tel 01246 565300
www.chatsworth-house.co.uk

Devon

Plymouth
www.plymouthgin.com
Paignton – Oldway Mansion
www.torbay-online.co.uk/paignton/paignton-oldway
Bideford
www.beautiful-devon.co.uk/tarka-trail
Greenway NT

Dorset

Poole – Brownsea Island NT
Monmouth's Ash
Map 195, ref SU *060 070*
Godmanstone – Smith's Arms
Map 194, ref SY *668 974*
Moreton – Clouds Hill NT

Durham

Causey Arch
Map 88, ref NZ *202 559*

Essex

Bradwell-on-Sea – St Peter's Chapel
Map 168, ref TR *031 084*
Greensted Log Church
Map 167, ref TL *539 030*
Kelvedon Hatch Secret Nuclear Bunker
Crown Buildings, Kelvedon Hall Lane, Brentwood, Essex, CM14 5TL
Tel 01277 364 883
www.japar.demon.co.uk

Gloucestershire

Sodbury
Map 172, ref ST *759 829*
Sudeley Castle
Tel 01242 602308
www.sudeleycastle.co.uk

Hampshire

New Forest – Rufus Stone
Map 195, ref SU *269 125*
Farnborough Abbey
Map 186, ref SU *873 565*
Watership Down
Map 174, ref SU *496 568*
Beacon Hill
Map 174, ref SU *455 573*

East Meon Court
Map 185, ref SU *682 224*

HEREFORDSHIRE

Whitbourne Church
Map 149, ref SO *725 569*

HERTFORDSHIRE

Standon Green End
Map 166, ref TL *364 198*
Markyate Cell
Map 166, ref TL *059 173*

HUNTINGDONSHIRE

Hemingford Grey Manor
Tel 01480 463134
www.greenknowe.co.uk
Holme Fen
Map 154, ref TL *457 727*

KENT

Sheppey – Muswell Manor
Map 179, ref TR *043 694*
Great Maytham Hall
Rolvenden, Cranbrook,
Kent TN17 4NE
Tel 01580 241346
Eastry Court
Map 179, ref TR *312 548*

LANCASHIRE

Rainhill – Skew Bridge
Map 108, ref SJ *490 914*
Hoghton Tower,
Nr Preston, Lancs PR5 0SH
Tel 01254 852986
www.hoghtontower.co.uk
Hall i' th' Wood,
Green Way, off Crompton Way,
Bolton BL1 8UA
Tel 01204 332370
www.boltonmuseums.org.uk/html/hall-wood-museum.asp
Carnforth Station
Map 97, ref SD *707 497*

LEICESTERSHIRE

Loughborough – War Memorial Tower,
Queens Park, Granby Street
Tel 01509 263370

LINCOLNSHIRE

Bowthorpe Park Farm – Oak tree
Map 130, ref TF *067 154*
Coningsby Clock
Map 122, ref TF *223 580*
Boothby Pagnell
Map 130, ref SK *969 307*
Harrington Hall
Map 122, ref TF *367 717*
Woolsthorpe NT

MIDDLESEX

Bruce Castle
www.haringey.gov.uk/leisure/bruce_castle_museum
Stanmore – Bentley Priory
Map 176, ref TQ *155 934*

Grim's Dyke Hotel,
Old Redding, Harrow,
Middx HA3 6SH
Tel 020 8385 3100
www.grimsdyke.com

NORFOLK

East Lexham Church
Map 132, ref TF *859 173*
Houghton Hall
Tel 01485 528569
www.houghtonhall.com

NORTHAMPTONSHIRE

Sulgrave Manor
Tel 01295 760205
www.sulgravemanor.org.uk
Deene Park
Tel 01780 450278
www.deenepark.com
Rushton Triangular Lodge
Map 141, ref SP *831 831*
Lamport Hall
Tel 01604 686272
www.lamporthall.co.uk
Naseby Obelisk
Map 141, ref SP *684 799*
Nene Valley Railway
Tel 01780 784444
www.nvr.org.uk

NORTHUMBERLAND

Bamburgh Castle
Tel 01668 214515
www.bamburghcastle.com
Alnwick Castle
Tel 01665 510777
www.alnwickcastle.com
Horncliffe
Map 75, ref NT *934 511*
Flodden
Map 74, ref NT *889 373*
Cragside NT

NOTTINGHAMSHIRE

Newstead Abbey
Tel 01623 455900
www.newsteadabbey.org.uk
Annesley Hall
Map 120, ref SK *504 524*
Gotham
Map 129, ref SK *536 301*
Laxton
Map 120, ef SK *723 670*

OXFORDSHIRE

Caversfield
Map 164, ref SP *581 253*
Kelmscott
Tel 01367 252486
www.kelmscottmanor.co.uk
Radcot Bridge
Map 163, ref SU *286 994*
Headington Hill Hall
Map 164, ref SP *537 066*
www.headington.org.uk/history/listed_buildings/headhillhall.htm

RUTLAND

Tolethorpe Hall
Tel 01780754381
www.stamfordshakespeare.co.uk/tolethorpe.htm
Tickencote
Map 141, ref SK *990 095*

Shropshire

Boscobel House – The Royal Oak
Map 127, ef SJ *838 081*

Somerset

Athelney – Barrow Mump
Map 182, ref ST *359 306*
Culbone Church
Map 181, ref SS *842 483*
Tarr Steps
Map 181, ref SS *868 322*
Sweet Track
Map 182, ref ST *427 414*
Orchardleigh Park – Lake Church
Map 183, ref ST *774 509*
Quantocks – Coleridge Cottage NT

Staffordshire

Stoke-on-Trent Potteries
www2002.stoke.gov.uk/museums
Izaak Walton – Fishing Temple
Map 119, ref SK *128 589*
Calwich Abbey (ruins)
Map 128, ref SK *127 434*
Great Heywood – Essex Bridge
Map 127, ref SJ *995 226*
Flash
Map 119, ref SK *026 672*
Alton Towers
Tel 08705 204060
www.alton-towers.co.uk

Suffolk

Orwell – Freston's Tower
Map 169, ref TM *176 397*
Fitzgerald – Boulge House
Map 156, ref TM *254 528*
Denington Church
Map 156, ref TM *282 670*
Flatford Mill

Surrey

Brooklands
Tel 01932 857381
www.brooklandsmuseum.com
Iron – Quality Street, Merstham
Map 187, ref TQ *289 536*
A23 Harps Oak
Map 187, ref TQ *286 546*
Dean Lane Bridge
Map 187, ref TQ *290 567*
Mitcham Station
Map 176, ref TQ *274 682*
Outwood Windmill
Map 187, ref TQ *329 457*
Stoke D'Abernon Church
Map 187, ref TQ *129 585*
Shalford Mill NT

Sussex

Uppark NT Church
Map 187, ref TQ *302 362*
Charleston Manor
Map 199, ref TQ *522 007*

Warwickshire

Handsworth – Soho House
Tel 0121 554 9122
www.birminghamheritage.org.uk/sohohous.htm
Tolkien – Sarehole Mill
Tel 0121 777 6612
www.bmag.org.uk/sarehole_mill

Westmorland

Luddesdown Court
Map 178, ref TQ *669 662*
Grasmere – Dove Cottage NT

Wiltshire

Fonthill Abbey (ruins)
Map 184, ref ST *922 308*
Sevenhampton Church
Map 174, ref SU *209 904*
Box Tunnel – east portal
Map 173, ref ST *858 694*
Crofton Beam Engines
Tel 01672 870300
www.croftonbeamengines.org
Bowood House
Tel 01249 812102
www.bowood-house.co.uk
Lacock Abbey NT

Worcestershire

Harvington Hall
Tel 01562 777846
Map 139, ref SO *877 745*
Madresfield Court
Map 150, ref SO *809 475*
Inkberrow – The Old Bull
Map 150, ref SP *014 574*
Tardebrigge Locks
Map 139, ref SO *989 690*

Yorkshire

Londesborough
Map 106, ef SE *868 464*
Goodmanham Church
Map 106, ref SE *889 433*
Bradford – Oakworth Station
Map 104, ref SE *039 384*
Haworth Parsonage
Tel 01535 642323
www.bronte.org.uk
Tan Hill Inn
Tel 01833 628 246
www.tanhillinn.co.uk
Brontë Birthplace,
Market St, Thornton,
Bradford BD13 3HF
Tel 01274 830849
www.brontebirthplace.org.uk
Brompton Hall (School)
Tel 01723 859121
Kirklees Priory
Map 104, ref SE *174 215*

Index of People

Index of Places